GIRL WITH A GUN

Love, Loss and the Fight
for Freedom in Iran

DIANA NAMMI & KAREN ATTWOOD

For all the Peshmerga women who lost their lives and continue
to do so for the safety and freedom of others

With love to Tara, Yasmin and Isaac

Contents

Notes

Diana was born in the Kurdish region of Iran. Kurds are an ethic minority in the predominantly Persian Iran. The national language in Iran is Farsi, also known as Persian. The Kurds have never had a permanent nation state and live as minorities in the mountainous region straddling the borders of Turkey, Iraq, Syria, Iran and Armenia. When we refer to Kurdistan in the book, we are generally referring to the Kurdish region of Iran.

Peshmerga are Kurdish freedom fighters and you can find various direct translations into English, such as 'One who faces death'. Our preference is 'One who sacrifices his or her life for others', as this truly explains what a Peshmerga is prepared to do.

Prologue: A Wedding

Your wedding day should be the best day of your life. For Kurdish women, when I was growing up, it was often the worst day imaginable.

My earliest memory is of an arranged marriage between a bride, not more than fourteen or fifteen, and a groom twice her age. Ahmed, the groom, was a huge man who used to work in my father's bakery. He had pockmarks all over his face.

It was the 1960s. I was not more than four years old but I remember vividly the dazzling beauty of the bride in her red and gold wedding outfit. Amina had long, shiny black hair, delicate features in her bronze-coloured face and enormous black eyes lined with kohl, which made them shimmer. She also wore a look that I recognised as fear.

Like all Kurdish weddings at that time, the celebration lasted for three days. On the first day, Amina went to the hammam, the public bath, with her bridesmaids, where she was washed and made beautiful. On the way to the hammam and on the way back, one of the bride's friends held a large mirror in front of her, to represent brightness and happiness for the future. On the second day, she had the palms of her hands and the bottom of her feet elaborately painted in henna at her home. This was a girls' only party with lots of laughter. On the same night, at the groom's house, the music began and the guests of the groom came together to dance. This continued the next day with the Zizi brothers – a group of three brothers well known in Saqqez, the small city in the middle of Iranian Kurdistan where I lived – singing and beating a huge drum. The music was joyful, rapid and loud, as everyone held hands dancing in a circle. The younger guests began to show off and move faster and faster. I felt dizzy just watching them. The guests took turns in leading the dance. I felt proud as my handsome father held a glittery scarf aloft, a sarchopi, to lead the dancers round and round.

The bride's family brought Amina to the ceremony in a car through the city. Her father handed her over to Ahmed, who was traditionally dressed in a white shirt with a blue suit, the coat and trousers known as kava and pantol.

The dancing and singing continued into the night until suddenly, as though the lights had gone out, the atmosphere changed.

My mother took my hand. We went into the dark bedroom, which was smoky from herbs being burned over charcoal, a wedding tradition to bring health into the marriage and drive out misfortune. The bedclothes were all in disarray, with just one dimly lit lamp in the corner. I could see a long white piece of material lying on the mattress and a beautiful rug on the floor. In a corner sat the lovely Amina, holding her knees and crying quietly. She was trying to cover herself with her long dress. Her long black hair tumbled all around her body.

Ahmed was standing towering above the bride, his expression cold as ice. He appeared completely unmoved by his new bride's distress. Amina's mother was also down on the floor, holding onto Ahmed's legs, crying: 'Please don't send her back home; her father and brothers will kill her.'

Gripped with fear, I tried to hide myself behind my mother's dress. Men all around me were shouting while the women were crying. Some were calling Amina names I had not heard before, like slut and whore, while others were more sympathetic and were muttering 'Poor girl!' or 'What has she done?'

'She couldn't have imagined this could happen,' one said.

Imagine what? Although I couldn't fully grasp what was happening, I knew that this was a dangerous situation, a matter of life and death. Some of the wedding guests were clamouring to have the girl killed, while others stood in stunned silence. This could end in a so called 'honour killing.'

Into the midst of the crowd, which was building up into an

animal frenzy, my father stepped forward and in a loud, calm voice proclaimed: 'No one deserves to be treated like this. Accidents can happen to any girl.'

Turning to Ahmed, he said: 'If you send this woman back to her family then you have to leave the city too. This matter is not more important than her life. You must accept her as your bride.'

With these words, the tension dissipated. Everyone fell silent. My father was a respected member of the community. He was also Ahmed's boss. I don't know how long we all waited in silence but eventually Ahmed said to my father: 'I respect you and your words. I will accept her. I will not send her back to her family.'

The bride immediately began to sob loudly while her female relatives jumped up to thank my father. Other guests were muttering how lucky she was. After some discussion, the music started up again and the festivities resumed.

I would later learn that it was Kurdish tradition for the wedding to be consummated on the evening of the third night, while the wedding guests waited in the next room. A representative from the bride's family, usually an older woman, would stay behind the bedroom door and afterwards she would present white material with blood spots to prove the virginity of the bride. This material would usually be carried ceremoniously on a tray for all of the guests to cover it with money. It was a symbol of happiness and pride in the bride's virginity. Amina had failed this virginity test. There was no blood. This discovery could have led to her being murdered in a so called 'honour killing'. Of course, this can happen for all kinds of reasons other than a girl having had sexual intercourse, but this was not common knowledge in my city at that time.

Although her life was spared, Amina was forever treated like a slave by her husband because he had saved her honour on that day. However, she did go on to bear him four children. This brought her a measure of happiness. From that time, she always called my father 'Father' and my mother became a second mother to her. The couple lived nearby. I used to enjoy going to their house and playing with Amina's make up. She always seemed so glamorous to me.

The events of Amina's wedding were to shape the entire course of my life. Although it was some while later before I fully understood what had happened, I started to question everything before me, beginning with the meaning of virginity. Why was virginity so important that a woman could be killed for it? I worried that if I grew up without my virginity, I might also be killed.

Amid these fearful thoughts, I had the light of happiness in my heart. I knew that my father would not kill me. He alone had stepped forward to save Amina's life.

From my father's action, I saw that a community can be persuaded to change its mind. I understood, in that moment, that one brave person can change the world around them.

Chapter 1

A Father's Love

My own story begins a few years before the marriage of Amina and Ahmed. I was born sometime after Ramadan, after the snows had melted. My beloved father, Abdulkarim, took great pleasure in recounting the story of my birth, telling me how he ran into the streets to give out sweets, dates and raisins to the neighbours so that they could share in his happiness.

'Congratulations on the birth of your son,' they all shouted, making this assumption because of his great joy. 'I have a daughter and I wouldn't change her for the world,' Abdulkarim told them. This story, repeated often throughout my childhood, gave me a lot of confidence. Brought up in a deeply patriarchal society, I knew to my very core that my father loved me as much as if I were his son. I would remain a daddy's girl all of my life.

I don't know the exact date of my birth and I'm not sure how old I am. On our birth certificates my sister and I share the same birthday, although the years are different. Mine is marked 1964 and hers is 1966. The certificates were obtained sometime after our births. It was the custom to put a girl's age as two years older than her real age so that she could be married younger. Parents preferred to marry their daughters before the age of sixteen if possible, before they started to find love by themselves. Romantic love could lead to all kinds of trouble and bring shame and dishonour on the family. However, I believe my birth certificate is one or two years younger than my real age. I don't know why this would be, and my mother cannot remember. Maybe my father wanted me to stay at home longer with them.

My mother, Fatem, was my father's third wife. Abdulkarim's first wife had died during the birth of their son. Sadly, the baby only survived two weeks because there was nobody to breastfeed him. My father's second wife could not have children and so my father divorced her after one and a half years. This may seem harsh but was quite normal in my culture. My father was desperate for a child. He didn't believe in polygamy, even though this was a common practice in our region, as in many Muslim countries. When I came along, three years after the death of my father's first born, I was a long awaited and much wanted child.

I was named Diana by my father but given the nickname Galavezh, which is the Kurdish word for 'morning star'. For my father, I represented a bright new future after years of heartache and loss. Little could he know that this name would be on the Iranian government's 'most wanted' lists by the time I was a teenager.

Abdulkarim was fifteen years older than Fatem. He had light brown hair and hazel coloured eyes. He was tall and handsome, with an athletic build, but his good looks failed to move my mother. Although my parents got along well and my father was a kind husband, I don't think my mother ever truly loved him. Her heart was already taken by her cousin, Aba.

My mother would talk openly about this love. It was a family joke, and my sister and I would laugh about it. Aba and Fatem had grown up together and were childhood playmates before becoming sweethearts. Aba proposed to Fatem but my grandmother rejected him and he never fully got over this. Practical Malika didn't want my mother to marry someone with no prospects.

I often asked my grandmother why she would force her daughter into a union that she didn't want.

'But, Galavezh, Aba had no job!' my grandmother would say.

Not long after Aba's proposal, my mother, a beauty with her olive skin and big eyes, caught my father's eye when she was out buying fruit in a corner shop. My father asked the shopkeeper who she was and immediately sent his uncles to Malika to ask for permission to marry her.

As the main baker in Saqqez, then a trading centre due to its central position in Kurdistan, Abdulkarim was deemed middle class and was therefore a more attractive proposition for Malika.

Aba did eventually marry someone else, but she died while giving birth to their daughter. For much of Aba's twenties and thirties, he lived with his mother and daughter. My father obviously trusted my mother with Aba; we saw them often when I was a child. Aba was tall and handsome, though not as good looking as my father in my eyes. A long time after his first marriage, Aba did remarry, and the couple had three children.

Malika was a formidable woman and an important figure in my life. Slim with blue eyes, she always wore traditional clothes, usually a hat and a chador, a long thin piece of material that can cover the whole body, which Iranian women would wrap around themselves. The chador does not have any fastening and some people hold the ends at their neck.

Malika was deeply religious, but her views were often forward thinking. She had lived through many hardships, including the British and Russian armies' attack on our region following their invasion of Iran in 1941. The British government believed that the Shah, Reza Shah Pahlavi, who had ruled Iran with an iron fist since seizing it in a military coup in 1925, had sympathies with the Nazis. They also wanted to secure our precious oil fields.

Everyone fled to the mountains from the cities and villages, frightened by the reputation of the invading forces. There was nothing to eat. Malika volunteered to go back to Saqqez to fetch flour to make bread. She asked for someone to accompany her.

'Not one man stepped forward, just one woman, and we had to make this perilous journey several times, risking everything at the hands of the Russian and British soldiers,' Malika told me. 'I brought back flour and made bread for everyone to share.'

Malika bore her husband five daughters but no son, so my grandfather took a second wife who gave birth to a son and a daughter. After siring all these offspring, he died, leaving the two women with the task of taking care of seven children. It was a time of dire poverty in Iran. My grandmother and the second wife, Habiba, who was like a sister to Malika, had to work hard to feed all of their children. Malika baked bread, while Habiba washed clothes for rich people in the city.

'We had six daughters and we had a difficult task to make sure that they went to their future husbands with honour,' she told me. 'This was a huge responsibility. It is for this reason that I arranged the marriages of all the daughters. I wanted them to make us proud and not bring shame on the family. All my other daughters were happy with our choice of husband. It was only your mother who wanted someone different.'

My sister Shaesta, whose name means 'worthy', was born when I was around two. My mother was weak following the birth and didn't have enough milk to breastfeed. Shaesta began to fade away. Everyone thought she might die.

Refusing to accept this, Malika went out to the yoghurt market in the town. This was full of women from the villages who came to sell their dairy products.

'I looked closely at all the women until I found one with full breasts who looked like she could feed another child,' my grand-mother said. 'When I found Aysha I knew she was the one. I offered to buy all of her yoghurt if she would come and feed baby Shaesta.'

Aysha readily agreed, as she could not normally sell all of her yoghurt. The pair hurried home, where they found everyone pre-paring hot water to wash the baby thoroughly once she was dead.

'Stop – she is alive,' my grandmother commanded.

With just a few drops of milk, my sister moved her lips, and little by little, she opened her eyes.

Aysha came every day to feed her. She had a baby boy called Karim. As they grew, the children bonded and were known as milk sister and brother. Much later, when Karim was a student, he came to live with us. There were no secondary schools in his village and because he didn't have any other family in the city, Aysha asked if he could lodge with us while he was at secondary school. He lived with us for two or three years and often helped my father in the bakery. At the weekend, he would go back to his village, or Aysha would visit us, laden down with honey, yoghurt, eggs and milk.

My grandmother doted on my sister. My mother, exhausted with me, a toddler, and a newborn, was happy to step back. My grandmother brought my sister up almost as if she were her own child. She would do anything for her. Shaesta was fussy about her food and my family all had to come up with games and tricks to make her eat little morsels. Grandmother would make or buy special treats for her.

Once when she got sick, the doctor told my father and mother that Shaesta must eat kebabs every day for two weeks. They were expensive but my father, of course, bought them for her. After a few days, Shaesta announced she didn't want them anymore. I was pleased, as this meant there were more for the rest of the family.

Both my sister and I had light brown hair like our father, which was often commented upon as it was unusual in Iran.

Shaesta and I used to sleep with our grandmother, curled up with her on a huge, thick, heavy mattress on the floor. Malika ironed my sister's part of the mattress to make it warm. I would quickly jump into her space, as my side of the mattress was always freezing. Despite this favouritism, I was never jealous of my sister. I sensed that she had not had an easy start. She needed this extra care.

At night, Malika would tell us stories of scary stepmothers and one about three girls who ran away, taking shelter in a cave with a one eyed giant inside. This one-eyed giant wanted to eat the girls, but they managed to kill him and eventually married princes. She also recounted the tale of Snow White and sometimes told us terrifying ghost stories.

Malika would also talk to us about her own life. She described how Reza Shah's guards used to tear women's scarves from their heads in the streets. My sister and I couldn't imagine this. In the 1960s we were accustomed to modern dress. Reza Shah had banned women from wearing the chador and the hijab in 1936 when most women still wore traditional clothes. While the chador could cover the whole body, the hijab mainly refers to the head covering.

For my grandmother's generation, being made to remove their chador felt like a violation. It was as though they were being made to undress, and religious groups and imams, of course, hugely criticised this. The Shah wanted a secular regime, not a religious one. The imposition of the law made some women fearful of leaving their homes.

At that time, in my community, the tradition of mutilating female genitalia persisted, due to the belief that uncut women were unclean. Although Malika had arranged her daughters' marriages, she did not allow them to be cut. She had gone through this herself, along with the majority of women of her age. She knew how painful and debilitating it was.

'Those people are disabling women,' she told me once. 'God created us in that way and he does not want us to change this. It is just their way of controlling women.'

Malika was horrified at what had happened at the wedding of Amina and Ahmed.

'They didn't murder women for not being a virgin when I was a girl,' she told us later. 'Instead, they would shave the bride's head, put her on a donkey sitting backwards and ride her through the city to shame her.'

Chapter 2

Family

Our city, Saqqez, had a long, winding bazaar right through its middle, with dozens of little shops. My father's bakery thrived at the centre of this activity. He was the city's only sangak baker – sangak was a special one-metre long bread, baked flat like a pizza over stones in an oven. It usually had sesame seeds and nigella seeds on the top.

My father would get up at around 4 a.m. to get everything ready at the bakery. Then he would return home to do push-ups and exercises with his heavy metal weights and wooden clubs before eating breakfast.

From when I was about four, Abdulkarim would wake me and my sister up to exercise with him. He would do fifty press ups with the pair of us sitting on his back before chasing us around the garden until we collapsed with laughter.

Although my father worked hard, he spent whatever he earned on good food and fine clothes. He never saved any of it. He was always well dressed, with lots of different outfits made from the finest materials. He was equally generous with the rest of our family's clothing allowance.

'You should always dress smartly,' he would tell us. 'Do not let people think you are poor.'

My mother would complain from time to time: 'We need to save for a house instead of renting. Why are you spending all our money on clothes?'

Our rented home was in a two-storey building, which over-looked a shared courtyard with a fountain in the middle, encircled

19

with beautiful potted plants. Every morning my mother would join the women from the building to sweep the garden and to water the soil to stop the dust from getting everywhere. Some days I would wake up early with my mother just so I could smell the wet soil. Even now the smell of wet soil takes me back to my home in Saqqez. Later, the women would come together to do the washing and housework.

In the afternoon, the women would gather in the garden to make tea and traditional yoghurt soup with rice, herbs and chickpeas. Sometimes they would pass the hot afternoons eating roasted sunflower seeds while the children ran around playing games with apricot stones. We counted them up excitedly at the end of the day to see who had the most. Another favourite game was collecting broken glass in blues and yellows and greens. This was great treasure that we used to play house, cooking or shopping.

Nobody had any money for toys from the shop, so we all had dolls made from material. Our mothers sewed cloth around a coin to make the faces and created mouths and eyes with cotton stitching.

Three of my mother's sisters lived in villages near to Saqqez and we would visit them regularly. Compared to our city court-yard, their gardens were huge, with apricot and almond trees running up the side of the mountain.

We would spend the whole day in the farms, picking fruit and swinging from the trees until late into the afternoon. Two years after my sister, my brother Anwar was born.

He had straight, light brown hair and hazel eyes, just like my father. He was loved by everybody, but especially my mother. A boy in my culture was really the mother's prize. Just before his second birthday, my parents bought a tricycle for Anwar from the city. It was a hot summer's day and he was so excited to cycle home on it. I can see him now, riding around the garden, laughing and laughing. He looked so happy but, suddenly, without any warning, he stopped breathing. Anwar had croup, an inflammation of the larynx and trachea, but nobody knew what to do. The hospital was too far away. He died almost immediately.

I saw my father crying for the first time that day. My mother, who was in her early twenties, was broken with grief. Her face was covered in scratch marks from her own nails.

After the funeral, she started taking me to the graveyard. It was a little way out of the city and she would sit crying over the grave, talking to Anwar. I looked on, feeling utterly helpless, knowing that I couldn't do anything to comfort her.

About two weeks after the funeral, we saw a man hiding behind the graves about four or five metres away, staring at us. He had thick black hair and a moustache and frightening looking eyebrows. Thinking he was a rapist, my mother jumped when she saw him. We ran all the way home.

Later on, I wondered if this man had been sent by my father to scare my mother. He could easily have caught up with us if he had followed us. My father was so worried about my mother's mental health that I think he feared she would kill herself. From that day forward, she went only once a week to Anwar's grave, always accompanied by my father.

The beginning of the recovery from deep grief only came with the birth of another son, Asad, who also had light brown hair just like Anwar and my father. Asad looked like me, although he had bigger eyes. When he was old enough, I loved holding his hands to spin him round and round while my mother shouted at me.

'Stop, Galavezh, you are going to break Asad's arm!'

One day, I was spinning him so fast that his elbow joint popped out. I was so scared of my mother's anger that, before Asad had time to scream, I popped it back in. Asad was so shocked that he remained silent.

Sometimes, when my mother caught me teasing Asad, she would say: 'Your brother is your shepherd. You must treat him with respect.'

I couldn't contain my laughter. 'We don't need a shepherd. Asad is younger than us!'

When my mother said things like this, she was often laughing herself. I think, because of our traditions, she felt it was her duty to explain that a women's role was to always be under some man's thumb. This was the society we lived in, which was extremely male-dominated.

My own father was open minded compared with other men, but everywhere we went, we were reminded by others of how a girl should behave. Girls should be modest, pure, speak quietly and not laugh in front of men and the elders. They should not even drink water outside. A girl must obey her male relatives, even those younger than her. Everywhere we went – in the mosques, in the home, the street, in schools – this is what we were told by neighbours and imams and friends in the community.

The message from the radio, TV, education, literature, poems and songs, was that women were not equal to men. The Shah, in a TV interview, admitted that he thought women were less intelligent than men.

The September after I turned five or thereabouts, I began school. The usual starting age was six, but my father said he sent me off at around five as he wanted me to be 'the youngest and the toughest in the class'. I was excited and proud. I was the first member of my family who was going to receive an education; my parents were both illiterate. I promised myself I would teach them everything I learned. My classroom was rectangular with two windows on one wall. On my first day, I noticed two long green sticks balanced on one of the window ledges. I couldn't stop looking at them. What were those for?

Our teacher, Miss Nastaran, was tall and dressed in a stylish modern skirt and top with high heels. Her hair was piled up on her head.

She started to talk to the class in Farsi, the official language of Iran. This took me and my classmates by surprise. We only spoke Kurdish at home. When we replied in Kurdish, we quickly found out what the sticks were for. Miss Nastaran took them off the window ledge and started to beat us.

'This is the last time you speak Kurdish,' Miss Nastaran said, continuing to strike us on the palms of our hands and also on our legs. It was so terrifying that a couple of my classmates wet themselves.

I had had no idea until this moment that there was anything wrong with speaking Kurdish in public. Although my classmates and I couldn't speak Farsi, we could all understand enough to get the gist of what she was saying. My father used to listen to Radio Iran and BBC News in Farsi all the time. Many people in Kurdistan spoke both languages.

On my second day, I walked to school with my mother, but as soon as she left and the other children went inside, I ran to hide with two friends behind the mosque. We were frightened of being hit again. We did this for five or six days until the school sent a letter home to my parents. As they could not read, they went to the school to find out what this was all about. They found us three girls sitting in the dirt behind the mosque.

'Galavezh! Why are you here?' my father asked. I burst out crying and explained what had happened.

'I will do everything to ensure that you can study,' he said. 'Nothing will stop you from going to school. Understood? You must go to school and no more hiding.'

I nodded my head while I cleaned my tears with the blouse sleeve of my white school uniform.

My father immediately went to speak to the teacher to put a stop to the violence. As he had not had the opportunity to go to school himself, my education was of the utmost importance to him. There were no more beatings from the teacher, but if we were late for school, the deputy head would strike us with a ruler. She used the side edge to make it especially painful. I made sure that I was not late very often.

My father was the eldest of four children. His parents had died when he was a teenager and so he had looked after his two brothers and sister from when they were young.

After running his bakery successfully for a number of years,

Abdulkarim went into business with his brothers, Ali and Mohamed, and they set up a grocery and grain store in Saqqez. The store had so much success initially that my father closed his bakery and the brothers expanded the business into a wholesale market in Karvansara, the main market in the centre of Saqqez. It was in a good position, as traders travelled from all over the region to reach this grain market.

After a couple of years of running the business together, Mohamed fell out with my father and Ali over money. My father accused him of wanting to take over the business. This is exactly what happened in the end, as Ali and Abdulkarim left the business entirely. Ali opened a bakery in Saqqez, but the row had been so bad that my father decided to start a new life in the small city of Baneh, where there was no sangak bakery. Baneh was close to the border of Iraq, and surrounded by mountains.

Nowadays, you can get from Saqqez to Baneh in twenty minutes through a tunnel that has been cut through the mountains, but in the late 1960s we had to take the beautiful and scary winding mountain roads going through deep valleys and over high peaks, through villages and across rivers. My father rented a jeep taxi. It was winter time and there was thick snow everywhere. The journey took us around four hours. Asad rode up front with my father and the driver. There was an oil heater lit in the back to keep me, Shaesta, my grandmother and my mother warm as we snuggled together under blankets.

At one point the snow was so thick that we couldn't move for an hour. We had to sit in the freezing cold until a huge snowplough arrived to clear it. There were only a few other vehicles on the road. In one car, I noticed a boy aged about eight, who looked as though he was also moving with his family to Baneh. We exchanged smiles for a brief moment with no inkling of what we might mean to each other one day.

Chapter 3

Where is God?

After living the first six years of my life in a bustling trading centre, it felt strange to be in a small city surrounded by farms, with cows and lambs walking in the streets. To the west of Baneh there is a huge mountain called Arbaba that overlooks the whole city. It has one tree on the top, which can be seen on clear days all the way from where we lived. A belt of vineyards runs around the lower slopes of the mountain.

For the first few days we stayed with a family we knew while my father looked for a room and a kitchen so that he could set up another sangak bakery. We rented a home and the business quickly became a success. We settled into our new life. During the winter the snow was so thick my siblings and I could safely jump from the third floor of our building into the soft blanket on the top of the snow hill below us. We used plastic bags in place of sledges to slide down the slopes. During the hot summers, after having breakfast and helping Mum with the house-hold tasks, we ran out to play hopscotch or with a rope and ball with our friends. We were never indoors.

In the February after our move, I started at the school in Baneh. My father bought me a lovely thick winter coat. It had a check design in red and grey and black. It was the best coat in the whole school. How I loved that coat! Knowing that my father valued me gave me great confidence. I made many friends, worked hard and became one of the best students in my class. After I had been at school for a year or two, I taught my father how to count and how to write his name. I began to help him with the bakery accounts. I got even better at literature and maths because I was helping my father with his work.

My mother, who never learned to read, saw the Arabic alphabet in pictures. She tried to help me remember the letters by telling me what they looked like, so N – ن – would be a bowl; L – ل – was like an upside down walking stick.

When Shaesta started school, she was more hard-working than me. She was also quieter and better behaved. Sometimes I paid her to do my homework.

In school, I noticed that the girls' behaviour was being policed by the teachers and even other students in a way that the boys' behaviour was not. If a girl laughed loudly, the teachers would say: 'Be quiet! Girls should not laugh in such a manner.'

Although we spoke only Farsi in school, at home and in the playground we would speak in Kurdish. As a child, it was not difficult to learn both languages. We got used to switching between the two. However, the experience of not being able to speak my own language in school made me start to question authority. Why was it wrong to speak Kurdish? Did this mean the Kurdish language and its people were not good? I knew this wasn't true and nobody could explain why it had to be forbidden. Why were Kurdish people being treated differently? There was something deeply unfair about these rules.

Around this time a number of incidents led to my questioning the existence of God. My classmate Kolsum's mother died, and I felt so sorry for her. She had nothing to eat at home and she used to take food from the school to give to her siblings. My family had fresh bread every day and I would cry to my mum: 'This poor girl has only food from school to take home for the children.'

I sometimes took bread to Kolsum, and my mum used to give me potatoes or eggs for her. I would smuggle them in and give them to her in secret so that the other children wouldn't see. I didn't want to embarrass her.

We lived next door to a rich family with a huge home, but our neighbours on the other side were so poor they had to go door-to-door asking for something to eat. My family lay somewhere in the middle due to my father's profession as a baker. How could one family have so much while another went without? I couldn't understand it. I started to talk to others about this, but all they would say was: 'It's God will; he tests his people. The more they suffer, the more likely they are to go to heaven.'

'God wants children to pray,' my grandmother told me. 'God will listen to children, as children are clean from sin.'

If I prayed five times a day and covered my head with a chador, God would protect Kolsum's family and provide for them, she told me. I covered myself for fifteen days. I prayed for my friend's family to have enough food and for all of the buildings to be the same height, for everyone to be happy and safe, and for there to be no more poverty. To my disappointment, nothing changed.

When I was seven or eight, Mostafa, the son of our neighbour Mama Amena, was arrested. Mama Amena was the local midwife and was well-known and loved. She had helped to deliver everyone's babies. Mostafa was a Peshmerga, a Kurdish freedom fighter. Kurdish Peshmerga are now famed around the world for fighting ISIS, but at this time they were just beginning as guerrilla forces in Iran.

In previous years, any Iranian Kurds who wished to become Peshmerga had had to go over the border to Kurdistan in Iraq to join one of the different groups fighting against the Iraqi regime. We knew about them in Saqqez. Iraqi Peshmerga would come over the border from time to time; however, in these early years in Iran, not many people wanted to join them. The Peshmerga carried with them an aura of death. The name is Kurdish for 'one who sacrifices his life for others'. As a child, I expected anyone who joined the Peshmerga to die shortly after.

Mostafa was a Peshmerga for the underground Democrat Party, one of the many opposition groups that had started up in protest against the Shah's regime. They wanted autonomy for the Kurdish region.

The old Shah, Reza Shah Pahlavi, had been forced to abdicate in 1941 by the invading British forces. His son, Mohammad Reza Shah, had replaced him on the throne. Thirty years later, and the son was hated by many people across Iran for his repression of his opponents. The prisons were full of those who had dared to speak out against him. People often simply disappeared. SAVAK, the Shah's feared secret police, had been given tremendous power and would arrest people for the slightest provocation. If someone criticised school food, they would be considered a political activist. There was no freedom of expression or freedom to protest. Anyone thought to be part of an opposition movement could be arrested. This included any Peshmerga. Stories of the torture in SAVAK prisons leaked out, tales of whippings with copper wires and branding with hot wires. The execution of political activists became more and more frequent.

Mostafa had paid a secret visit to his family with a friend and the authorities had found out. He was known by the regime to be a Peshmerga. Both the son and friend were arrested and taken to a garrison not far from the town. We could see from our rooftops that there were people moving in the base, but we couldn't make out what was happening. Mama Amena cried all day long asking God to intervene.

Several days later we heard gunshots.

'Please God let these boys be alive!' I shouted.

Our prayers did not save them. The boys had been executed following a military trial, my father explained. I was devastated.

The day after the execution, I said to my teacher, Mullah Mohamed, 'I heard that God can change everything but nothing changes. What is God?'

'Shut your mouth!' the mullah said, with a startled expression. 'Never ask this again!'

The next day, two men with black suits came and interrogated me at the school.

'Who taught you to ask such questions?' they demanded.

'Nobody told me,' I replied, honestly. 'I see all these problems all around us, yet nothing changes when we pray to God.'

Shortly after, the men arrested my father. He was questioned for several hours at the base for the secret police. When he was released, my father told me the men were from SAVAK.

'Don't ask such questions again,' he warned me. 'Every wall has a hole and inside the hole there is a mouse listening.'

From the moment of the boys' executions, I didn't believe in God any more. However, I thought that if I said it out loud, some catastrophe, such as a flood or earthquake, would befall my family and community, so I kept my thoughts to myself. Instead, I used to practise saying it in my mind: There is no God . . . There is no God.

When I was about nine, I decided I needed to break my fear of hell. For a long time I had been saying, There is no God to myself. God was supposed to be all powerful and able to read my thoughts, yet nothing had happened to me, my family or my neighbours. What difference would it make if I were to say this out loud? One night, in bed with my grandmother and sister, I decided to find out.

'There is no God,' I said.

There was no response from God, but my grandmother reacted like a volcano. She ran from the room screaming: 'Disaster is upon us!'

Coming back to our bedroom, she started to read the Koran rapidly, while blowing over my face.

'You are possessed by evil spirits who are making you say bad things,' she said. 'If anyone had said such things when I was a girl they would have been beaten black and blue to get rid of the spirits.'

Malika was getting angrier and angrier. 'You shouldn't have stopped praying; this is why this is happening to you.'

It was difficult for me to stop myself from laughing at her hysterical reaction. My father and mother came to see what all the fuss was about.

'What happened? Why are you so angry and upset?' my father asked. My mother was too stunned to speak.

'Galavezh has questioned the existence of God; she is a disbeliever, and we have to do something urgently!' cried my grandmother.

My dad turned his head to me, waiting for my response.

'Grandma, I have tried hard but I don't believe there is a God,' I muttered.

My father said, calmly, 'Let's just talk about this tomorrow.'

I think my grandmother thought that my father was bewitched as well. My sister was so scared of my grandmother's reaction that she remained lying down in shocked silence while my mother cried: 'Oh my God! Oh my God! God forgive her. She is young and naïve; she has been brainwashed by someone.'

'It's OK,' my father said, giving me a hug and leading my mother out of the room.

The next day, my father asked me how I had come to this conclusion. I told him I had been saying, There is no God in my mind for quite some time, yet nothing bad had happened to us. I had prayed, yet nothing had changed. The world was so unfair and yet God did nothing.

'If God can see everything and everyone,' I asked him, 'why does he tolerate all of this injustice and discrimination?'

'Galavezh, my dear daughter, it is fine to think such things but please keep these thoughts to yourself,' my father said.

I'm sure my father did not believe in God either, but he did not want to admit this to me due to the danger this might place the family in. Although the Shah wanted a separation of the state and religion, the main religion of the country was Shi'a Islam and the Shah had a good relationship with some of the Shi'a mullahs and imams. Although he expelled some religious leaders who spoke against him, he wanted to keep others on side and he allowed them to continue their activities. In fact, those who questioned religion were seen as a threat to the government. The Shah's secret police would link anyone who was not openly religious to communist and leftist organisations and this could lead to imprisonment.

During Ramadan, my mother would fast and pray but my father didn't. One year during Ramadan, my father was in the bakery drinking water when a customer asked him: 'Why are you not fasting, baker?'

'That's easy for you to say, but God created me to be a baker, working in front of this burning hot oven on this boiling summer day, and I am expected to not drink water,' my father replied angrily. 'Do you want me to be thankful for this?'

One year my father bought a cow to sacrifice for Eid so that he could offer the meat to the neighbourhood. I watched as the men painted the cow's face with make up and put a tiara on her head so that she looked like a bride, as was the custom. I was too frightened to watch her being sacrificed in the Muslim way, with her throat being slit, but I could hear the horrible sound, like a baby crying.

'I will never forget the way that cow looked at us,' my father later said. He never made such a sacrifice again.

Following this revelation that God did not exist, I knew that I must search for meaning in this life and not in the heavens. I continued to question everything. Muslims are expected to be charitable to the poor, but I felt that this in some way justified extreme poverty. I began to understand that poverty was rooted in the capitalist system and religion was a way of making people accept this. We are conditioned to believe that we are created as God intended and that we will be rewarded in Paradise. Religion asks us to tolerate the intolerable, instead of protesting against the authorities to demand what we need in order to live. It became clear to me that the idea that we must put up with all manner of indignities with the promise of a better afterlife was created entirely for the benefit of men and the wealthy. It was not for women. It was not for the poor.

I had shocked my grandmother by shouting my thoughts out loud, but I felt free for the first time in my life. A great burden lifted from my shoulders.

Chapter 4

Political Awakening

My first crush was on a boy who lived in a house on the top of a hill about 200 metres from my home in Baneh. I never saw the boy outside his home but I would catch glimpses of him from the windows. I believed that I was in love with him. I spent a lot of time trying to find him in the shadows.

One winter day, when the water was frozen and the only working pipe was down the hill in between our two houses, I was sent to collect water with a large jug. The boy must have been watching out for me as he jumped down from a window on the first floor. He handed me a letter before walking quickly back inside the house.

I started to shake. My mother and the guests at my home had witnessed the boy giving me the letter. When I arrived home, they called me over before I had a chance to put the jug down.

'Galavezh! What does it say?' they demanded.

'What are you talking about?' I said quietly, setting the jug down on the floor.

I couldn't breathe. My throat was dry as I looked down at the missive written in Farsi. I could see that the boy was declaring his love for me. As my parents and their guests couldn't read Farsi, I made a show of reading the letter, but I changed the words and said that he was asking me how I was. Even so, they all started shouting at me for taking the letter, saying this boy was Persian and I should have nothing to do with him.

'He is not even Kurdish! You will bring shame and dishonour on the family,' one said. 'You should have thrown the letter in his face.'

This was the end of my first love story.

I didn't know much about love, or about growing up and the changes that hormones would bring about in me. I was unaware that my emotional needs would be transformed along with my body.

One day when I was in secondary school, I had the sensation that I had wet myself. Embarrassed, I quietly looked down on the floor, but I couldn't see anything. What on earth had happened? I was scared and didn't move from my bench at the end of the school day.

My friends asked me why I was sitting so still. As they gathered around me, I confessed that I had wet myself. They asked me to stand up. As I slowly did so, they noticed that my dress was all bloody.

'It's your period,' one said, as they all rushed to help me. We went to the toilets and washed my tights and dress. They couldn't explain exactly why this was happening, but they tried to assure me that this happened to all women.

When I got home, I told my mother I had been bleeding. She swooned with horror and started to pray, saying: 'Which boy did this to you?'

I began to panic, thinking this must mean that I had lost my virginity. Amina's wedding day was always at the back of my mind. I tried to remember which boy had looked at me on the journey to school. Which one had taken my virginity without me knowing?

Fortunately, my grandmother stepped in.

'What are you thinking, Fatem?' she muttered. 'She has started her period. That is all.'

My mother was too worried about me bringing dishonour on the family to explain what this all meant. Without going into detail as to why, my grandmother told me that this would happen every month. She gave me folded material to use to line my underwear. This was a few years before disposable pads were introduced. She also brought a mattress and laid it on the floor near to the heater. She told me to rest and covered me with a heavy duvet. She cooked a sweet meal with dates and egg. I was extremely grateful for having my grandmother take care of me. My body was so tired and needed this rest. A little while later, my mother came and gave me a hug and some advice on what I would need to do every month.

I was to finish high school around the age of fourteen and had to decide what to do with my life. Above all, I wanted to support my father and family financially.

The Shah's attempts to modernise the country had led to an expansion of education and the country needed more teachers. To deal with Iran's high illiteracy rates, a new curriculum was introduced in schools and adult education classes were starting up around the country. The government announced that it would pay students a good salary to train as teachers. This was a great opportunity for me.

I decided I would try to win a teacher training place in a boarding school in one of the biggest cities in Kurdistan, several hours away from my home. I would be able to help my community and give most of the 500 toman training salary to my family. My parents also thought this was a good plan for me.

I had to send my application before the end of the school year and sit a test at the beginning of summer. On a sweltering hot day, my father accompanied me to the school by bus with several other girls and their families in order to take the entrance test. We stopped on the way to have a tasty lunch of chicken kebab and rice in a traditional restaurant.

I was successful and the offer of a place at the teacher training school marked a huge change in my life. From being a daddy's girl, I would now be without my parents and live an independent life with girls my own age, supervised only by school staff.

Eleven other girls from Baneh, including my friends Sadat and Pari, set off for the school at the same time as me. It was an early morning in September. My mother invited all of our neighbours over to see us off. She and her friend held Korans above our heads and we had to walk under them to be blessed. As the bus pulled out, the women threw water after it for 'good luck'. My mother and her friends began wailing as though somebody had died, which I found both hilarious and upsetting. Although I loved my parents dearly, I was too excited to be sad at leaving them. Sadat's mother had died a few years before, and, as it was her duty to take care of the housework and her five sisters before her father remarried, getting away from home meant real freedom for her. We cheered as the bus pulled out to take us to our new lives.

The primary teachers' training school stood within an enormous compound in the north of the city, surrounded by walls about five metres tall and topped with barbed wire. It had more the air of a prison than a school. Inside, however, it was modern and beautiful. There were several large buildings and lots of greenery.

On arrival, we were taken by a group of second year students to a huge room, rather like a military dormitory, with eighty bunk beds. We were hungry after the journey, so we quickly left our belongings and made our way to the self-service canteen. On the way, Sadat and I and the other girls from Baneh laughed and jumped in the air. It was like a dream. We all felt so grown up and independent. We were going to be teachers!

In the canteen, we were served Istanbuli polo, a traditional Iranian meal of rice and cubed potatoes with meat and green beans. We took our food and tried to find somewhere to sit. There were two enormous rows of tables and chairs, enough to seat what seemed like 300 girls, but the canteen was crowded and we couldn't find enough space for twelve to sit together. Some older students were finishing up and called us to take their seats.

It was so noisy in the canteen we could hardly hear anybody speak except for one voice screaming. The voice got louder and louder until eventually the whole canteen was silenced. I tried to see what was happening but I couldn't make it out at first.

Eventually, I saw a short, thin woman walking along my row

yelling and swearing.

Somebody must have done something wrong and she is angry, but who is she? I was thinking, when to my surprise I found her in front of me.

The woman had cropped black hair and big eyes with lots of make up. She was wearing a black skirt and high heels. She appeared to be shouting at me but I couldn't understand why, so I assumed she was talking to someone else.

'You slut,' she said. I looked around and saw that everybody was bent over their plates, trying not to catch the angry lady's eyes. It seemed as though everyone was holding their breath.

'Are you talking to me?' I said.

'Shut up, you slut!' she replied.

I wondered what I should do. I hadn't done anything wrong, yet I felt ashamed and could feel myself blushing. I thought that if I accepted what she was saying I would have to keep my head bent down forever at this school, but if I shouted back they could have me sacked. I would lose my chance to be a teacher.

Ah, I don't care if they sack me; my family love me, I thought. I picked up my plate and slammed it back down on the table, spilling the food.

Immediately, the silence was broken. All the girls in the room started to bang their forks and spoons on the plates. It was so noisy. Everyone was screaming. The woman ran from the room with two guards following her to her office on the ground floor.

I was still in shock when students from other cities came over to our table.

'Hi, I'm Alia from Ilam!'

'I'm Fariba from Kermanshah. Where are you from?'

'We are from Baneh,' I replied.

'I guessed so,' said Fariba.

'Who was that angry lady?' I asked.

'She is Miss Azari.'

'Why was she so angry with me when she has never met me before?'

GIRL WITH A GUN

'This is just how she behaves, especially with new arrivals. Are you a member of the Mojahedin?' This was an Islamist political opposition group. Their full name was Mojahedin e Khalq or the People's Mojahedin of Iran.

'I'm not religious,' I replied.

'Of course not. Are you a communist?'

'No, I don't know what that is.'

'Then which party do you belong to?'

'I don't belong to any party.'

'Mm, you are hiding which party you belong to as it's obvious you are a socialist,' one said. 'How brave, standing up to her like that on your first day here.'

I understood for the first time that I was not alone in my questioning of authority, of religion and the state. It was an exhilarating feeling.

Sensing a kindred spirit, the girls crowded around me and started to talk about politics and the Shah's regime. This was 1976 and the seeds of the Iranian Revolution were already in the air throughout the country. The school was no exception.

The girls talked about how fed up they were with the widespread poverty, repression and the secret police. We were living in an atmosphere of complete political suffocation.

'This capitalist regime does not look after the Iranian people,' Fariba said. 'Instead they arrest us and kill us.'

One girl told us she had a boyfriend who was in prison because of his political activities. Another said that her brother and sister-in-law had been executed because they were members of a political party.

Fariba informed me that Miss Azari was the deputy head and she was openly working for SAVAK. She was the only teacher to live on the premises and she was always accompanied by two guards.

'Galavezh, you must be careful when speaking to her,' she warned. The other teachers at the school were mostly left wing but could not speak about this publicly because of Miss Azari's support of the Shah. Some of the teachers had brothers or sisters who had been imprisoned or executed.

The day after the plate banging incident, Miss Azari called me to her room. She looked a little embarrassed about the previous day's scene but nonetheless she attempted to frighten me.

'Galavezh, I have a huge organisation behind me. You cannot go against the system.'

'Whatever system this is, I don't care about it,' I responded, looking her straight in the eyes. 'We have our system too and you have to treat us with respect.'

Over the following weeks, we settled into the school, meeting our lecturers, the head of the school, who seemed kind and approachable, and some of the other staff. We quickly got used to the timetable. We were allowed to go out for just a few hours with friends on Thursday afternoons, which was also the day our parents could visit us.

One day, Miss Azari asked me to go to her office. She told me that we Baneh girls must move into separate bedrooms with just three of us in each one, together with nine other girls we didn't know. She feared that my group of twelve troublemakers was going to work with other political activists and influence all the other girls in our eighty bed dorm. Thankfully, Sadat was in my room.

The other girls in my dormitory turned out to also be rebellious, apart from a few led by a student called Fatima. Everyone in the school wore modern style clothes, but Fatima and her group chose to wear a full-body chador and hijab. Her body was covered from head-to-toe with black material. We could only see her hands and face. We assumed she belonged to the Mojahedin and was part of the Islamic movement. I later learned that this was just her disguise. She was working with SAVAK through Miss Azari. She was there to spy on us. She always looked at us with hatred in her eyes.

Our group grew bigger and bigger. Fariba was a clever girl with lots of ideas, and she invited five of my friends to set up several secret societies. Each society would have five or fewer people.

It was important to keep the numbers small in case anyone was arrested and might be forced to give up their comrades' names under torture. The plan was to organise activities such as bringing in banned books for us to read in a kind of book club and connecting with other activists outside the school.

Some of the students had links to other colleges and universities and would smuggle in fliers and forbidden books, such as Sadegh Hedayat's The Blind Owl, Maxim Gorky's The Mother, which is about revolutionary factory workers, and Samad Behrangi books such as One Peach, A Thousand Peaches. Behrangi used folk tales to avoid censorship. One of my favourites was his children's book, The Little Black Fish. It is a political allegory about a black fish that, against the warnings of his mother and the threats of his elders, leaves his stream and makes it out to the open sea. We also read Marx, Engels and other philosophers, along with books about the Russian Revolution and the Paris Commune of 1871. We had to be vigilant when smuggling in such books because of our spy.

Fatima would surprise us by coming silently into the room and immediately looking under the bed. We always had to be on the alert and ready to move everything to another room. We put books in holes in the walls and constantly changed our meeting rooms. We knew that if Fatima found anything and reported us, we would have been arrested by SAVAK. We could have been imprisoned or even executed. Nevertheless undeterred, we held our meetings and would sing along to guitars, plotting our own revolution. Many times Miss Azari herself visited our rooms unannounced with her guards. She would ask us to leave the room and leave the cupboards unlocked, so they could search our personal belongings and under beds for any papers, books and letters. She was desperate to find evidence against us and we knew it.

Every morning at 5 a.m., the whole school was woken up and we were made to listen to the national anthem and do exercises. The secret society decided that 5 a.m. was far too early. Inspired by our political heroes, such as the socialists and communists who had been imprisoned for their beliefs, we decided we would go on a hunger strike.

We carefully wrote out our demands:

One extra hour in bed.

Exercise to be voluntary.

Searches of our cupboards to stop.

The school to provide clothes for those wishing to exercise.

The last demand was a nod to equality. Exercise clothes were expensive and some of the girls couldn't afford to buy them.

Our hunger strike did not quite go to plan. On the first day, we managed to avoid eating any food but we did drink water. On the second day, our will was failing us rapidly and we gave money to some other students to get food from outside. On the third day, we went secretly to the kitchen to get supplies when no one else was there, but we were seen by a member of the kitchen staff, who informed Miss Azari.

Furious, she called the strikers into her office.

'I know about your hunger strike and that it is not working because you are taking food from the kitchen,' she sneered. 'I have looked carefully at your requests. I will accept your request to wake up at six a.m. and for exercise to be optional, but that is all.'

A partial victory.

The secret society's next project was to write slogans in red onto the grey walls. The school would wake to find 'Iranian oil is cheaper than French water' or 'The Shah must go'.

Since oil had been discovered in Iran, foreign powers had exploited our successive weak governments into allowing foreign companies, chief among them the Anglo Persian Oil Company, to control oil extraction. This had not changed under Reza Shah Pahlavi and his son, Mohammad Reza Shah. Our great natural resource was sold to the West to enrich our rulers while the Iranian people died from cold in the winter.

Fed up with this abuse of our national wealth, the politician Mohammad Mosaddegh had begun a popular political move-ment in the 1940s that had led to the nationalisation of oil by parliament in 1951. Mosaddegh was elected as prime minister shortly after and, during his time in office, the Shah had only nominal power.

The British wouldn't stand for the loss of their oil profits. Sanctions were imposed on Iran by the United Nations, which nearly crippled the country. In August 1953, Mosaddegh was overthrown by a military coup orchestrated by the CIA and British intelligence services, and the National Iranian Oil Company was founded as an international consortium.

The Shah, who had fled to Italy for several months while Mosaddegh was in power, returned to Iran and continued to sell oil abroad to line his own pockets. He lived as an international millionaire while his people starved. In the 1970s, oil remained a huge issue throughout the country as the gap between rich and poor widened ever further.

The day after a slogan appeared, Miss Azari would ask everyone to help to clean it up. After scrubbing off the red, the grey came off too, leaving the slogans in white underneath.

The whole school began to talk about the slogans. Everyone was excited. Some of the teachers even brought them up in class and wanted to discuss the issues they raised, but my group made out that we didn't know anything about them.

Miss Azari asked everyone to go to the main yard.

'I know we have some troublemakers in the school who want to create a riot, but I will identify them one by one and they will face the system,' she warned.

We just laughed at her threat and went for lunch. When we returned to our afternoon class, I noticed Masti, one of my classmates who was newly married, sitting laughing in a corner at the end of the room. We all gathered excitedly around to ask her about her wedding and what her wedding night had been like. Although my friends and I felt that we knew a lot about worldly affairs, on the subject of love and marriage we were complete novices.

'It's like hammering a nail,' Masti told us, leaving me none the wiser. We were all laughing but deep down I felt terrified.

During the school year, we went home a few times and our

families also visited us. One day, Sadat had a visitor at the school. It was her father's younger brother, Abdullah, who had just been released from prison. He had been incarcerated for three years, accused of being an opponent of the Shah. Sadat's family were wealthy landowners in Baneh, and owned a whole village. Although I had spent many nights at Sadat's home in Baneh and was close to her family, I had not been that aware of Abdullah when I was growing up.

Abdullah was twenty-six but he seemed much more worldly wise than that. He dressed in dark grey Kurdish trousers and a light grey shirt. He was not so tall and not that handsome, but he was incredibly charming, calm and confident. I was attracted to him immediately.

Sadat's grandfather had two wives, one of whom was Sadat's aunt, her mother's younger sister. This meant that the older sister had married the son, while the younger sister had married the father! They were a big family. About sixty relatives lived together in a huge house. It was one of the biggest in the city and had four floors. There were always dozens of children running around the house. It was many months into my friendship with Sadat before I worked out who was married to whom, and how people were related.

Abdullah was a high ranking member of the underground left-wing Working People's Organisation, set up by a group of Kurdish revolutionaries, intellectuals and students studying in Tehran. This would go on to become the political party Komala, one of the main opposition parties in Kurdistan. Abdullah was a military commander in the Working People's Organisation's Peshmerga. He had been the first person from Baneh to do military training overseas before coming back to Baneh to train others.

More Kurdish people were joining up to be Peshmerga in Iran. There were different Peshmerga groups allied with different organisations and parties. All Peshmerga groups had two key aims: to overthrow the Shah and to have basic human rights for Kurdish people, rights that had long been denied. Some Peshmerga, although not all, also wanted a separate state of Kurdistan. Divided between Iran, Iraq, Turkey and Syria, Kurdish people had never had their own homeland. Although they still had their aura of death, my opinion on the Peshmerga had changed since I was a child. I now felt that they were angels coming to save the Kurdish people.

In June 1978, I was due to sit my final exams after two years of teacher training. Miss Azari wanted to prevent the twenty girls from the secret societies from qualifying as teachers and she decided to ban us from doing the exam.

Fortunately, her plan was foiled by other teachers at the school. They said they would go on strike in support of us. They refused to let the other students take the exams without us. As this would have meant no qualified teachers for that year in our region, Miss Azari was forced to back down. Our rebellious actions were taken into consideration, however, and we were given the lowest marks possible for behaviour. Although we got good marks for all the other topics, this dragged down our averages.

I didn't let this bother me for long. I spent the summer with my family in Baneh, and met up with Sadat and Pari from time to time. My cousins came to visit me and we had a lovely summer. My mother was proud and my grandmother was so excited to have her grandchildren grown up and happy. 'A house without youth is dead,' she would say.

We were newly qualified teachers ready to unleash our knowledge on the world. Before we finished our teacher training, we had been offered jobs with the option to go to a village or stay in the city. I chose a village and, with Sadat and Pari, planned to move to Upper Boeen, about thirty minutes from Baneh, to become a primary school teacher. This would be the beginning of an idyllic couple of months of calm in the countryside before the storm of revolution engulfed the country.

Chapter 5

Village Life

Sadat, Pari and I needed to go to Upper Boeen to find a room for us to rent. Sadat's uncle Abdullah offered to give us a lift in his jeep. Sadat and Pari chattered to each other all the way there. We were all so happy.

On the journey, Abdullah and I talked about the Shah's regime, the possibility of a revolution succeeding and how poverty was killing people around the world. The revolution we dreamed of was a workers' revolution.

'Rights are not given, you have to take them by force,' I proclaimed.

'Revolution is the only way to gain rights,' Abdullah replied. 'The workers and farmers must come together. We need big changes to happen.'

Sadat, Pari and I moved to Upper Boeen in the middle of August 1978, a few weeks before the new school term. About seventy villagers, mainly men and a handful of women and children, came to greet us, led by the elderly mullah, who stood tall in his white turban. They were all curious to see the new teachers.

The mullah led us to our school, which comprised three rooms and a small corridor. Our classroom had two big windows and was flooded with sunshine. I was excited and hoped that I could make a real contribution to the community.

After a tasty lunch of chicken and rice with the villagers, we were taken to our new lodgings, a single room shared between us in the home of Amena, her farmer husband Abda and three daughters, aged sixteen, thirteen and seven. They also had an elder boy who was no longer at home.

'Our home is your home,' Amena smiled as she hugged us.

Amena was a strong character who was clearly in charge of the household and her husband. She took care of us like a mother. We liked our independence, however, and we got into the habit of cooking for ourselves on a tiny oil burner in our room. We made simple meals of rice, potatoes and chilli, usually with some stew. The rice would take an age to cook, so we had to try to remember to put it on early.

Amena's eldest daughter Masuma had never studied. Instead she did most of the housework. The younger daughters Mastura and Nasrin were in year five and year two at school. They spent most of their free time on the farm and cleaning out the waste from the cows and sheep. Despite this gruelling work, they always had lovely smiles on their faces. They would run to hug us when we came home.

At first it was mainly boys who enrolled in the school. Amena was unusual in sending her young daughters to school, but she believed in their education. Most of the villagers didn't want to educate their daughters. They thought school was a waste of time; the girls would soon be married and preoccupied with housework and farm work. Some villagers were worried that if their daughters learned to read and write, they would bring shame and dishonour to the family by writing letters to boys. It would open their eyes to the world. They didn't understand the value of education for a girl. Sadat, Pari and I spent several evenings going from house to house to persuade the parents to send their daughters to school.

Primary education had been made compulsory by the Shah for boys and girls, but not everyone was able to attend and the ruling was not enforced. Tuition fees were high, and families also had to find money to pay for books and other materials. None of this was provided by the government. In many cases, children themselves were the only breadwinners in a family.

'It is so important for women to learn to read and write,' I would tell the villagers. 'They will be able to understand more about all the changes that are happening in the country now. It will enable them to help their own children in the future.'

DIANA NAMMI AND KAREN ATTWOOD

The villagers were mostly illiterate, and because we were educated and came from the city, they gradually started to respect and trust us. By the end of the first month we had sixty boys and twelve girls in the school. This felt like an incredible achievement. I became the teacher for years three and four, while Pari taught years one and two and Sadat took year five. We shared the role of headmistress between us.

Although we talked to the children in Kurdish, we had to teach them in Farsi, as all of the exams would be in Farsi. We were also worried that if we taught in Kurdish, SAVAK spies might find out and we would be sacked. At the beginning, the children laughed when we spoke in Farsi but they got used to it quite quickly, just as I had when I was a little girl. However, we certainly didn't beat them if they spoke in Kurdish!

Our first few months in the village were filled with joy. Upper Boeen's 150 families produced wheat, onions, cucumbers and melons, which they would take to the city to sell. Their gardens were filled with apricot, walnut and apple trees. On sunny days, we would accompany the villagers into the mountains to gather wild mushrooms. We dressed as they did, in traditional dress.

The girls usually wore long dresses in the evening but wore pantol for work and their days in the mountains. Pantol are baggy trousers made with lots of material, narrow at the ankle, flowing around the legs and tied with a drawstring at the waist. They are really comfortable. It was impossible to work in a long, wide dress.

The boys and girls sang traditional songs as we walked. We had to be careful of snakes, as the mushrooms would be in the middle of lots of greenery. Some of the mushrooms we found were as big as a coffee table and half of the village would share one between them, fried, or grilled on a fire in the mountain. I have never since found any mushrooms that taste as good as these.

The boys would often make jokes at our expense.

'We would be happy to exchange our girls for you if your father would like another wife,' one said.

'This is not possible,' I laughed. 'We don't believe in exchanging wives and certainly not polygamy!'

We treated this as a joke so as not to offend, but bride exchanges were common in the countryside and the girls would have little say in the matter. It was a way of avoiding paying a dowry. If a family had no money, they could instead exchange one girl in their family for a girl from another family. Child marriage, although it still existed in the cities, was far more common in the countryside.

The villagers would sometimes find husbands for their daughters when they were only nine, or in some cases, a girl would be promised as soon as she was born. The girls could then be forced to marry someone they didn't care for and this could lead to fights between families. Girls always went to the home of her husband's family after marriage. If a marriage from a bride exchange didn't work out and one wife returned home, the other marriage would also be automatically ended.

Sadat, Pari and I decided to speak to the villagers about early marriages to try and persuade them that it was not a good idea until a girl was at least sixteen.

'But what can we do?' one father told me. 'We cannot afford to feed all of the family. This is one less mouth to feed.'

Hearing this was heartbreaking. Talking to the villagers made me realise that it was a lack of education and wealth that determined a girl's life chances. Poverty was suffocating.

We sometimes joined the girls when they went, without the boys, to collect water from the fountain in the middle of the village. This was their time to be free together, to laugh and chat and put on make up. They applied white powder on their sun-kissed faces and kohl round the eyes. They seemed so innocent to me.

During the long days of late summer and early autumn they would linger, splashing in the water. We would gossip with them about who they had feelings for. At first they were shy, but gradually they opened up to us.

'Promise me you will wait until you are sixteen to get married,' I always implored.

Along with our school activities, we also started education

classes for adults, in particular for the women. Word spread and people from the nearby villages started coming to our classes.

One day we invited all of the women to come to the main room of the mosque to discuss women's rights. Initially there were objections from the mullah, who insisted that women were unclean and could not go in there. After a few days debating, the women overruled him by the sheer strength of their determination. Their husbands accepted that allowing them in the mosque would probably not lead to anything bad happening.

We worked hard with the villagers to try and solve some of their problems. We also helped them by giving out painkillers for aches and pains from our supply from the city. The villagers accepted us as their daughters and felt that we were there for them. They told us we were the best teachers they had ever had.

When we first arrived, one side of the village would not talk to the other because they were arguing about access to water. After talking to families from both sides, we wrote out a schedule dividing the week into days when each side could access the water. I realised that this kind of problem needed a village council. We got the idea from Abdullah, who had studied many books about the Russian Revolution and different socialist systems.

Traditionally the landlords and the mullah made all of the decisions on behalf of the village. We knew that a council made up of men and women, including representatives for the farmers, would be more effective. Bringing the community together to discuss the water issue openly had been a success. We wanted to capitalise on that. The mullah and the landlords were resistant to the idea of a council until Amena put herself forward. Amena was respected in the village and her brother-in-law, one of the most powerful people in the village, gave her his support. The idea started to take hold but it took many more months of discussions to get off the ground. Amena persuaded other women to join and the council was formed by the villagers nominating each other. Although the mullah had been against the council, he joined in from the first meeting. He didn't want any important decisions to be made without his input.

The council became an effective way of solving problems, such as scheduling farm work. If one farm didn't have enough boys to help at harvest, the council could sort this out. The villagers quickly learned that it was beneficial for everyone. People even began to plan weddings at the meetings. The word spread to other villages and our council generously advised them.

Sadat, Pari and I didn't have our own car, but the village had two Land Rovers. This is what we would usually use for transport. On Thursdays, we would get a lift home in the Land Rover taxi to visit our families for the weekend. The driver was an amusing man who loved women. He would entertain us with stories on our journey. However, after a few weeks we got into the habit of getting a lift home with Sadat's uncle Abdullah and we began spending more and more time together.

From time to time, Abdullah would take us all to see other towns in Iran. We would drive up the winding roads into the mountains and look down on the tiny homes below us. We could see the smoke coming from the roofs, where villagers were baking bread and cooking food. All we could hear was the gentle braying of animals. Abdullah rarely spoke about his time in prison. Everyone knew that prisoners were tortured by special guards who were trained to be harsh without mercy. They wanted to force the prisoners to confess. I could not imagine what he had gone through, and I didn't feel comfortable asking him about it. I didn't want to remind him of his suffering.

Just once he told me it had been unbearable.

One day, Sadat suddenly told me that Abdullah loved me. I was embarrassed. I didn't want to discuss my feelings with her. However, I did eventually admit to her that Abdullah was the only man who had captured my mind. Abdullah and I saw each other every weekend during these months but we never spoke directly about our feelings. He was not a talkative man, but I enjoyed being in his calm presence. We never touched one another other than to shake hands, but we both knew how the other felt. I was elated whenever I saw him.

We didn't want to make our families too conscious of our growing feelings for each other, so we never stayed too long in a different town, just enough time to have lunch or dinner with Sadat and Pari.

Sadat, Pari and I knew that we were coming to the marriageable age. Soon we would have to think about that, but in those first few months in Upper Boeen I didn't have a care in the world.

However, while we were living our countryside idyll, demonstrations were building up throughout Iran. The outside world would soon invade our sanctuary. Our future was about to be snatched from our hands.

Chapter 6

Revolution

In order to appease growing discontent across the country, the Shah had implemented reforms from the early 1960s, which he called his White Revolution. This so-called revolution was supposed to transform the country without violence, and the education that I had benefitted from had been one of its pillars. Land reforms were another important part of this modernisation effort. The Shah wanted to divide land between farmers and the landlords and give some power to the farmers. This was really a way of him wresting power from the landlords, who did not always support him. In some areas, the landlords were forced to sell land to the rich cronies of the Shah. Their workers lost their jobs. These former agricultural workers were among those flooding into the cities to find employment in the burgeoning industries of Tehran and Shiraz in the 1970s.

However, the cities in Kurdistan were completely ignored in terms of development, new factories and job opportunities. The regime clearly wanted to keep Kurdish people in poverty. Although Baneh had two main roads made of asphalt, the road to Upper Boeen was just a dirt track, as in almost all Kurdish villages.

Across the country, the Shah's reforms came too late. The prisons were overflowing with political prisoners. The people would be silent no more.

Opposition groups had grown in strength. We began to hear more stories about the Fedai Guerrillas, a secular left-wing organisation, and the Mojahedin e Khalq, the Islamic group that had been fighting with the army in other parts of Iran. The workers in the newly industrialised cities organised themselves into underground groups, which were full of socialist and communist members. They demanded better wages and conditions. In the countryside, farmers were tired of being treated like slaves by the landowners.

This was also the time of the hippy, in Iran as much as the rest of the world. The young people who travelled from Upper Boeen and other villages into the cities to work in the new factories came back with long hair, flowing outfits, flared trousers and bold ideas. They would climb onto the roofs in front of the mosque and play loud music and tell stories about big, beautiful cities with huge buildings and factories.

Whereas before ordinary people had been terrified to speak out for fear the secret police were listening, it became commonplace for men or women to openly criticise the regime in the street. This led to gatherings, led by student groups and workers' unions, which turned into demonstrations, which grew bigger and bigger. School pupils were often in the front line of these demonstrations.

All the time we listened to the news. It came through the loudspeakers at the mosque. People would stop what they were doing and gather to listen together. As well as Iranian radio, we listened to the BBC and to US, Israeli and Albanian stations, which all broadcast in Farsi. Different countries reported different incidents. We could put reports together to form a picture of what was happening around the country. We also received newsletters from the various political groups which were growing in numbers throughout the country.

In September 1978, we heard that hundreds of workers in Tehran's main oil refinery had gone on strike. Hundreds of thousands of people came into the street in the capital shouting: 'The Shah must go! Death to the Shah! The Shah must go!'

The government was broken.

A few days later, this strike spread to five other cities, triggering a strike by government officials. By October, a nationwide general strike was declared, with workers in all industries walking off their jobs. Demonstrations continued throughout Iran with riots in Tehran.

The response from the regime in some cities was rapid and terrible, with the military firing on the crowds from helicopters while foot soldiers shot people indiscriminately. Thousands were killed and injured. The funerals would themselves turn into demonstrations. The cycle of violence would start again.

Political parties started to take over military bases in some areas. In others, the military joined the revolutionaries and gave up their bases voluntarily.

In October 1978, after I'd been in Upper Boeen for a couple of months, I set up a teachers' council in Baneh with a number of other teachers from the surrounding villages and towns.

Shortly after, Sadat, Pari and I organised a demonstration with our students from Upper Boeen. We marched in the streets from the school all the way to the education authority in Baneh. It was a hot, sunny day, but even the youngest children, at six or seven, seemed to bounce all the way there, they were so excited. They felt like they were on an adventure.

The parents chanted: 'We have the right to wear Kurdish clothes. We have the right to talk Kurdish in school. Our children deserve a good education.'

The slogans on our banners demanded more nourishing food for the children, better classrooms and newer benches and blackboards. We even carried some of our blackboards with us so we could show how old they were. It took us half the day to get there. When we arrived, we were tired but exhilarated. We started to shout in front of the education authority for the leaders to come down and meet with us. They refused, so we threw stones at the window. This brought them down. Sadat, Pari and I were called into the education authority office where, following a brief meeting, they accepted all of our demands. They gave us new benches there and then and ordered a bus to take us home along with a feast of hot kebabs.

We were jubilant after our success, but we knew that this was not simply because of our demonstration. The situation in Iran was so fragile that all local authorities were frightened of further protests with increasing demands that would lead to the whole world collapsing around them.

Religious demonstrations took place in the holy city of Qom, the Shi'a Muslim heartland, and in some other cities. Although I did not know this at the time, some of them were held in support of the exiled religious leader Ruhollah Khomeini, who had been banned from Iran due to his denouncing of the Shah's White Revolution reforms. All of the demonstrations that I attended in Kurdistan, and many more in much of the country, were secular and left-wing. Some of the fundamentalist religious groups wanted to participate in our demonstrations wearing religious dress, but they were not allowed. Our revolution was not about religion but about human rights.

'You're not welcome here in religious dress,' the people of Baneh shouted.

In Kurdistan, we had not heard of Khomeini.

The education system began to collapse as demonstrating against the regime took over people's lives. My school was almost shut completely by the end of October. It was just used to organise demonstrations. I moved between Upper Boeen and Baneh and concentrated full time on overthrowing the regime.

During these heady months, I didn't see Abdullah much. He was busy with his work with the underground Working People's Organisation. Instead, I joined in with fellow activists from Baneh. We held meetings, organised banners and wrote slogans. We would spend all of our time together in different houses, in a friend's basement or on a roof garden, and would all fall asleep in the same place, exhausted by our activities.

Students played a huge part in the revolution. Shaesta, still at high school, was the representative for her class on the students' council, which met weekly, and was made up of five boys and five girls. The council wrote banners and fliers, and planned and often began Baneh's huge demonstrations. Council members would be joined by their friends until almost the whole city was out. They got their courage from their friends and family, Shaesta told me. My mother worried constantly about the pair of us.

In November it seemed like the whole of Baneh came out to demonstrate every single day. Everyone opened their doors so that those fleeing from the police could get to safety. The police and military service personnel in some cities did attack demonstrators, and many were killed, but in Baneh the police didn't want to fire on their neighbours. They gave up quickly and joined in with the protests. The police who joined the revolution were welcomed with flowers.

All of the shops were closed but the store owners would donate to the activists, and everyone shared everything that they had so that essential supplies were accessible to all. We also had donations from the farms around Baneh. My father brought bread and fresh kebabs to wherever the activists were based.

The border with Iraq was not open during these months, but smugglers would bring a steady supply of food into the city. Smuggling continued to be one of the main incomes for Baneh.

On 16 January 1979 I had gone back to Upper Boeen to fetch some supplies when about fifteen men from the village came to the school with old guns.

'Where did you get all these?' I asked.

'We've had them hidden in the mountains for years,' one said. 'We're ready to defend ourselves.'

'We must return to Baneh,' another said. 'The Shah has gone.'

I caught my breath. The Shah had gone?

In the same instant, I felt incredible joy but also fear for the future. Would this lead to war? This was a victory for the revolution and we had to celebrate, but I also felt sadness that so many people had been killed before witnessing this day.

I went with the armed men quickly in the Land Rover towards the city. It was a beautiful afternoon. By the time we arrived, the sun had gone down. The atmosphere was electric.

The Shah and his wife, Farah, had fled Tehran for Egypt, never to return. Although the Shah had had a great relationship with Western countries, including the USA, at first none of them allowed him and his family to enter their country. It was Egypt that gave them asylum.

The whole city was dancing in the streets. They were full of colour, as many women were dressed in their traditional Kurdish clothes. At the roundabout, the traffic had ground to a standstill. Everyone got out of their cars and joined in the dancing. A man had a small pistol in his hand that he was using in place of a sarchopi, for Kurdish-style dancing. I joined the circle of dancing, and the men from Upper Boeen quickly got lost in the crowd. It was a day full of joy and excitement for all of us.

It was too crowded for me to find my family, but later in the evening I went back home. My grandmother was happy that the hated Shah had gone, but she had been through many changes of government. She was apprehensive about the future.

'It's important to have a new regime, but we have got rid of people before,' she said.

My mother was also worried. As well as Asad, she also had a new baby boy to look after, my little brother Aras. My father was both excited and concerned. That night he told me that he had once been a Peshmerga. It had been for several months in 1945 during the time that the Kurdish leader, Qazi Muhammad, had formed and headed the Republic of Mahabad, an independent Kurdish state in the city of Mahabad, which had been supported by the Soviets.

Independence had been short-lived and Muhammad was executed by Reza Shah for treason in 1946.

'We have to be strong or this freedom will be taken from the people,' my father warned me. 'In Mahabad, the military came with huge tanks to end our independence.' I was shocked. He had never spoken of his months in Mahabad before; he had been afraid of other people finding out. It was hard to imagine my father, the baker, as a Peshmerga. I was even more proud of him.

'This time it will be different,' I said. 'We are ready.'

I may have sounded confident to my father, but in reality I had no idea what the future held. I believed in socialism, but I didn't see the Soviets as the right example to follow; they were as imperialist as the US.

Iran had been united in wanting the Shah to go. Now he had gone, what would come in his place?

Chapter 7

The Kurdish Resistance Movement

Two weeks before the Shah was forced to leave Iran, the leaders of the US, UK, France and West Germany met on Guadeloupe Island in the Caribbean. Revolution in Iran was high on their agenda. They knew that the Shah could not stay as their Western puppet but, with the Cold War at its height, they were frightened that Iran could fall under Soviet influence. The Guadeloupe Conference would change the direction of the revolution.

Khomeini is known throughout the world as the leader of the Islamic revolution of Iran, but I first heard of him on BBC Radio. As protests built up throughout Iran against the Shah, Western reporters started to interview the religious leader, who was at that time exiled in Paris. Khomeini had been arrested in 1963 by the Shah's secret police for denouncing the White Revolution and again in 1964, after which he was exiled. He had lived in Turkey, Iraq and finally France, until 1979.

In recent years, more has been discovered about the contact Khomeini had with US president Jimmy Carter via intermediaries, with documents detailing how Khomeini promised that Iran would continue to sell oil to the US. Although the level of engagement is in dispute, what is clear is that the West could not accept a left-wing movement. They supported Khomeini's return to Iran, ensuring that the Iranian army, over which the US wielded significant influence, would not rebel against their new leader.

The left-wing and secularist movements, which in many ways were stronger and more popular than the religious movements among the people, had not organised themselves in the same way as the religious groups to take power. The religious groups had not been driven completely underground by the Shah. Although some leaders had gone into exile, others had remained and had been able to educate people about Sharia law in the mosques. Religious nationalism was close to many Iranian people's hearts. Shi'a Muslims felt that their religion had been oppressed during the Shah's rule.

The truth is that all of the many secular and socialist parties and organisations who fought so hard during the revolution failed to seize power. There were no plans put in place for what to do once the Shah left, and no obvious leaders from the socialist parties came forward to take control. This was a huge gap identified by the West. Khomeini came in and filled it, returning to Iran on 1 February 1979. Millions of his supporters came out to welcome him.

Khomeini's new Islamic government immediately started to change the constitution of the country.

Sharia law replaced secular law. Although Kurdish Iranians were generally Sunni Muslims, religion wasn't the dominating force in Kurdistan. What had been far more important than religion for Kurdish people was the struggle for freedom from oppression. Kurds, as well as many Iranians throughout the country, had wanted a secular regime. This was a hijacking of the revolution we had fought for, and we had no idea then that Islamic fundamentalism would eventually try and suffocate everything of beauty in Iran and all that we had worked for.

The regime banned music, dancing and colourful clothing. Gender segregation was enforced everywhere: in schools, on buses, on the beaches and even in queues for food at the shops.

Women and girls were ordered to cover themselves from head to toe in all public places. Guards enforced the wearing of the hijab by throwing acid on women's faces or any parts of their body that were not covered. They cut women's lips with knives and razors if they were spotted wearing lipstick. Women could no longer work in key roles, such as in the judiciary. To continue in jobs like teaching or banking, one had to pass a Sharia test.

Restrictions on polygamy were removed, according to Sharia law. The legal age for marriage was reduced to nine years of age. Executions in the street became commonplace. Women were stoned to death for adultery. This was a return to the Dark Ages.

The first public protest against the Islamic Republic was the magnificent women's protest against the hijab on 8 March 1979 on International Women's Day in Tehran and other cities. More than 100,000 women marched, carrying banners with slogans such as 'No to hijab!' 'Women's freedom is the measure of society's freedom.' 'Women's rights aren't Eastern or Western, they are universal.' 'We didn't have a revolution to go backwards.'

The regime began to arrest members of opposition groups. They attacked all other religions, including members of the Baha'i religion, Christians, Jews and Sunni Muslims. Any activities believed to be against the regime were banned. No more than three people could gather at once.

In the first half of 1979, this newly formed Islamic government didn't yet have full control over all of the country. In Kurdistan, the revolution continued; the people had power. All anyone could talk about was the revolution and about how we, the people, could rule. We would not let the Islamic Republic take over. A Kurdish resistance movement was born.

Day by day, this resistance movement grew stronger and stronger. With the collapse of local government, our cities and towns were being run by different political parties, through elected neighbourhood, village and city councils. We had volunteer guards, who were not Peshmerga, patrolling the neighbourhood at night. During the day, the Peshmerga would defend the city.

The people, especially the young, began to organise themselves into neighbourhood councils, which were called jameayat, which means 'group', or benkeh, which means 'meeting place'. These jameayat and benkeh ensured that the city continued to function. First thing in the morning everyone would head to the jameayat and benkeh to find out what the activities were for that day and how they could get involved. There, everyone would be excitedly talking about the latest news and developments. Guns were smuggled into Baneh and anyone could easily get their hands on them. These weapons would be dangerous if not used properly. In the jameayat and benkeh we talked about this issue in depth, and decided to organise gun safety training. Iraqi Kurdish Peshmerga who had come into the cities were invited to provide this training, and we asked everyone to take it seriously.

Some political parties, such as the Democrat Party, tried to take complete control of the cities for themselves. However, the momentum of the people's movement was so strong, and there were so many different parties and ideas, that no single party could rule in the region.

Little by little membership of political parties grew, including that of Kurdish nationalist organisations wanting khodmokhtari, which means a self-governing Kurdistan. Other left wing parties also jostled for power, such as the Marxist and Maoist groups; Fedayeen Khalq; Peykar; the communist Tudeh Party and the religious group, the Mojahedin. There were also smaller parties led by imams, such as Ahmad Moftizadh, a Sunni Muslim who led a fundamentalist religious movement in Sanandaj which wanted Sunni Muslim rule in Kurdistan while being pro-Khomeini. Khbat was a small Islamic group in Baneh. Sheikh Ezading Hussaini was a progressive imam in Mahabad, who was a moderate and for a free Kurdistan.

The Working People's Organisation that Abdullah belonged to was no longer an underground movement. It had evolved into the political party Komala. Many of its leaders, imprisoned under the Shah, had been released in 1979. There was a lot of discussion within Komala as to whether Iran's system represented feudalism or capitalism, or a mixture of the two, and whether the revolution should start from the villages or the cities. Komala was a populist organisation. All of its educated party cadres and high-ranking leaders spent time labouring alongside the workers in the villages.

By this time, although I was a fervent Komala supporter, I was not a member. There were only a few members of Komala, and the process to become one was extremely difficult. You had to prove yourself and your loyalty. Potential members would first be made pre-members by the party leaders and regional committee.

I was one of many volunteers working on creating a more equal society. We oversaw the running of first aid training and education, and arranged for teams to go to hospitals to help the nurses and doctors. We learned how to inject medicines, dress wounds and stitch up patients. This training would be extremely useful to me later on.

I became one of the key organisers of both the Women's and the Teachers' Movement. We wanted teachers to have an active role in a new society and for our voices to be heard. We wanted to review the curriculum and base it on equality and human rights.

Pari and Sadat reopened the school in Upper Boeen. Whenever I visited, the classroom discussion was always about what was happening in Kurdistan. At this time, the villagers were free to get on with their lives and to come and go from the cities with ease.

In a team, I started to go to different schools, taking fliers with information about what teachers could do in this revolutionary situation. We had regular weekly meetings and study teams. There were little or no salaries, so doctors, nurses and teachers had to work voluntarily. There was so much energy around that nobody complained.

The activists organised reading teams or book clubs in different neighbourhoods all over the city for illiterate women. As almost all books were in Farsi, we had them translated into Kurdish. Once they were translated we could discuss the issues covered in the books or articles.

We had book clubs for activists, where we studied political works by Karl Marx and revolutionary books that the communist Tudeh Party translated, known for their white covers. Books in different languages, many of which had been forbidden under the Shah, appeared from all over the place. We were overjoyed to experience the real freedom of being able to read any books that we wanted to for the first time.

We were free to speak in the Kurdish language and wear Kurdish clothes. We organised Kurdish poetry and theatre nights with Kurdish songs and music. We had classes with teachers from Iraq who came to teach us how to read and write in Kurdish. They brought with them many Kurdish poetry books. After years of only writing in Farsi, it felt so comfortable for me to be able to read and write in my mother tongue. I mastered it quickly and found that I could be far more creative in my writing. Over a period of several months, hundreds of thousands of visitors from all over Iran and other countries came to Kurdistan to witness for themselves the real freedom we were living. They wanted to learn from and experience people power. They called Kurdistan 'The Museum of Freedom'.

After years of living under the Shah's regime, this was a new beginning. For the first time, we could talk freely and have different opinions and beliefs. We all took care of each other and treated everyone like a member of the family. Everyone seemed joyful and full of energy. During these few heady months, Kurdistan felt like a democratic and truly revolutionary environment. It was exhilarating.

Chapter 8

Engagement

I had turned sixteen and my father started to receive marriage proposals for me. As soon as Abdullah heard through Sadat that other men had asked for my hand in marriage, he sent his sister and sister-in-law around to propose.

'I don't like the idea of you marrying into this family,' my father fretted. 'They are a big family and they may not be kind to you.'

My parents, my siblings and Malika formed a tight-knit unit and I was my father's beloved eldest child. He was scared of Abdullah's huge sixty strong tribe of uncles and aunts with their endless children everywhere. I tried to placate my father.

'Abdullah is political. He is not like other men. His family accept his politics and will support us.'

'I have always said that I would allow my daughters to marry the man they want,' my father said. 'You must marry the person you choose. If you love him, I will respect your wishes but on the condition that you marry quickly.' A long engagement was frowned upon. It could bring shame on a family due to the temptations for the betrothed.

Our wedding was planned for a day close to New Year in 1979, which in Iran is the first day of spring, or 21 March. For Kurdish people, it is the main celebration of the year.

After we announced our engagement among our families, Abdullah's parents sent presents to my home, but I was not interested in gifts.

With weeks to go before the wedding, fighting broke out between landlords and farmers in Mariwan, a neighbouring city.

The landlords and tribal leaders were heavily armed and had the support of the Islamic Republic. The landlords wanted to take back lands that had been divided up and given to farmers during the Shah's White Revolution.

Komala supported the farmers and, as the fighting escalated, Abdullah and a number of Peshmerga went to Mariwan to help them.

I celebrated New Year's Day with my family. We had lunch together and, in the evening, we had baghali polo ba mahiche, which is lamb shanks stew with rice and broad beans, cooked by my mother, a New Year tradition in our family. My father brought fireworks home for us and we gave some out in the street. Everyone started to set them off. The streets were full of people celebrating. Some even set off small hand grenades, which made a huge bang as they exploded.

There was a feeling of freedom, hope and optimism in the air. My excitement about what the future held for Kurdistan was doubled by my joy about my wedding. I was so happy that I had found someone so capable and committed to political action that I could spend a meaningful life with.

My only concern was my virginity. I had not had the opportunity to talk to Abdullah about this. I always remembered what had happened to Amina on her wedding day and I did worry in case I didn't have my virginity. I still didn't know what it was despite the fact that I was about to be married.

However, my fears faded when I thought about Abdullah and his calm nature. I knew that this would be an unusual kind of wedding because it was in the middle of the revolution. It would be an opportunity to break taboos. Instead of a traditional marriage, we could have a real partnership of equals.

A couple of days after the New Year celebrations, I went back to Upper Boeen with New Year gifts: pens and notebooks for the school students.

It was a sunny but cold day. The top of the mountains glistened with snow, which was beginning to melt, and the village was green and beautiful. I was walking over a tiny wooden bridge when I saw Rahim, a Peshmerga friend of Abdullah, coming towards me. I waited for him on the bridge. There was a Peshmerga base nearby so it was not uncommon to see the fighters in the village. I was excited to see him but when I saw his face I could tell instantly that he had bad news.

'Hello, Galavezh. I'm so sorry to tell you this but Abdullah has been shot.'

I started to shake but managed to stop myself from crying. I had to be strong. I was a revolutionary woman. I should not cry in front of a Peshmerga.

Abdullah had been shot in the head and was unconscious. He had been taken to a hospital in Tabriz, a large city in northwest Iran, where there was much better medical equipment. It was a several hours by car from Mariwan. Following a week long battle, the farmers and Peshmerga had managed to take over all of the twenty farms in the area. It had been a success with no injuries on the Peshmerga side. The fighting was over, night had fallen and it was raining heavily. The company was returning to a safe place to rest when Abdullah was shot in the head by a sniper hidden somewhere behind him. He had been shot on New Year's Day while I had been celebrating with my family.

In a state of shock, I returned to Baneh and waited at Sadat's house for news. We told each other that Abdullah was alive. He would come back to us. We knew that a head wound was a serious injury but, for those few days, we kept up hope that he would recover.

It was difficult waiting in his busy home. Everyone was crying all the time.

Twelve days after Abdullah had been shot, another Peshmerga came to the house in the early morning. He told us that Abdullah had died without ever regaining consciousness.

I was distraught. However, I also kept thinking that because this was the revolution and so many people had already lost their loved ones, it was important for me to not show my feelings.

Sizdah Bedar is the thirteenth day after the Iranian New Year and marks the end of the long festive break. A few weeks before the celebration, everyone plants wheat or lentil seeds on plates decorated with red ribbon. By the time of Sizdah Bedar green shoots have sprouted on the plates. These shoots represent all of the ill health, misfortune and unhappiness in the home. On Sizdah Bedar everyone goes into the fields or the mountains for a picnic, carrying their shoots so that they can throw them into the river to make wishes and to wash misfortune away. It is the first day that families and friends can all get together after New Year to enjoy nature in all of her springtime glory. It is a wonderful time.

This year, instead of spring sunshine, it was raining heavily. On Sizdah Bedar, hundreds of cars went in a convoy to bring Abdullah's body back home. I travelled with his family in one of their Land Rovers. Only close family members could go and visit Abdullah's body in the mosque. Seeing him lying there, covered by a white cloth, I began to cry for the first time since hearing that he had been shot. I did my best not to make a noise so that other people couldn't hear me.

As military commander for the Baneh Company, Abdullah had been the highest ranking Peshmerga to be killed from Baneh during the revolution. Thousands of people came into the street for the funeral. All the roads leading into the cemetery were full of black umbrellas.

After the funeral the weather changed and the sun came out. I went to Abdullah's home to welcome the guests with tea, biscuits, dates and halwa, which are sweets made with sugar, water, oil, rose water and flour. The house was full of people.

Abdullah's stepmother hugged me tight. 'You were his bride,' she said with tears in her eyes.

I stayed in Abdullah's family home for a week and tried to support them. It seemed like all of the city came to visit. It was hard for me to hold in my emotions all this time, but I didn't cry when people came and hugged me and wept over me. Instead

I would try and comfort them and say: 'We should be proud. Abdullah is a martyr.'

A few days after the funeral, Komala held a big public meeting as a memorial to Abdullah. Many of the organisation's leaders spoke about him.

'All of his life Abdullah made sacrifices to end poverty,' one said.

It was my turn to stand in front of all those gathered. This meeting was the first time I had had to speak in front of a large audience. I was nervous but I also felt empowered by the Peshmerga inviting me to talk.

I stood and read a Kurdish poem called 'Aram', which means calm. This had been written for a socialist Peshmerga from Iraq.

For me, this poem perfectly represented Abdullah. One of its lines read: 'You were so calm that calmness is missing you.'

This event helped me to deal with my emotions. Everyone treated me with such respect and expressed their condolences directly to me. The political leaders told me that I was brave and that Abdullah was proud of me. Each time someone told me I was brave, it gave me more strength.

Finally, I went home. My father, mother and grandmother held me for a long time. I hadn't allowed myself to let my emotions out; I had kept them in for a whole week. I went to my room and started to properly sob. Once I started, I felt as though I would never stop crying. Abdullah and I had had no physical relationship. It had all been based on unspoken feelings. Our connection was sparked by our strong political beliefs, something that was common during the revolution. I don't know whether, if we had been living a normal life, I would have loved him in the same way. I didn't question my feelings at the time. It's not something I will ever know.

I didn't have an older brother and I felt that Abdullah had played that role for me. He had been my guide and mentor. I know he would have always taken care of me. We would have been strong together. Every girl wishes to have a life filled with such a love. With Abdullah's death, I knew I had lost that opportunity, possibly for ever.

For several days, my grief felt overwhelming. I missed Abdullah terribly. I could not believe I would not see him again. I kept thinking about our last meeting, when he'd given me and Sadat a lift back from Upper Boeen. That was before our engagement. I'd had no idea that it would be the last time I would see him. Would I have done or said something differently that day if I had known?

This was a difficult time for me, but I had to remind myself that in a revolutionary situation you need to be brave and not bring your feelings to the surface. I knew Abdullah had died for a cause he believed in. I had to concentrate on helping other people instead of drowning in my own sorrow.

In the weeks following Abdullah's death, I often sat quietly on the roof of my home to watch the sunrise. Each morning the city was wakened by the lovely sound of the cock crowing, followed by a chorus of birdsong. I would breathe in the fresh air all around me as I began to watch the vibrant city come to life.

I looked down on everyone walking to work and the children in groups heading to school, some happy, others crying after their mother and father. Young people going off to start their daily activities. I couldn't be prouder of the Kurdish people.

At these moments, I experienced the profound beauty of life. At the same time, I had a sharp pain in my heart thinking about Abdullah and all the other people who had lost their lives in our fight for freedom.

Chapter 9

Kurdistan Under Attack

On 30 and 31 March 1979, Khomeini held a referendum. It was announced with fliers everywhere. The only question on the piece of paper was: 'Do you support an Islamic Republic?' The only possible answers were 'Yes' or 'No'.

I was in Baneh, at home with my parents, when the referendum papers came through the door. As soon as I read them, I ripped them into shreds. Apart from those few who belonged to religious groups and were pro-regime, Kurdish people boycotted the referendum. It was even banned in parts of Kurdistan by various political parties, including Komala. Kurdistan did not accept the result of the referendum, which stated that 98 per cent of people had voted in favour of an Islamic Republic.

This had not been a real referendum. We knew the result was always going to be 'Yes'. The Islamists already had power and a temporary government operating. They would not have accepted another response.

Witnessing what was happening in Kurdistan with its freedom and burgeoning democracy, Khomeini warned Kurdish leaders against trying to break away from Iran.

Many people from every corner of Iran had joined this continuation of the revolution in Kurdistan. Khomeini and his government could not tolerate this.

In Kurdistan, we also knew that the neighbouring countries of Turkey, Iraq and Syria, with their large Kurdish communities, would not accept the freedom that was happening in Iranian Kurdistan. They would see this as a threat and think it might encourage Kurdish revolts in their own countries. None of these countries wanted an autonomous Kurdistan.

In order to bring Kurdistan under control, the goverment put sanctions on the region. This made it harder for people to find food and feed their families. Basic items were already too expensive. We were facing a food crisis and had to rely on smuggled goods. Smugglers were often shot coming across the border from Iraq.

In August 1979, I was sitting with my father listening to the BBC when Khomeini's voice came on the airwaves. He was declaring a holy war against what he called 'Kurdish rebels seeking autonomy or independence'. The government was issuing a fatwa, which is a legal opinion on a point of Islamic law, to begin jihad, or a holy war, against the Kurdish people. Khomeini made his now infamous command: 'Attack Kurdistan via earth, sky and water.'

'Iranian Kurdistan hasn't got any border to the sea,' my father smiled sadly.

I shivered as I heard Khomeini's words. What could our Peshmerga do with their guns against the Islamic regime with its aeroplanes, jets, tanks, rockets and missiles? For our rejection of an Islamic Republic, Khomeini was unleashing the hounds of hell upon us.

The assaults on Kurdistan were barbaric. The same horrors we have seen in Syria carried out by ISIS in recent years were perpetrated by the Islamic Republic of Iran on its opposition and on the Kurdish people.

On 2 September 1979 an horrific attack happened in Qarna. A small village of around eighty families who had not been involved in any fighting, Qarna was marched on by a group of one hundred Islamic Revolutionary Guards with tanks and cannons.

The Islamic Revolutionary Guards Corps, or pasdaran, had been founded in April 1979 by the order of Khomeini. While the Iranian Army, which was made up of conscripts, defended the country's borders and maintained order, the pasdaran were established to protect Iran's political system. They were religious fanatics who had volunteered to be pasdaran. Ideologically driven, they wished to be martyred for their cause.

In Qarna, the pasdaran beheaded many of the villagers with knives, and shot others. They killed children by stamping on their heads. Not even the village mullah was spared. His decapitated body was found among dozens of other dead. The guards believed that if a girl wasn't a virgin she could not get to heaven, so they raped some of the girls before murdering them. The only people alive after the attack were those who had been away from home that day.

It was the same story in Qalatan. The pasdaran killed everyone and burned the village. We heard about a disabled woman who had been trapped inside a home. The pasdaran left her to burn alive. There were similar stories coming from the villages of Sarv e Kani and Chaghal e Mostafa.

Qarna and Qalatan terrified the Kurdish people. We were shocked that Iranian forces could attack an innocent village and burn it down. It was seen as a direct result of Khomeini declaring war.

Qarna and Qalatan might have frightened us, but it also enraged us. Men, women and children got ready to defend themselves.

Komala's Baneh Regional Committee was headed by three young men: Baqi, who was Abdullah's cousin, Azad and Babak. They needed to prepare the city against an attack by the government. Volunteer activists were split into small teams. I was put into the community team with four other teachers: two women, Rabe and Nasrin, and two men, Azimi and Rahman. Our work was to help people from the city to escape ahead of any potential government attacks on Baneh.

On the first day we were each given a small pistol and five minutes' training in how to use it, along with the instruction: 'Fire if you need to.'

We had to do our best not to be captured, I thought. Capture was worse than death as it would mean torture and also rape for any woman. Holding my own gun for the first time, I had mixed feelings. I felt a measure of relief that I now had the means to defend myself, but I was also nervous. I hoped there would be no need to use it.

My team travelled to different parts of the city to persuade families to flee to the villages, which were safer. The villagers warmly welcomed those fleeing, finding homes for them in the mosques, the schools and in their own homes, sharing any food that they had. These villages quickly became overcrowded.

We visited two or three villages a day to update people with any news from Baneh and to encourage the villagers.

I always wore pantol, mainly for reasons of practicality, but also because wearing the traditional men's trousers gave me an air of authority. I felt more confident and the villagers took me more seriously.

We had to be vigilant for helicopters all the time. We heard that the Islamic Guards had started to kidnap people from the villages and farms, so everyone was terrified of helicopters. On a number of occasions one would fly over us just as we were making our way from one village to another. Each time we were lucky enough to be close to the village and we ran quickly to take cover. Baqi and Babak sometimes came to meet with us so that we could inform them of our activities. They both seemed so fearless to me.

A short while after Qarna and Qalatan, I arrived with my community team at a village. We invited everyone to the mosque. I wanted to encourage people, but morale was low.

'We need to be prepared to defend ourselves against the pasdaran,' I said. 'We need to support each other against the government's attack. They have no mercy for any of us, not for children and not for elderly. They kill everyone, raping young women before killing them.

'We must not allow Qarna and Qalatan to be repeated. The Islamic forces are heartless and bring with them darkness and destruction. Your village council needs to get everyone ready.

Teach everyone to use a gun and make sure you have access to first aid.'

One villager stood up to speak. 'We will defend our villages and our families. We will not allow another Qarna to happen.'

The regime bombed Kurdish cities and villages from the air. On the ground, they attacked Sanandaj and Mahabad with large army columns, moving westwards towards Saqqez, almost upon Baneh.

In November 1979, we heard that fifty-two Americans were being held by a group of extremist students who had stormed the US Embassy in Tehran. I knew from listening to various overseas radio stations that the regime was negotiating with the US over oil and future business and cooperation. I wondered whether the hostages were being used as a front. Khomeini's slogan was 'Death to America'. The regime wanted to show people that it was against any dependency on Western countries. This slogan against the US was used to control people, particularly women, to prevent them from engaging with Western culture, which was deemed too loose and which gave women too much freedom. Yet at the same time, they were negotiating with the West. It was complete hypocrisy.

My community team did a final tour around Baneh to persuade any remaining families to leave for the villages before the heavy bombing started. The city was like a ghost town.

We went to my own home, which had already been hit. One of its walls was partially destroyed. To my astonishment, I found my mother and father and two brothers all living down in the basement, in the darkness, without any windows. I was shocked and distressed at seeing them all huddled together, desperate for help.

My father jumped to his feet, relief on his face at seeing me. 'Galavezh!'

'How are you?' I ran towards him and hugged him.

'I am fine, we are fine,' my father said.

'Why are you still here? What are you doing here in this basement? You should have left the city by now.'

'We're safe down here,' my father replied. 'The walls are so thick. We can manage this.'

'This is not just about the walls – the bombs come through the roof. The roof is not thick. There will be many bombs and the noise will be always in the children's minds. Other cities have been destroyed. You have to leave.'

My father thought that it would be just a few days of rockets. He didn't realise this government would be so cruel it would send massive bombs by military jets to obliterate us.

'You can't go to our family in Saqqez, the army is already there,' I told him. 'Go to Upper Boeen. Go to the school or the mosque and tell them you are my parents. You will not have a problem finding somewhere safe to stay.'

They left that day for Upper Boeen. They were one of the last families to go. Just days later, our home was hit again by a large rocket launched from the garrison base. The regime managed to take over all Kurdish cities apart from Bukan and its outskirts and suburbs, which remained in Peshmerga control. After the Islamic guards seized Baneh, the bombing stopped and, little by little, families moved back home.

This marked the beginning of a strange period in Baneh. Although the Islamic guards were in control, they were not organised sufficiently yet. It didn't feel as though they had real power. Pasdaran would come into the coffee shops and we could debate quite openly with them and tell them they were wrong to attack Kurdistan. The Peshmerga had fled to the mountains, but in the evenings they would come back to the city to visit their homes and families.

Shaesta's student groups continued to organise demonstrations to protest against the prospect of an Islamic Republic. Many of these demonstrations ended with Khomeini's pasdaran spraying tear gas or shooting at the activists.

During one protest, Shaesta and her friend Layla only just escaped from being shot by running to take cover in the garden of the richest man in Baneh. They made their way from his outer garden into a second garden closer to his house when the man shouted to them: 'Don't bring fire into my home,' which means: 'Don't bring trouble into my home.'

Hearing his words, Shaesta and Layla went back into the first garden, nearer to the street, where they could hear loud shooting outside the man's house.

The man's own children had been among the protestors and eventually he felt sorry for Shaesta and Layla and he allowed them into his house. Shaesta was shocked to see his home absolutely full of people escaping from the shooting. The man's family offered her and her friends lunch, but they refused. They were too upset at having been denied entry the first time they asked.

The Kurdish were angry. The situation across the region was so unsettled. In Saqqez, the people rose up with the Peshmerga against the army and were able to defeat them. In Sanandaj, the people took over the radio and TV station under the leadership of Sadiq Kamangar, a judge and well-known politician.

Through a series of small battles, the Peshmerga gradually took back control of the cities and the military bases throughout the government controlled part of Kurdistan. For three or four months Baneh remained in the hands of the Peshmerga. The activists worked hard to organise the city.

With the Peshmerga controlling the region once more, the government asked for negotiations with Kurdish leaders from Komala, the Democrat Party and Fedayeen Khalq. Although Komala wanted a socialist government and did not support an Islamic Republic, they wanted to find a way of gaining some autonomy for the Kurdish community, while the Democrat Party wanted self-rule in Kurdistan with the cooperation of the central government.

As time went on, it became clear that the new regime would not grant any freedoms at all. Equality and human rights for Iran and for the Kurdish people had not been important to the Shah and were even less so for the Islamists. The referendum had made no provision for regional autonomy. Kurds would not be given any seats in the Assembly of Experts, which was responsible for writing the new constitution.

Chapter 10

Second Attack

Khomeini had become Iran's Supreme Leader in November 1979. The position of Supreme Leader was created under the new constitution and was more powerful than president. Khomeini's hard line advisor Abolhassan Bani Sadr became the first president of the Islamic Republic in February 1980. Bani Sadr and his followers had given Khomeini shelter from the Shah's secret police when the religious leader had sought exile in Paris. Khomeini's support ensured Bani Sadr's victory in the election for president.

In the spring of 1980, I heard Bani Sadr on the radio ordering the Islamic Guards: 'Tie your shoelaces! We are invading Kurdistan to end the Kurds.' He was commanding the soldiers to get rid of people power and the Peshmerga, and take back control of the region.

The Islamic regime launched a ferocious second assault on Kurdistan, attacking the cities of Sanandaj, Mariwan and Mahabad with full force. This time the Peshmerga were better prepared. They had built up larger military bases since the first attack. The battles were more protracted, as the Peshmerga were able to hold on to their bases for much longer.

Most families fled the cities and villages, but there were people who couldn't get to safety and had no choice but to stay in their homes. Around 40 per cent of the young people from Baneh came together to help. Activists, including my sister and I, remained in the city. Several teams went from house to house to ensure that those who remained had enough food. One group found a family who had disabled twins. The parents decided to stay at home as they couldn't carry them out of the city. In another home, the team found an elderly couple who had stayed behind as they couldn't walk. They didn't want to be an extra burden to their children, so they had insisted on remaining.

By the time the military got to Baneh, we had learned from the battles in the other cities that there would be no mercy from the government. They executed anyone they captured, including patients in the hospitals.

Komala had become a strong, popular organisation with several military bases in the city. Hundreds of people were armed and organised to defend Baneh. We were ready for the attack, but we couldn't get everyone out before the bombing. Many people were killed in the streets, including Baqi's mother, Amena.

Shaesta was in the first aid team. Their role was to go house to house, carrying medicines with them, to check if people were alive and to make sure the injured and disabled were taken care of. They also went to the Peshmerga trenches, which were made from rocks, alongside the roads and on the tops of the mountains. They brought the injured to the hospital and health centres manned by voluntary doctors and nurses.

One day, Shaesta arrived at a house and could sense that it was not empty. She went through the front door with the team, shouting 'Hello' in Kurdish so as not to frighten anyone inside. After a short while a woman emerged. She took the team into the basement. There, in the dark, was a profoundly disabled boy of around eighteen years old. The rest of the family had all left to avoid the bombs, but it was impossible to transport the boy safely and the mother could not abandon her son. She told Shaesta she had some bread, rice and potatoes and didn't need any further help. Shaesta visited them whenever she could.

Another day, the first aid team passed the home of Shamsi, one of its members.

'Let's go and visit my home,' Shamsi said. They found that the neighbour's house had been hit by a rocket and Shamsi's garden was full of broken glass. She immediately started to clean it up until Shaesta stopped her.

'What are you doing? You can't worry about cleaning in the middle of a war!'

'But what if my mother comes home? I need to clean up. She will be shocked.'

I continued my work in the community team. The two girls who had been in my unit during the first Baneh war didn't want to come back to the city. They stayed with their families in the village of Bejve, close to a Peshmerga base. I carried on working with the two men. Azimi and Rahman were funny and brave. Despite the hardships we were going through, they always made me laugh.

One of the main meeting places for activists was the home of my sister's friends Leyla and Farasat. The first time I visited the small house, around thirty people were crowded into the living room and garden. Several people were printing fliers in the corner of the room. I joined a group in the garden making home-made hand grenades from glass bottles, foam, wicks and petrol. We used to break the hard foam that you find in packaging to protect electrical devices into small pieces and mix it with petrol in a bottle. This could be lit and thrown into tanks and military vehicles.

Leyla and Farasat's mother was a lovely woman.

'I'm so worried,' she would say. 'You are all so young. You might get really hurt – you must be very careful.' We laughed at her.

'The whole city is at risk,' someone said. 'We need to defend ourselves, otherwise the government will take control of everyone's lives.'

'I will pray for you,' she said.

'Oh, prayer doesn't work!' another replied. 'Doing this work is the only thing that will help us.'

She laughed with us and busied herself with cooking. It was difficult for her, as they were not a wealthy family, but she still fed us all whenever she could.

Leyla was the same age as Shaesta, but didn't get so involved in our revolutionary activities. She was beautiful, clever and chatty and more into love stories, intrigue and make up. She was the youngest child, so she was much cherished.

With my community team, I travelled to the villages around Baneh to ask for their help, to try and improve morale and to ensure that they were giving their support to the Peshmerga. It was much harder for the villagers to cope during this second war with all of the people flooding in from the cities. Everyone was distraught. We knew it was a much more serious attack than before.

Sometimes those displaced from the cities would tell us they didn't wish to stay in the villages any longer. It was part of our job to inform them that the Peshmerga were still fighting. It was too dangerous to return home.

One warm, sunny day, I went to visit my family in the village they were staying in, and we went to a nearby farm to collect food to bring to the people sleeping in the mosque. The weather was so beautiful it almost seemed like a normal day. I forgot the war for a brief moment until two helicopters appeared. We were used to them swooping on the farms to arrest people, but this didn't make it any less frightening each time it happened. We were terrified they would shoot us.

My mother, grandmother and I tried to show the helicopter pilots that we were in women's dress and didn't pose any danger, but they continued circling over our heads for around ten minutes. They were most likely gathering information and intelligence about how life was set up outside of the city. The helicopter pilots were themselves taking a great risk by coming to the villages. The farmers were armed and could easily shoot down a helicopter. I wondered how this pilot could be so ready and willing to shoot innocent people.

When it was time for me to go, I was surrounded by my family, imploring me to stay: 'Don't go back to your work. You need to be more careful.'

'I will be careful,' I promised, hugging them goodbye. There was no point in me hiding myself away with my family in a room. I would rather die trying to help others to change our situation. This was the last fight for freedom in the city.

Midway through the battle for Baneh, the Islamic regime sent special commando forces to capture Mount Arbaba, which is a key strategic point overlooking Baneh and many villages around the city. Arbaba also overlooks the main roads from other cities to Baneh. The Peshmerga, hidden in ambush, allowed the helicopter to land before surrounding it and capturing the fourteen special commandos on board. They would later be exchanged for political prisoners. The seizure of these commandos boosted people's morale. It showed what the Peshmerga were capable of. Immediately, many more people from Baneh asked to join Komala.

Back in the city, I caught up with Shaesta. Every day there would be between eight and ten helicopters constantly shooting bullets down into the city while aeroplanes rained down missiles. Whenever we saw a helicopter, we had to take refuge in a building or behind a wall. At night time we usually remained in the city with the other activists, sleeping in basements. Sometimes Shaesta and I would be together at night, but usually we were with our different teams. Most bombing happened during the daytime, but sometimes bombs and rockets fell at night. Anyone who remained in the city had to cover all windows so that none of the electric light could be seen by the bombers. The noise of the military jets as they came over the city sounded like extremely high-pitched thunder. We waited without speaking for the bombs to drop. We hoped they would not hit any houses with people or animals inside. One night, one of Shaesta's classmates was hit by a rocket and blinded. Her friends drew up a rota and took it in turns to visit her and look after her.

The battle in Baneh lasted twenty-eight days. By the time the regime forces had completely taken over, every single building had been hit. Many were reduced to rubble. Baneh was a dead city.

The Peshmerga left for the villages and mountains, and families started to return to try and rebuild their homes and shops. I came back to Baneh with my parents to find our home had been partially destroyed.

Despite the stress of the war, I was happy to spend time with my family. I always missed them so much when I was busy with my revolutionary activities. I felt desperately sorry for them because of the house, but their lives had been saved, which was the important thing.

For the first few weeks, we slept together among the rubble. Nobody had insurance, and of course, the government didn't help with any reconstruction work. Instead, everyone, from business people to widowed women and my father with his bakery, had to start from scratch. As always, the community rallied around each other. We helped to rebuild homes along with lives.

Chapter 11

Going Underground

After this second attack on Baneh, my community team went their separate ways. Azimi decided to join the Peshmerga while Rahman rebuilt his home and started a new life in Baneh. I knew that I could not have a normal life. I wanted to continue my political activities and wondered how I could do this best.

Komala had been following my work closely. In late summer, 1980, I was invited to a meeting at their small base in the valley of Chom Razen, where the organisation had a number of tents housing around seventy Peshmerga in a field next to a village.

I met with Baneh's regional committee, Babak and Baqi, whom I knew from my work during the wars, and Azad, who was the older brother of Farasat and Leyla, my sister's friends from Baneh. I was excited to meet Azad because I had heard many stories about his bravery in combat. Azad was known for always being on the front line. Once when on a mission to take over a regime base, a large pasdar had grabbed one of the Peshmerga with Azad. Azad had jumped on the back of the pasdar and made him release the Peshmerga.

Azad smiled at me when we had a moment alone after our meeting.

'It is so good to meet you,' I said. 'I have heard many stories about you.'

'But can you not remember where we met before?' he said.

Azad was charming and strikingly handsome. His eyes were his most impressive feature. So dark brown they were almost black, they sparkled when he spoke to me.

I laughed as I could not answer him. 'I don't know.'

'I saw you one day in Komala's red Land Rover with Abdullah. He had been to Upper Boeen to pick you up. But I met you before this. Can you really not remember? Take your time and think about it.'

I shook my head, still smiling.

'I saw you on a snowy day when we were children, in your car with your family. The day we both moved to Baneh.'

I was astonished that he had been that boy from all those years ago and surprised, and also flattered, that this well well-known Peshmerga had recognised and remembered me.

Azad, Baqi and Babak put me into a team with three other recruits: Halala, whom I had worked with in Baneh during both wars, and two young men, Mahmood and Habib, whom I had not met before. Our mission was to establish an underground committee and organisation in Baneh for Komala and to help rebuild the city physically and emotionally.

I had complete faith in the Peshmerga and I was thrilled to be put in this team. I would have done anything for Komala.

Halala was from the landowning class. Although Iran had become a capitalist country after the White Revolution and the feudal system had collapsed, in some villages its grip was still strong and it effectively remained in place. She had lost her two older Peshmerga brothers during the battles in Baneh. I felt that her class position gave her a lot of confidence, but it was her brothers' deaths that fuelled her political activity.

Habib was from Sanandaj, and was relaxed and friendly. He was always making jokes. When we returned to Baneh, I would often find him at my home, standing laughing with my father.

Mahmood came from the city of Bukan from a large tradi-tional tribal family. He had studied in Tehran and was the most respected animal vet in Baneh. At first he appeared to be more standoffish and serious than Habib. He was tall and undoubtedly good looking, but he seemed uncomfortable whenever he had to speak to women.

In one of our first meetings together, I asked Mahmood to come over and talk to me.

'Why are you always looking at the floor when you speak to me?'

'I don't know,' he smiled.

A few months later, Mahmood confessed that he had been terrified about what I was about to ask him that day. He had been brought up to interact with girls in this aloof manner. He had never had his behaviour questioned before.

The four of us stayed in Chom Razen for around two weeks. As part of our training, Halala and I were sent to work with the women in the village and Mahmood and Habib had to work in the fields with the men. As socialists, Komala believed we had to be equal to the villagers and experience true village life. It was important to join in with them and experience their hard work and their suffering. One of our tasks was to help the women milk the cows and goats. We also had to clean out animal waste, which would be recycled and used for fertiliser and fuel. The villagers loved us because we worked for them without any expectations and we talked to them about a world free from discrimination and violence.

Komala's supporters were encouraged to wear simple, old fashioned clothes to show that we were serious-minded and equal to the workers. However, I was my father's daughter. I always tried to look my best even in the basic items that we had.

While hard at work, I found myself thinking about Azad and what he had said to me about us meeting as children. For some reason I couldn't explain, I felt as though I had always known him. I hadn't experienced such an immediate closeness before with anyone else. I knew that I wanted to see him again and I realised I was attracted to him. However, this was not the time for such thoughts. I tried to push them to the back of my mind. I had to be more reserved toward him.

Back in the city, my team set about organising the under-ground committee. We wanted to ensure that all of those who had lost Peshmerga sons or family members in the war would receive visitors with gifts, which we collected from other families. One of the first people we collected food and clothes for was a mother living on her own in utter poverty. She had lost both her sons.

We created the underground committee with a pyramid structure. Halala, Mahmood, Habib and I were at the top. Directly underneath we had two deputies: Mastoreh and Naji. Mastoreh was a lovely, charming girl with big black eyes. She was always so calm and we got on well together. Naji was kind-hearted. Nothing ever seemed too much trouble for him.

On the next layer down, we had the men's and women's committees with five people in each. We couldn't mix the teams because it was difficult for mixed gender groups to meet together under the strict rules of the Islamic regime. Men and women who were not related could be arrested simply for walking along the street together. Below this layer, there were several other teams with about five or six people in each. This structure continued for several layers. Shaesta belonged to the students' committee. One of their key tasks was organising protests against the compulsory wearing of the hijab.

This had not been enforced in Kurdistan while we were under the control of the people's councils and the Peshmerga. Now that the regime forces were running the city, this had changed. In a reversal of the Shah's decree of the 1930s, when women had their scarves forcibly removed, women could be dragged from the streets and whipped for not wearing the hijab.

There were about 150 people in total in the underground committee. The most important element of the pyramid structure was that nobody should know the identity of the people in the other teams, apart from the team leader. Each team leader would know the identity of one person from a committee above and would report to him or her at regular meetings.

It was for the same reason we had kept numbers down in our secret societies back in teacher training school. If a member of the organisation was arrested, it would limit the number of names that person could give up if tortured.

Even the leaders at the top of the pyramid were not to know the identities of the people in the teams on the lower levels. We only knew who was in the men's and the women's team on the next level down. We were only ever in direct contact with our deputies. But in truth, it was a small city, so I was aware of some of the activists on the lower levels and they knew me.

All of the teams spent time on education. We read books on revolutions, history and philosophy and also discussed Komala's views and programme.

One of our main tasks was to find the locations of military bases and identify their equipment. We had to draw up maps showing exactly where the regime soldiers were, so that the Peshmerga could make plans to attack them. We identified those who were working with the government and drew up lists, addresses and any other related information that could help Komala arrest them and put them into one of their prisons.

We collected clothes, money and medicines to send back to the Peshmerga bases. We distributed party publications and recruited new supporters. We communicated by sending tiny letters to each other. We used pseudonyms so that we could not be identified. Mine was Mineh, which is a man's name.

The Central Committee for Komala wrote our socialist manifesto and part of our work was to raise awareness about this. The party had both a long-term and short-term strategy. We wanted a socialist regime to come to power and guarantee freedom and equality for all Iranians. We knew that given there had been communist revolutions in China and Russia, the same was possible in Iran. We were aiming for a classless society but we didn't want to follow the Russian and Chinese models. We knew they could be equally oppressive.

Despite our rocky start, Mahmood and I found that we had a lot in common and we quickly became good friends. Like me, he was an atheist and he constantly questioned the huge gap between the rich and poor. His mother had died when he was young, and soon after his father had married a woman called Tajieh, who had brought him up as her own son alongside her two daughters, Behjat and Nosrat.

Mahmood's father had died when he was about five, so Mahmood became the only man in the house. He inherited some land from his father, but his uncle took control of it, leaving his stepmother and sisters without access to the money. The family had little when he was growing up, but when Mahmood turned eighteen, he won back his inheritance after taking his uncle to court. Finding himself newly wealthy, Mahmood was shocked to discover that suddenly everyone wanted to be his friend. This reaction profoundly changed Mahmood. It made him angry about the injustice that he could see all around him and determined to do something about it.

Mahmood's family had been living in Baneh for about two years. The meetings of the underground Baneh committee leaders were often held in their home, as the sisters gave our team the cover we needed. It was difficult for a man to visit a woman who was not his relative, but we could say that we were visiting Mahmood's sisters. Habib lived with his sister next door to Mahmood, so they could easily meet up every day.

Mahmood was well known in Baneh. Being a vet was highly valued, as people were dependent on their cows and lambs. His job also proved useful for our underground work. Mahmood had to travel to all of the villages around the city to care for animals, which meant he could take messages to the Baneh Regional Committee without drawing any suspicion.

Behjat had two young children. Her husband, Farogh, was a Peshmerga on the main Central Committee for Komala, living in the Bukan area.

Nosrat worked for Komala delivering their tiny secret letters between Baneh and Bukan. She had spent time in prison after being caught with a carton of Mahmood's books. Mahmood loved books and made a point of reading every day. He had been proud of having his own collection in several boxes, including works on Marx, Engels and Lenin and other history books. He had received a message that the pasdaran were arriving and had managed to run away and hide two cartons of books in a building site. Nosrat was found with the other carton and arrested. She protested that she was illiterate and had simply found the books, but she was imprisoned for three months. Nosrat refused to give up Mahmood and had been willing to sacrifice herself for him. When it became clear that she was not going to be released, Mahmood went to the prison himself and said the books were his, but they didn't believe him and they didn't release Nosrat for several months.

Although we were an underground group, in reality almost everyone in Baneh knew what we were doing. Although Mahmood was not known as a Komala supporter, I was well known as an activist and our meetings with the teams under us were always held in each other's homes. It was usually enough for me to just say north or south to a taxi driver to be driven to the correct place. One day I got in a taxi on the way to a secret meeting. Without me needing to say a word, the driver took me directly to the correct place.

From time to time we would have meetings with the Baneh Regional Committee in the mountains or in Lower Najneh, a beautiful village in a valley where the Peshmerga had a base in the old school. The seventy Peshmerga living there had a close relationship with the villagers. They were well looked after by them.

Many women had moved to Najneh to seek shelter as activists or with their brothers, husbands and other family members. Najneh was the first village where I saw a large number of Peshmerga relaxed and able to talk freely together. In Baneh, you always had to be careful. If identified and reported on by somebody, you could be in serious trouble.

The first time we went to Najneh, Halala and I travelled separately from the two boys to avoid being arrested for being accompanied by someone of the opposite sex. Halala was originally from

Najneh and had many uncles and cousins living in the village, so it was easy for her to organise a driver for us. Lots of the cars that went out of Baneh to the villages were shot at or bombed by the helicopters always hovering above, so it was nerve-wracking when we reached the checkpoint. We told the guards that we had to go to the village to see Halala's family.

The first person I noticed when I arrived at Najneh was Azad, who was all full of smiles as he shook our hands. He asked us to go to one of their rooms to wait for Mahmood and Habib to arrive before we all went to dinner in one of the villagers' homes.

All of the Peshmerga were friendly whenever we visited Najneh. There would be a lot of joking around and we always felt so welcomed.

In our meetings with the regional committee – Azad, Babak, Baqi – they would ask about our activities in the underground committee. They would tell us what they needed, whether it was money or medicines or clothing. We would talk about what we had discovered about the regime's military bases and look together at the maps we had drawn. We talked about our underground organisation and our policies before making plans to return to the city.

We went back to Najneh every three or four months. Whenever we went by car, we brought pastries and sweets from the city. At other times, the regional committee members would come to the villages near to Baneh for our meetings.

One day Halala and I wanted to take a large parcel of clothing that we had prepared for the Peshmerga. We couldn't go by car as they would have asked us at the checkpoint what we were doing with the clothes. We decided that the only thing to do was to walk. Our backpacks weighed about fifteen kilograms each and we had to trek through the mountains. It took a whole day hiking in the summer heat. We didn't have proper shoes or clothes for such a walk, but we were exhilarated when we arrived. The Peshmerga were so happy to see us that they made it all worthwhile.

I began to notice from the way that Azad was always so elated to see me that he was also developing feelings for me, but neither of us wanted to bring this up. We were ideological people. Our beliefs and the party were everything to us. Komala believed that party members and supporters, and especially the Peshmerga, shouldn't have romantic love for each other. Between Abdullah and I it had been different. I had been younger and not so involved in Komala's activities. By the time I was falling for Azad, it was an unspoken rule that any private life should be sacrificed for the good of the party. Komala arranged marriages for political reasons and we were encouraged to put the party above all else.

Chapter 12

Explosion

As soon as he had taken power, Khomeini had begun the process of brutally murdering his political opponents all across Iran. During the 1980s thousands of people – students, political activists, anyone who dared whisper against the regime – were arrested in a wave of extreme oppression. They were accused of being anti-revolutionary or apostates.

Many of those detained suffered horrendous torture, sometimes daily abuse for years, with the worst punishments reserved for political prisoners. Stories came from the prisons of men and women forced to crawl on their hands and knees while being whipped. We heard of those hung by chains with their arms twisted behind them, their feet beaten until they were unable to walk, their teeth smashed and broken. Some were put inside coffins and deprived of food until they talked. Those who confessed to avoid execution were known as tavvab, penitents, and many tavvab women were forced into marriages with pasdaran. Others collaborated with the regime, writing reports for them and giving up the names of fellow dissidents.

Many prisoners were shot by firing squad. Virgins were systematically raped before execution to ensure that they didn't go to heaven. In the first eight years of the Islamic regime, between 20,000 and 30,000 people are believed to have been executed in prison.

The regime tightened its grip on Baneh. The pasdaran began to arrest many of the young people who had been involved in demonstrations and political activities during the revolution.

Seven times the pasdaran came for me and my sister. Komala informers inside the government usually managed to warn us before they got to our home, and we moved out quickly to various safe houses.

One day we were at home when the pasdaran arrived. Shaesta and I had to jump from the flat roof of the house onto our neighbour's roof to escape.

During this period, my father was arrested a number of times and held for several days while the guards questioned him about our activities. The guards did not treat him with the respect he deserved. My father denied that we had been involved in any political activities.

One night we were all at home when the house was surrounded by pasdaran. Six came through the garden up to the house accompanied by a man wearing a white mask over his face. My sister and I began to shake. My mum, close to tears, got up to hide our photo albums under her clothes before the pasdaran entered. The guards used to take pictures from albums in homes for their files to help them to recognise people later on. We didn't have any pictures with guns, just normal family photos, but these could still be used to entrap us.

'I hear that you have a gun in this house,' one of the guards said to my father.

'We don't have anything more dangerous than a needle,' my dad replied calmly.

'We know your children are helping the Peshmerga,' the guard continued.

'That's not true.'

The guards looked at the man in the mask. I recognised him as a member of the Tudeh Party. His sister was a friend of mine and a Democrat Party member. He looked at us and silently shook his head.

It seemed as though the guards were at our home for several hours, but it was probably only about fifteen minutes. When they finally left, we wept and hugged each other with relief.

Shortly after, a feared Islamic revolutionary judge arrived in Baneh with Chamran, one of the founders of the pasdaran. Wherever he went, this judge executed people. He had been in exile in Baneh during the Shah's regime but he had no mercy for anybody, not even for former friends and neighbours who had helped him during his time there. Shaesta and I had been warned of the judge's imminent arrival and we managed to escape to a safe house, where we hid out for several days.

The judge ordered the guards to surround the neighbourhood. They swarmed over the roofs of the houses to take people by surprise in their homes. Thirty teenagers were dragged into the square. The judge decided simply by looking at them which ones should be taken to prison and which ones executed.

One day I was on my way to meet Mahmood and Habib when a huge government military car containing about twenty soldiers went by. I was wondering what this might signify when there was a loud explosion right in the middle of the street market where I was standing. I was blown off my feet.

At first I thought that it was the car that had exploded, but I realised that a man next to me was bleeding. I tried to stand up to help him but I couldn't move. I looked down. My clothes were soaked in blood. I had fallen in front of a shop belonging to the Hosseini family. The two Hosseini brothers came out straight away with their black and white scarves, known as jamaneh, in their hands, which they used to tightly bind my hand and leg to stop the flow of blood pouring from them. A car arrived immediately and I was whisked off to hospital. I will never forget those who helped me that day.

Twenty nine people were injured in the attack, including several children. Thankfully, nobody was killed. Later some people said it was the Democrat Party that had thrown a grenade at the military car, but others said it was the guards who had thrown the grenade into the crowd.

Shrapnel had gone between the bones of my forearm, which caused heavy bleeding. I couldn't move my fingers. My tendons had been damaged but fortunately the metal had missed the bone, so it had not been shattered. My knee had a lot of shrapnel inside it, which made walking painful for some time after, but it was too deep to remove. I still have this shrapnel in my knee.

My parents came to the hospital to visit me. My mother was crying but I started laughing softly. I was in pain but I was pumped full of adrenaline and in a good mood. I wanted her to know that I was fine and not traumatised by my injuries. My parents were so thankful that I had not been killed.

Nobody was arrested following the attack. It was not a good time to arrest anyone. Everyone was so angry that a grenade had hit the community in the middle of the main street full of women and children, and tensions were high. The government was fearful that if they tried to arrest anyone there might be violent demonstrations.

I remained in hospital for two days. When I returned home, I received a tiny secret letter from Mahmood and Habib. They had heard about the explosion and were worried, when I didn't turn up for my meeting with them, that I had been caught up in it.

The whole community rallied around to help. Our home was full of guests every day. Even people who didn't know my family came to visit. As one group went out, another came in. I sat in the large guest room with my leg stretched out while visitors sat on rugs on the floor around me.

'Don't cry for me,' I told them. 'I am alive. I am fit and well.'

I didn't cry, but my mother cried enough for both of us. She prayed to God to save me and for nothing more to happen to me.

For about a week I had to remain stretched out, but little by little, I started to move my legs until I could walk again with a slight limp. After several weeks, this limp had gone.

I resumed my activities, but Komala warned me to be careful. The attack had made me even more well known as an activist. My name was already on the guards' list of the most wanted in the city. My public appearances were cut down.

Chapter 13

Escape

At the end of the summer of 1980, Mastoreh, one of our deputies on the underground committee, was arrested in a raid at her home and taken to prison. I found out through Komala's network of insiders that Mastoreh had confessed after being tortured. She had given up the names of the leaders of the underground committee, also of Naji, her fellow deputy, and all of our pseudonyms.

My father received a message that the pasdaran were on their way to arrest me. I immediately got ready to run. As I stood to go, my father, his face wrought with anguish, put his two hands on the door to prevent me from leaving.

'Please don't go,' he said.

'If I don't go, I will be executed.'

He put his hands down to allow me to leave. We both knew I had no choice. I will never forget the pain in his eyes that day as he begged me to stay.

For one night, I stayed in the home of Parvin and Asso, two sisters who had been on the student committee. Their brother had been killed in the war and their parents were fearful for their daughters' safety. Their father was strict and didn't want them involved in battles and dangerous activities. Sometimes he hit them and imprisoned them at home. This meant they had to do everything in secret. Despite this, both parents seemed to like me and they wanted to help.

I slept there one night but their mother stayed awake the whole time. She was terrified about the pasdaran coming. It wasn't fair on the family for me to stay any longer.

I went next to the home of Nosrat Khanom, a widow with no independent income. She was a lovely woman with three sons and two daughters, but had recently lost one son in the war. He had been married and had a beautiful baby girl. The baby's mother had returned to her family home after his death and was no longer living with Nosrat.

Nosrat's daughter Shahnaz was married to Azimi, who had been in my community team during the Baneh wars and had since joined the Peshmerga. Azimi had always been so kind when we worked together. I had a lot of respect for him. Shahnaz was heavily pregnant with the couple's first child.

While I was staying with Nosrat, I found out that Habib had been arrested before he had a chance to get away. He had been tortured and executed within days. His family were asked to pay for the bullet.

I was devastated at this news. We had all worked so closely together on the underground committee and had become good friends. Habib was just about to get engaged. This should have been a time of celebration for him and his family.

I was frantic with worry about the rest of the organisation. Who would be next? I had to try and get messages to everyone else to tell them to get away from home.

Habib's family were in Sanandaj, so there wasn't anyone from his family close enough to be able to pick up his body. Mahmood was not as well known to the regime as the others in the city, so he decided to collect the body and take it back to Habib's parents. On his way back to Baneh, Mahmood received a message from friends to warn him that the pasdaran were coming for him. Instead of going home, he went to a safe house.

Mahmood met with other members of the underground committee to warn them. He went to Naji's home to persuade him to leave Baneh with him.

'No, they won't come for me,' Naji said. 'I will continue my activities here.'

I'm not sure why Naji didn't leave at that time. Perhaps he

underestimated the extent of the attack from the regime, but I believe he also trusted Mastoreh.

Unable to persuade him, Mahmood left the city. Two days later, Naji was arrested on his way home by a pasdar calling him by his pseudonym. He was imprisoned and executed a few days later.

Within Komala, there was a large debate about tavvab. It was our belief that nobody should be imprisoned and tortured because of their political ideas. I did have some sympathy for the tavvab, although this is not something that I could express among Komala comrades. Lots of people close to Mastoreh, including her sister and several cousins, were members of the Peshmerga. She was seen in our community as a great betrayer and was isolated after this. She was later forced to marry one of the Islamic Revolutionary Guards.

For me, I was young and idealistic and loved Komala with a passion. I strongly believed that I would never have given up the party and my comrades under torture. Mastoreh was a teenager, yet so were many of the people who had died and not betrayed their friends. I knew of many comrades, some younger than me, who had stayed in prison undergoing torture for years, or who were executed when it was clear that they would never confess. I did ask myself what if the torture was so bad that it would break anyone, no matter how strong your beliefs?

Would I really have been that strong? Fortunately, I was not put to the test.

Nosrat Khanom looked after me for a whole month, treating me as a member of her own family. She was so helpful and protective of me. I knew that I was putting her family at risk by being there, but it was a relief to have a place of calm after hearing about all of the executions.

I discussed with Nosrat, in great detail, the different choices facing me. I considered going underground to various different cities, but my picture had been circulated by the regime and it wouldn't have been safe. I could not return home, as I faced certain death. I could not sit and wait in Nosrat's home until the guards discovered me.

If I wanted a chance to stay alive, I had run out of options. I had to join the Peshmerga.

Once I had made this decision, I had to wait for the right time to make my escape to Peshmerga controlled territory. On the road that I needed to take, there was a large checkpoint. There was no way to avoid this checkpoint and the guards took great care in scrutinising everyone against photos they had in their files. They arrested anyone whose name or photo was on their list. I spent a lot of time talking with Nosrat about how I could get through this checkpoint.

At first, Nosrat wanted me to wait until Shahnaz gave birth so that we could all leave together with the baby. In the end, we decided that it would be safer if Shahnaz joined us later. After the birth, she would have all of the customary visitors; it would be too difficult to keep me hidden. One of the regime's spies might spot me there and report me.

Eventually, Nosrat came up with a plan for me to borrow her deceased son's baby daughter, Kvestan, who was now about two months old.

'You can pretend you are my daughter in law,' she said. 'I will come with you and get you through the checkpoint and out of the city. As long as we get through the main checkpoint we will be OK. They will not be strict on a baby.'

I knew that this was a good idea but also extremely risky. I would still have to go through the checkpoint where they would likely have my picture and name. I wasn't worried for Kvestan, though; if anything happened to me, Nosrat could take the baby. The plan was for me to get the bus to Saqqez, where my grandmother was now living, and rest there a while before heading to Peshmerga territory.

On the day of our departure, I dressed in stylish Kurdish clothes and took Kvestan in my arms. It was 6 a.m. and the sun was coming up over the city. My mother came to the bus garage to say goodbye and to bring some clothes for me. It was dangerous for us both to be seen together. I got down off the bus to hug her quickly. She was clearly stressed.

'Don't stay, don't stay,' she said. 'I just want to see you onto the bus.'

She cried, started to pray and waved me goodbye.

I took Kvestan onto the bus and she fell asleep in my arms. As the bus pulled away, I had to work hard to keep my emotions to myself. I was worried about leaving the city and my family and joining the Peshmerga. This was a new world for me. I also knew how painful it was for my mother and father. I was their much wanted first child, still a teenager, having to go and live with freedom fighters in order to stay alive.

To try and keep calm, I stared at Kvestan. She was sleeping so soundly. Bright morning light shone on her beautiful little face. I didn't want her to wake and I tried to keep it out of her face with my chador. The bus started moving through the city. Apart from the military, there were not many people out. All of the shops were still closed, apart from the bakeries, which were opening to morning customers. Around the square, young jobless men waited in groups for builders and other contractors to choose them for the day. They always picked the fittest and strongest men.

'Don't worry, you will be fine,' Nosrat kept saying. 'You are young; you have got the baby.'

'I'm just going on a trip with my mother in law,' I repeated to myself.

We arrived at the checkpoint and time stopped still. If I was arrested, it was certain death.

I watched the pasdaran stop the bus but I couldn't hear much. The door was opened and a tall, armed pasdar came up the bus followed by two others.

They asked everyone to get off with their birth certificates and belongings. Nosrat waited until all the other people got off before calmly walking down. I decided to stay where I was until I was asked to move. I could hear the footsteps of the guard coming towards me.

Eventually I heard his voice: 'Your pass!'

I looked up at him. I could see that he was an extremely hand-some man but all I could think was that in his mind he was intent on killing innocent people.

I was wearing a traditional Kurdish black glittery waistcoat. My birth certificate was in my waistcoat pocket. I motioned with my hand to the guard that I was trying to get my birth certificate but I didn't want to disturb Kvestan, whose head was on top of the pocket.

The pasdar looked closely at the baby. 'That's OK, sister,' he said, with a calm voice. 'Don't wake her up. You can remain here. What is your name?'

'Nasreen,' I replied.

I was allowed to stay on the bus while Nosrat got off along with all of the other passengers. They were put into a line. One by one, the guards searched them and also examined each piece of luggage thoroughly. They checked their birth certificates and their names were matched against those they had on their list. When they called out Nasreen, Nosrat told them that I had remained on the bus because of the baby.

After around thirty minutes, Nosrat got back on the bus. Several people had been arrested and taken away. As the bus pulled away from the checkpoint, I continued to worry. I knew they could still stop the bus, but it carried on moving on toward Gardaneh Khan, the highest mountain in the region between Baneh and Saqqez. I had been extremely lucky to have met with such a kind guard. I started to breathe.

Chapter 14

Joining the Peshmerga

The bus climbed to the mountain ridge overlooking Baneh. I looked down on the streets where I had grown up, the whole city spread out before me. It looked golden in the morning sun. I could see the road from Lower Boeen to Baneh quite clearly and the queues of cars at the military control points.

From afar all seemed calm, but I wondered how many mothers and fathers were crying for their children in those homes at that moment. How many were mourning children who had died? How many hearts had been broken? We had escaped for now, but there were many young people who could not leave the city. I had warned my friends to be careful, but it had taken me a while to get out. I wondered if I would ever see them again.

When we arrived in Saqqez, Nosrat put me in a taxi to take me to my grandmother Malika's home.

'You are an angel!' I told little Kvestan. I kissed her forehead before handing her back.

'I will make arrangements for you to get out of the city soon and bring Shahnaz when she has given birth to join you,' Nosrat said, hugging me goodbye.

Malika had moved back to Saqqez not long after the Shah left Iran. She had wanted a peaceful life away from mine and Shaesta's political activities. She also wanted to be near to her other daughters, who all still lived in the city. She rented a small room in a large house with a garden. She had no income and was dependent on the support of her children. She held me tight when I arrived at her home. As usual, she was wearing traditional

Kurdish clothes and a hat. She was by now around seventy and she looked very elderly to me.

I split my time between Malika's house and several of my aunt and uncle's homes for two weeks before Shaesta came to join me.

Following my escape, the pasdaran went several times to our home looking for my sister and me. It was no longer safe for her to stay. During the daytime, she went to school as usual. The pasdaran did not want to come to the school to arrest the students as they feared this would lead to demonstrations. Instead they would come at night to take them, one by one, from their beds. Shaesta had had to start sleeping in our neighbour's home in order to avoid arrest.

One evening, while it was still daylight and she was just finishing her dinner, our mother told her: 'You must go next door now!'

'It's too early,' Shaesta replied, but our mother insisted. Five minutes later the pasdaran raided our home. Our neighbour came to our home to see what was happening before returning to Shaesta.

'You were lucky!' she said. 'They have just been for you.' My mother could no longer cope with the fear of Shaesta being arrested. She decided to take her to join me.

For the bus journey, Shaesta wore her best traditional Kurdish clothes, a light pink dress, so that she would not draw attention to herself. This was instead of her usual simple revolutionary uniform of a dark dress and a chador. During the revolution, we believed that our clothes should be made from the same materials as poor people's clothes. When they came to the checkpoint, Shaesta pretended that she was feeling ill so that she and my mother were allowed to remain on the bus. Their papers were not even checked.

My mother only stayed for lunch with us in Saqqez. On her way home, she was arrested at the checkpoint. The pasdaran demanded to know where Shaesta was. My mother insisted she didn't know where her daughter had gone and she was released after two hours. The next day the pasdaran arrived at my home and during the daytime they lay in wait there for the whole week. They were hoping to catch us and our friends and comrades in their trap. Over the moon with having Shaesta back with her, Malika invited all of the grandchildren who were our age and living in Saqqez to her home for a little party. It was noisy with our chatter and laughter in the small room.

Malika cooked rice and chicken and said how proud she was to have all of the grandchildren with her.

'I dream of you both getting married and having a happy life,' she said to me and Shaesta. 'Please take care of yourselves.'

We were used to coming to Saqqez to visit our family, so for Shaesta it felt a little bit like a summer holiday. We told each other that we would only be away from home for a short while. We believed that it would not be long before the Islamic Republic was defeated. We never imagined that we would be away from home for the rest of our lives.

We kept in touch with Nosrat via Komala's tiny letter system. We heard from her that Shahnaz had given birth to a baby boy and both were well. Shahnaz needed to leave to join the Peshmerga as soon as possible.

We received a brief letter from our comrades in Saqqez telling us to get ready to join the Peshmerga. We packed all of our things and left Malika's house, but a battle broke out with government forces close to where Nosrat needed to travel from. The route was blocked and she couldn't get to us.

Shaesta and I came back to my grandmother's house. Malika was at the door resting her head against the door frame. We realised that she was crying. We knew her eyesight was bad and we decided to walk past her to see if she could recognise us. We went right on by before turning back to hug her.

'I didn't realise it was you!' she said in surprise. 'I was watching you and thinking of the lucky family who have their daughters safe with them. I was hoping that my two granddaughters would come back to me like those girls.'

We didn't have much extra time with Malika. Nosrat contacted us again and told us to prepare for our departure. This time it felt certain. Shaesta and I spent a long time at the doorway hugging Malika. I worried that I might not see her again.

Nosrat had arranged for around twenty young men and women, including Shahnaz, to join us. We left on a cold night in November 1980 for the village of Torjan, where the Peshmerga had a base. We were tightly packed into a trailer on the back of a tractor. It was pouring with rain and the trailer filled with water. We were all freezing cold and wet. Shahnaz's baby cried throughout the entire two hour journey. He wouldn't calm down at all.

When we arrived in Torjan, my sister and I were sent to one of the houses for Peshmerga women, while Shahnaz went to one of the villagers' homes. The host's wife told her the baby's nappy was wet and that was why he had been crying so much. Shahnaz changed him and fed him and he immediately quietened down and slept soundly all night.

Although I felt relieved to be out of immediate danger, my mind was full of images of my friends who had been executed. I was particularly upset about Naji. He had had the chance to escape and yet had chosen to stay. Had he believed that the regime would be merciful? Did he think there wasn't enough evidence against him?

I was tormented with guilt. I had managed to escape. I wondered what more I could have done to help my comrades. Should we have forced Naji to come with us? Habib and Naji were too young to die like this. Their lives were cut short by the government just because of their beliefs. Today it is still incredibly painful to think about what happened to them both.

Yet I also understood that by working with Komala we had chosen this life. We knew we were at risk. It was our own personal decision to demand a better life for everybody, free from violence, war, execution, torture and imprisonment. Iranian and Kurdish people deserved to be safe and to be free to express different opinions. We deserved the right to freedom of speech and equality. I couldn't remain silent in the face of such injustice. I felt I was born to fight for our rights. To become a Peshmerga meant that we would sacrifice ourselves for others. I knew that I was ready to give up my life for my beliefs and our people.

The first person I saw stepping outside the next day was Azad. He had been promoted to a top position on Komala's Central Committee and was now stationed in Hajji Kand, a village close to the city of Bukan, where his parents lived. He was in Torjan for meetings.

My feelings for Azad had grown during the time we had been apart. It was wonderful to see him. I felt safe for the first time in months.

'Why are you here?' Azad was equally surprised to see me. He heard that I had escaped but had not known I would be in Torjan.

'I had to leave the city and come through Saqqez to join the Peshmerga. Did you hear about Habib and Naji?'

'Yes, it is terrible news,' he replied. 'The attack from the regime is relentless. I am glad to see you alive. While you are here you will have to take great care. Cover yourself at all times.'

After a week in Torjan with the Peshmerga, Shaesta and I were taken by car to Najneh. When we arrived, we were excited to see many of the girls who had been part of the underground organisation in Baneh. They had managed to flee after Mastoreh's confession. Among them were Halala, and Azad's sisters Leyla and Farasat. Mahmood was also there.

We all hugged each other tight and swapped stories about how we had each managed to get out of the city. We were relieved and excited to see each other but also distressed about our comrades. So many people had been arrested. The organisation had been severely damaged. We were determined to rebuild it, but this would not be an easy task with the difficult situation in the cities.

In Najneh, the Baneh Company of seventy Peshmerga was stationed along with smaller squads of between twelve to fifteen people. Altogether there were about a hundred Peshmerga in Najneh. There were also four community teams with four or five Peshmerga in each, covering the north, south, east and west of the district.

As in other villages, there were also groups of people who were armed but not professional Peshmerga. They worked on their land in the villages but had been trained up and given guns, ready to defend Komala and their homes and families against a government attack.

One of the first things I had to do after arriving in Najneh was to meet with Babak, Baqi and Azad and give a detailed report about what had happened in Baneh.

Babak invited me to listen to a cassette recording. He pressed play and a voice I instantly recognised sent a cold shiver down my spine. I realised I was listening to Mastoreh's confession. It had been broadcast on TV and radio, one of the tactics used to break down the resolve of the activists and the community.

'Who is this? Do you know this voice?' Babak asked.

I confirmed to them that it was Mastoreh. They gave me the cassette to take away and listen to privately. Someone inside the government had sent the cassette to the Central Committee, via our underground network. It was hard to listen to Mastoreh giving up the details of our activities and the names of everyone in the underground committee. I couldn't believe what I was hearing.

She sounded distressed. Mastoreh was not someone to show her emotions and she usually appeared calm even when confronted with something she didn't want to do. Listening to her, I thought of her face. Two of our dearest friends had been executed because of this confession just for the crime of being thought a member of the opposition.

A few days passed. I was called once more for a meet ing with Baqi, Babak and Azad. This time they had happier news for me. I was to be made a pre-member of Komala for the exemplary work I had done for the party. I was the first woman from Baneh to be given pre-membership of Komala. Even some of the Peshmerga men were not pre-members. This gave me a unique position within Komala.

It was a huge honour. I was elated and proud of myself. Most importantly, it meant that Komala were happy with the work I had done for them in organising the underground committee and working for the women's movement.

Most of the other women from my Baneh team were happy with the decision and said I deserved it, but I did notice the attitude of a couple of them change after this. Following my elevation to pre-membership, one of my key tasks was to organise meetings with the other Baneh women. Together we decided that we would meet with the women in Najneh and its neighbouring villages to talk about women's rights and the issues of 'honour' killings, forced marriage, child marriage, polygamy and domestic abuse.

Like the rest of rural Iran, Najneh was deeply patriarchal. The village women worked extremely hard on the land along with their husbands, yet when they came home, they had to wash and cook and clean while their husbands took it easy. The wives didn't have a rest even if they were pregnant. They would continue working until the ninth month. There wasn't any village toilet for the women, and they would have to go to the fountain to wash and clean. They also had responsibility for bringing water back to their homes.

We wanted to persuade the men to support women in doing the housework. We had a lot of meetings in the mosque, attended by both men and women, about what we could do to improve their lives.

Initially, the men would laugh and say: 'It's women's work.'

When we argued that the men were capable of fetching the water, they would say: 'But the fountain is for women only.' They made lots of excuses. Eventually, we arranged for public toilets for women to be built in several villages – it took a long time to get going, but it did happen. We also tried to address domestic violence, and worked as mediators in violent marriages. Divorce was almost impossible for a woman. There were no shelters or safe refuges for women, and their families wouldn't have them back even if they fled a violent marriage. There was no social security benefit for anyone, and certainly not for women. Divorce was shameful, and divorced women would be called 'widows' and lose all respect in the community. Komala would give a warning to violent husbands and we would arrest them and put them in prison if they continued to be abusive.

Despite the party's recognition giving me more confidence in my abilities, I was conflicted. I felt strongly that as women we were not accorded the same respect as men.

I and the other women of the underground committee of Baneh had worked hard to establish an underground group. We had all nearly been executed and only just managed to escape with our lives. We now lived among the Peshmerga but we were not armed. We were not expected to fight on the front line. The women were instead left to organise political meetings and discussions, and to cook and clean for the Peshmerga men. This meant that only the men were considered true Peshmerga.

Every Friday we had a break from our work, when we had a social gathering called galta o gapp, which means jokes and discussion. This was an evening full of games, singing and dancing. On this night, we did not talk about politics. Instead everyone had to take turns in performing. Anyone who could sing would sing, and those who couldn't would have to read a poem or tell a joke. There was no choice in the matter. I had a good voice and I always preferred to sing.

We also had to take part in obligatory criticism meetings. If we had told a lie, or if our appearance wasn't as it should be, or anything else was against the understood rules of behaviour, we had to confess it in front of the group.

After I had been in Najneh for about two or three months, Babak came to speak with me privately. I assumed he had a question about work for me.

'Baqi loves you,' he told me. 'I've come here to ask for your hand on his behalf.'

I was surprised. I had had no inkling of this from Baqi. I admired him greatly. He was confident and brave, and as the military commander for Baneh, he was highly respected. The military was at the centre of everything the Peshmerga did, so the military leaders were accorded more respect than the political leaders. Baqi had always been kind and warm with me. I considered him a good friend but I had no desire to marry him.

It was the custom to say 'I will think about it' instead of saying 'No'. I told Babak I would think about it and I forgot about it completely.

A short while later, Baqi himself came to find me. He asked me to go with him into a private room and he asked me to marry him.

Baqi was visibly shocked when I told him that I wasn't interested. He was so loved and respected that he had thought it would be a simple matter, that I was certain to say yes.

'Why not?' he managed to ask.

'I don't love you,' I replied.

Baqi quickly made his excuses and left the room. He was upset and a few days later went to speak to Azad, who after Babak was his closest friend.

'Please go and speak to Galavezh and tell her I love her and want to marry her,' he implored.

Azad was reluctant to do this.

'Perhaps it is because you love her and want her for yourself that you won't do this for me,' Baqi accused him.

In Komala, friendship was extremely important. Friends would sacrifice their lives for each other, while a marriage was a matter for the party to decide. Azad knew he had to come and ask me to marry Baqi.

He came and found me in the girls' room and he told me of Baqi's love.

'I can't marry him,' I replied.

'Why?'

'There is no particular reason. I don't want to marry someone that I don't love.'

'Do you love someone else?' he asked me. 'Who do you love?'

At first I refused to answer, but he kept asking me and asking me for a whole fifteen minutes: 'Who do you love?'

Eventually, he said: 'Do you love me?'

I laughed at these words. I was embarrassed.

Finally, I replied: 'Yes, and that is why I don't want to marry Baqi.'

'I love you too,' he smiled. 'That is enough for me.'

We both fell silent.

I didn't see Baqi face to face again after turning down his proposal but I knew that my rejection of him was not accepted by some Peshmerga. Babak also stopped speaking to me properly. Some people appeared to hate me because of my decision. I knew that Baqi's friendship was important to Azad – it was a dishonourable thing for him to love me. It was a betrayal of their friendship.

A few days later, Azad left for Hajji Kand without us talking about our feelings again.

Chapter 15

Love

During the months that I had been on the run and escaping to Najneh, Iran had gone to war with Iraq. Saddam Hussein, Iraq's despotic president, had invaded Iran in September 1980. This led to a protracted war between the two countries, which had the effect of uniting Iran against a common enemy and lessening the internal opposition against Khomeini.

Many of the Iranian parties who had been opposed to Khomeini and an Islamic regime, such as the Tudeh Party and Fedayeen Khalq, dropped their opposition to him and began to support the Islamic government. Iran regained all territories lost to Iraq by June 1982, but instead of ending the conflict at that moment, Khomeini chose to go on the offensive, prolonging the war for a further six years.

Hundreds of thousands of soldiers and civilians would be killed on both sides.

Komala was strongly opposed to this war. This was a war between two capitalist governments that shouldn't be supported by the people and opposition parties. The party believed that the Iranian regime was using it as an opportunity to control the Iranian people and also export its version of Shi'a Islam around the world.

In the early years, the impact of the war was mostly felt in Iran's most southern border with Iraq, in Khuzestan, and Kermanshah in Kurdistan. However, all of the major Kurdish cities, including Baneh, were bombed by the Iraqi air force. Many parts of the city, rebuilt after Khomeini's assault, were demolished once more.

Fifty people were killed when the city park, where everyone used to walk with their families, was bombed. There was no place of safety any more. Normal life ended for everyone.

At first, the Iranian military services forced my father to bake for them. 'Your children are Peshmerga,' one pasdar said. 'They are supporting Iraq. If you don't bake for us, we will kill you.'

My father baked for the regime for about a week but he wanted no part in this war. Instead my family started to leave Baneh during the daytime, like many other families, to go and stay in the mountains and the villages close by. This meant my father couldn't work anymore. During the night, my family came back into the city and my father would bake to feed the family. My parents and brothers lived in this unsettled, hand to mouth way for many years.

Some people had to stay in the city. They had nowhere else to go. There was no water, electricity or heat. In an energy rich region, the people had no access to oil and gas. Many died from the cold.

I remained with my comrades from Baneh in Najneh until winter 1980, when we received a message that some of us were to go to Hajji Kand to be organised into new positions. This was the first time that Komala had had so many women from different cities come to join the Pesh merga, all forced to leave their homes due to the regime's crackdown on the opposition. The party was not sure at first what to do with us all.

Shaesta and I, and the other girls from Baneh, including Halala, Farasat and Leyla, travelled by jeep through several cities and villages to Hajji Kand. Although the area was under Peshmerga control, it was risky to travel through it. The Peshmerga were on constant alert for a government attack on the city of Bukan, close to Hajji Kand. At certain stages of the journey, we had to get out and walk. We stayed at Peshmerga bases in different villages each night.

On arrival in Hajji Kand, we were all split up. Halala and I were put together in one house and told not to come out much.

We might be sent back to another city to work undercover, so it was important that as few people as possible could identify us.

Shaesta was sent to the Komala hospital in Elmabad to assist the medical team there. We would have liked to have stayed together but we never questioned Komala's decisions on how they should organise us. We thought that they knew best and we were used to being separated. The hospital in Elmabad was located in a large house that had belonged to the village landlord. In each of the rooms there were four or five Peshmerga patients with a curtain separating each one. The operating theatre facilities were up to date because modern equipment had been brought from the hospitals in other cities. The doctors were experienced consultants, surgeons and anaesthetists who had volunteered for the Peshmerga. A team of Peshmerga patrolled the hospital at all times. At night, the nurses not on shift would get together to read and discuss the Komala manifesto.

When she first arrived, Shaesta received basic medical training. This included instructions on giving injections. The custom was to give injections in the backside. The rookie nurses practised with diagrams on paper and were told to make sure there was no blood coming out of the syringe. They were also taught how to take a patient's blood pressure and pulse and how to use a thermometer. They would take these measurements every day and write down the results for the doctors to look at on their rounds.

On one of Shaesta's first days at the hospital, twelve injured Peshmerga were brought in. One of them was disabled from the waist down, and had many bedsores because he couldn't move. He eventually died of a resulting infection.

One night around 4 a.m., when Shaesta was on shift, she noticed that the floor was wet and she could smell oil. She discovered that the oil heater was leaking. There were carpets in each of the rooms, so she called Peshmerga guards and they came and removed all of the carpets and beds. One match and the whole place would have gone up in flames.

Sometimes, the villagers would be rushed into the hospital.

Once a woman was brought in at 3 a.m. bleeding badly from miscarrying her child. Shaesta had to call the surgeon to come and do an emergency procedure to remove the baby.

Usually when injured Peshmerga were admitted, Shaesta and her fellow comrades would have to rush to the operating theatre. If someone had been blown up by a rocket or a mine, it was the job of the nursing assistants to take out the intestines and look for holes. It was important to sew them up. One time, Shaesta had to hold a Peshmerga's badly damaged leg while a doctor amputated.

Although Shaesta was only fifteen, she never felt scared in the operating theatre.

'It was a matter of life and death,' she told me. 'We had to save them. I didn't feel sick with the blood, not at all. We were revolutionaries. We wanted to help.'

Sometimes, the Peshmerga were injured so badly that they would die in the middle of the night and it would not be possible to move them to the mosque until the next day. On such nights, Shaesta would sit among the dead and reflect on their short lives and what they had been through. She would think about all the young people being killed every day.

Not long after my arrival in Hajji Kand, I was invited, along with Halala, to a meeting with two members of the Komala Central Committee to discuss the problems and challenges we had faced in Baneh. Mahmood had also arrived in Hajji Kand and joined us for the meeting. We talked about how our public work in Baneh during the wars meant that we were widely known as activists in the area. In hindsight, we had not been the best people for an underground role – everyone in the city already knew who we were. Baneh was small. The Tudeh Party and the Fedayeen Khalq had both been working with the government and had started to spy on us for them. Their members knew who all of our members were.

I was asked to attend a large public meeting in Hajji Kand with Komala supporters from lots of different cities, where I and several others had to cover our faces with white material. This marked us out as someone who could be sent back underground. It was important that we could not be identified by many others within the organisation.

In the meeting we discussed the extreme torture that had become the hallmark of the Iranian regime, which continued its attack on underground organisations, arresting and executing thousands more prisoners.

There was a wave of people becoming tavvab under torture and giving up the names of their comrades, which meant that a large part of Komala had been damaged due to their confessions. Everyone was scared of the regime. At the same time, the severe measures led to an increase in support for Komala. The party was looked upon to defend the dignity of the country.

I remained in Hajji Kand for a few months, but mostly stayed in the house as I had been told to. I kept myself occupied by reading books and the party's newsletter.

The best part of living in Hajji Kand was that I was able to see Azad frequently, as he was also based there. The first time I saw him after we had confessed our love, we avoided all mention of our feelings and instead limited our conversation to the political situation.

One evening he asked me to come and visit him in his room. While we were chatting about politics, he casually said: 'So what is your plan? Are you still thinking of working underground or staying within the Peshmerga?'

I was torn. I wanted to stay in Hajji Kand to be close to him. I had so much respect and love for the Peshmerga. They were like saints for me. It was good to work directly with them.

On the other hand, I knew that I was good at underground work and I was keen to get back to this role in another city.

'Maybe the party will let me go to the city, but it is risky for me as my picture is everywhere,' I said. 'I am also happy staying here.'

Azad laughed at me. 'You want both but you need to choose between working as a Peshmerga, which would mean we can see each other more, or going to the city, which would mean we would be forced apart.'

'I will think about it and will let you know,' I said. I stood up to leave. Suddenly, and without warning, he took my hand and kissed it goodbye.

It felt like I'd had an electric shock.

I had not expected this. Women could be killed for a loss of honour in Iran and a kiss on the hand could not be given lightly. I was worried in case anyone had seen us, as this would dishonour us both, but at the same time I was ecstatic. A kiss was almost a betrothal. It was a promise. We no longer had to hide our love; I felt able to talk about our feelings to others.

As they lived close by in Bukan, Azad's family visited Hajji Kand regularly to see him. I knew them already from my time spent in meetings in their home in Baneh. Whenever they came to see Azad, I would visit them. Azad's mother was always kind to me. I liked her very much. Both parents seemed happy with our relationship. I'm sure Azad must have discussed his intention to marry me with his mother, as she treated me in a special way. I kept thinking that I must inform my own parents soon, but Azad and I did not discuss what was happening in our relationship or make any plans.

While I was in Hajji Kand waiting for a decision to be made about my future, the party organised an economics training course with a wonderful teacher called Dr Dariosh, who had a Ph.D. in economics and finance. He was going to teach us Das Kapital by Karl Marx. Around fifty of us were sent to this class, but I was the only woman. I think this is because I was the only pre-member of the party that was available to take the class. I was so excited. I didn't really ask why there weren't any other women in the class.

In some lessons, Dr Dariosh divided us into small teams. We had to work closely together studying different parts of Das Kapital and later explain it to the rest of the group. Having someone as knowledgeable as Dr Dariosh to explain Marx to us was truly thrilling. I really enjoyed the class and found Das Kapital to be one of the world's greatest books for its explanation of capitalism, the class system and socialism.

I was in a group with a former mullah, whom we all called Mullah Osman, who was older than many in the class, and Siamand, who was my age. Mullah Osman was hugely popular and made a joke of everything. He was always talking about the time when he had been a mullah, and liked to joke about how a mullah organised his life by taking food and everything else he needed from the people without having to do any work.

'This is true capitalism in action,' he grinned and none of us could stop laughing for the rest of the class.

I grew up in a family where boys and girls were free to talk and laugh with each other, so it was normal to talk with boys in the classroom like this. However, one day the wife of a Central Committee member came to the class and saw me laughing with the men. She went back to the Central Committee and interrupted a meeting to say to Azad in front of the other members that I was 'shameless'.

'Comrade, you love this woman and she is laughing with those men,' she said. 'Who is this girl that you love? She doesn't deserve you. How are you going to marry a woman like this?'

Azad was so shocked and angry at the woman that he didn't know how to respond. He walked out of the meeting and came to find me.

I couldn't believe what he told me. I was distraught. It was my reputation she was threatening. I didn't know what to do.

I continued with my economics class but the atmosphere in the Peshmerga community started to change around me. This woman had a strong network around her and she started to gossip about me with other women. All of a sudden it seemed as though everyone was talking about me and my scandalous love for Azad. Who was I to think of marrying a Central Committee member?

I began to think everyone was against me.

No one in the party suggested that Azad and I get married. Instead, they did what they could to separate us. This was not a political relationship, it was personal, and most people thought I should overpower my own needs. It was a sin to have such feelings, in their eyes. They thought we should put our feelings to one side and sacrifice ourselves for the party.

The general feeling was that a marriage should be decided by Komala so that the relationship could benefit the party. The chosen couple would live together and carry out activities on behalf of the party. It was unacceptable to love anyone of your own choosing. If someone loved someone romantically, it meant they were putting their relationship above the party.

I was made to feel as though I should have married Baqi, even though I didn't love him, and not marry Azad, whom I loved dearly. However, I knew my own mind and I was certain of my feelings. There was no other man for me.

I felt utterly alone. Nobody seemed to understand me. I had devoted all of my life to this organisation. I had been so honoured as to be one of the first women to be given pre-membership. What did it matter if I was in love? It didn't mean that I didn't love the organisation first and foremost. My belief in the organisation and love for it had no end.

The situation became unbearable. I was in shock and worried about losing the person that I loved. With so many Peshmerga talking about me, I felt ashamed. Without honour and reputation, women were nothing. I had made a promise to my father that he would always be able to hold his head up.

As a man and a member of the Central Committee, Azad was protected. Despite all of the talk against me, he continued to visit me. Every day he sent me a letter, always several pages long.

In this suffocating atmosphere, I was invited to a meeting with the Central Committee. They informed me that I needed to collect my personal belongings and be prepared to move to the village of Kani Rash with Halala, where we could be hidden. Once we were there, they would decide whether to send us to a city to continue our underground activities or whether we would remain with the Peshmerga. I had to accept this. I thought it might be good for me to be away from all of the gossip and I hoped for the situation to calm down. However, I knew that I would miss Azad.

The next day Halala and I left Hajji Kand for Kani Rash, with a team of four Peshmerga men. It was a cold winter. As far as the eye could see, everything was white and glittering from the sunshine reflecting on the snow. It was beautiful, but I was heavy hearted. When we arrived in the village a few hours later, it was snowing heavily. There were no other Peshmerga living there in the village. Halala and I were given a room with an old woman and her husband. They were both extremely kind and treated us like their own children. They gave us their guest room, which had rugs on the floor, unlike their own room, which was bare and smaller. In the centre of the house was a large, smoky, windowless room with a stone ware oven in the middle and a hole in the top of the roof for the smoke to go out and for light to come in. The woman used to cook and bake everything in this room. She would make popcorn for us every night.

Halala and I had some first aid materials with us and, as we had been trained in first aid, we started to help the villagers by treating their headaches with painkillers and by giving them injections of medicines, such as antibiotics. We quickly became famous throughout the village because of our first aid work, and made many friends. We began to be invited to different homes every evening to dine, or sometimes villagers would send food to our house in support of our host.

Although we were being well taken care of, I missed Azad terribly and became extremely depressed. Every week he would send me, via a fellow Peshmerga, three-page letters full of his love. I lived for those letters. I felt only half alive the rest of the time.

One night, my sister Shaesta came to visit me and Halala along with a number of her friends, including Azad's two sisters, Leyla and Farasat. I was really happy to see them all and to get some news from Azad. After they had been with us for about half an hour, Leyla took me to the roof garden.

'I think you should stop thinking about Azad,' she said. 'He has told me that you have made up all this love story and there is nothing between you and no feelings from him to you. I have come here to give you this message from him.'

I couldn't hear her any further, although I knew she was continuing to talk. I felt my world turn upside down. How could he have kissed me? A kiss was a promise. How could he say all that about how much he loved me and change so suddenly?

I didn't doubt Leyla's words. She had no reason to lie to me. She was a friend and she was a Peshmerga. Peshmerga women do not lie to each other.

While everyone went to sleep, I filled about six pages of a writing pad in a letter back to Azad. I was in a state of shock and utter distress. I reminded him of our love and told him that he was a liar and that he had not been truthful with me. He had simply been playing with me.

In front of Leyla I didn't cry, but I cried all night while I was writing the letter. I sent it back with Leyla. The next day I received a one-line reply from Azad: 'Do as you wish.'

Our relationship was over, just like that.

My hopes for a happy future with Azad were gone overnight. After all I had gone through with the horrendous gossip about me, my love had now abandoned me. Even though I was surrounded by people, I felt completely alone. I didn't dare try and speak to Azad. I was proud and would not beg for his love. I was also deeply embarrassed. His letter was a full stop for me. Yet I knew that my love for him was so deep it would never end.

For a few days I was very ill. I couldn't bear everyone talking about me and calling me a loose woman. I couldn't imagine a life without Azad. I thought about committing suicide, but I knew this would bring dishonour to my parents. Instead I decided an honourable way to die would be to go and fire at a government military base so that the soldiers there would be forced to retaliate and shoot me dead. I would be a martyr killed in the war. However, I was stopped by the overwhelming thought of my father and mother receiving news of my death. They were so proud of me and my work with the Peshmerga. I knew this would crush them.

If I were to die, my reputation would be even worse than it was now. I would be for ever known as a weak, romantic woman and I would be forgotten after a while. I needed to stay alive and show the party that the people who were gossiping about me were wrong. I became angry with myself for considering suicide as a way out of my problems. What would killing myself have achieved?

I was not the silly girl the party thought I was. I was a strong revolutionary woman and must not lose my sense of pride. I would make them see who I really was.

Chapter 16

The Publishing Department

Towards the end of 1981, I was invited to a meeting with the Komala Central Committee. They told me that they had decided to send me to join the publishing department instead of to a city for underground work. They had arranged for Halala to go and work underground with a male comrade, in an arrangement known as 'home team', which would give them cover. We said goodbye not knowing if we would ever see one another again.

I moved to Sardarabad, a village with about a hundred families, which was approximately thirty minutes from Hajji Kand and twenty minutes from my sister in Elmabad.

There were around fifty people in the department, with a dozen women. I was introduced to everyone and warmly welcomed. Galavezh H, the daughter of one of the Hosseini brothers who had saved my life when I had been blown up by a grenade in front of their shop in Baneh, and her brother Jalal were both working there. I also recognised Mehri, who had been a year ahead of me at teacher training school. I soon settled into my new home, where I would spend the next year and a half as a senior editor checking spelling and grammar for Komala's series of newspapers.

It was an important job. All of Komala's public information for Kurdistan went through the publishing department. The party had one newspaper, which was of the usual size and distributed publicly. They also had smaller newspapers printed to the size of a box of matches, which were sent to the cities for our activists. These were read and distributed within the underground organisations. We had another newsletter that was for the eyes of members and pre-members only and circulated internally.

As editors, we received announcements, political articles, mainly from Komala's Central Committee members, and reports on Komala's battles and activities. These were sent in by each company's communications team and from the central committees for each city.

We also published details of the brutal and barbaric attacks by the government and long lists of the names of those who had been executed. If possible, we would include photographs of the deceased.

In addition, the newspapers ran information on Komala's communist manifesto, with political comment pieces on equality and our beliefs on free education, free health care and a separation of religion and state. We carried reports on how the country should be run by a mixture of central councils and local neighbourhood councils with each and every person having a say in their own community.

The office was located inside a huge house belonging to the landlord of the village. He had another equally large home that he shared with his four wives. Inside the mansion house, there were several big rooms housing all of the equipment for printing, editing and writing. Next to the house a Peshmerga base with around fifty men protected the publishing department. They took turns on guard throughout the day and night.

It was a lively place. We worked hard and often until late at night to meet deadlines. Once we had finished editing, our work would go to the printing department, who were regularly up all night getting everything ready for the various Komala meetings. My team would often go and help the printers. It was so noisy in the print room, and the printers' hands were always covered in ink.

The house had a beautiful garden that I enjoyed walking in; it was full of apple, peach and both sweet and sour cherry trees. I started to take care of a small jasmine plant. In the spring, I watered it every day. The smell was so fresh and beautiful, especially in the early morning and evening. Jasmine is yas flower in

Kurdish and the plant became known as Galavezh's yas because of the attention I paid to it.

In the winter it was extremely cold, and all of the girls would sleep curled up next to each other like sausages to try and keep warm. Most nights, we would sing songs before falling asleep. This was a good way to warm ourselves up and to comfort each other. My favourite was a beautiful song called 'Jane Maryam', which I still love to sing now.

Galavezh H became my closest friend. She had been with me briefly in Najneh and Hajji Kand, but it was in Sardarabad, where we worked side by side, that we truly became good friends. As we both had the same name and both hailed from Baneh, I became known as Galavezh Soor, or Red Galavezh, because of my face. Most of the girls had dark skin, but my pale face burned easily. Galavezh was known as either Galavezh H or Galavezh Yek, which means 'number one' as she had joined the department before me.

In the evening, the whole department would eat together in the Peshmerga base where there was a long sofreh, a plastic tablecloth that we put along the floor. The Peshmerga, both men and women, would take turns to cook for all of the department and the Peshmerga guards.

The first time that it was my turn to prepare the meal, I was too distraught to cook. I had never cooked for such a huge number of people. I was shocked to see the huge pans. I wasn't a good cook, in any case, and I wasn't sure what to do.

I was also thinking about Azad, and felt absolutely heartbroken. Galavezh H could see that I was troubled, as I was tearful and listless.

'Come with me,' she said. 'I will do the cooking for you. You can watch and learn.'

Galavezh H cooked for a hundred people that day all by herself. All I had to do was peel some potatoes. I was really grateful for her kindness and understanding.

Galavezh was the only daughter in her family. Her father

had always been cold towards her and they had never had much of a relationship. When she was fifteen she fell in love with a boy her own age but her family wouldn't accept him. When they found out she had romantic feelings for him they forced her into marriage with another man.

Galavezh H tried to stand up against the marriage but nobody in the family would support her. In the first few years of marriage, she left her husband several times. Each time she was sent back by her father.

Galavezh H gave up and decided to stay with her husband, a Democrat Party member, and make the best of her situation. Not long after she reconciled herself to the fact that she could never leave him, he was killed in battle. After his death, Galavezh H decided to become a Peshmerga with Komala, like her brother.

One evening, Galavezh H told me she remembered coming to my home in Baneh for a meeting and eating lunch with my family.

'We were eating rice and chicken and your father had a piece of chicken breast,' she said. 'You said to your father, "Could I have a bit of that breast?" I was astonished when he replied to you, "Of course, with all my heart." My father would never have spoken to me like that and I would never have dared ask for chicken. I thought it was normal for fathers never to speak to their daughters. Seeing you with your father made me question my relationship with my own parents.'

This story made me even more proud of my father and also so sorry for her. It had obviously been a shock to her to realise that a father could be so different.

Mehri had also been forced into marriage, but this time it was by the party, not her family. Her husband was a member of the Central Committee. This marriage was arranged for both of them.

At first, Mehri didn't care for her husband and was depressed about her situation. She went out of her way to avoid seeing him for the first few months of their marriage but gradually, over time, she accepted him. Eventually she started to love him.

DIANA NAMMI AND KAREN ATTWOOD

However, by the time that we were working together in Sardarabad, the husband had grown cold towards Mehri. Unsure of how to deal with this, she sent a close girlfriend to go and talk to her husband on her behalf. To Mehri's distress, this girl fell in love with her husband and started a relationship with him. At first the friend denied the affair, but later admitted to it. A short while later, Mehri's husband divorced her and married this other woman.

Galavezh H, Mehri and I spent many hours talking to each other about how unhappy we were with love and men. Talking was a form of therapy for us and we became extremely close. Our discussions helped me to process my feelings of betrayal and anger, and both friends were critical of Azad. They couldn't understand why he had ended our relationship.

'Don't worry, things will change,' Galavezh H said often. 'I was forced into a marriage and now look. I am free. Azad will regret his decision one day.'

Yes, but it might be too late for us by then, I thought. When we weren't in the publishing department, we would walk into Sardarabad or one of the other villages close by. Komala suggested that we talk to the villagers about equality and human rights and we gladly did so.

Zhn ba zhn was a common marriage practice in the region. This is when a young woman in one family marries a man in another, while her brother is married to her sister-in-law in a kind of exchange. It was rare for all four people to be satisfied with this kind of union. At least two of them would be unhappy and maybe all four of them. Usually at least one couple, and perhaps both, would have been forced into the marriage.

In other cases, if a father became a widower, he might exchange his daughter with another family in order to get a new, usually younger, bride for himself.

Gawrah ba bchook was another form of marriage, where two adults get married and at the same time two youngsters in the same families are promised to each other, even as tiny babies. These children grow up knowing that they are engaged to someone they are unlikely to love and more likely to hate. There have been many cases over the years where girls have committed suicide rather than marry the person she was promised to as a baby.

Forced marriage could happen at any age. In a forced marriage either the bride or the groom, or often both, have not consented to the marriage. Instead, physical and mental duress is used, such as blackmail or imprisonment. Sometimes the bride or groom are killed for not consenting to the marriage.

Women and girls are the predominant victims in these marriages, which were commonplace in the villages but also happened in the cities.

The practices of 'honour' killings and 'honour related' violence, such as forced abortions and being forced to marry a rapist, were acceptable in the community.

The victims would get little or no sympathy, and if a family member helped them by providing shelter, they would be at risk too. The perpetrators of such honour violence were usually family members or other members of the community. They were and are usually men, but there were cases when female family members were involved in harming or even killing the victim. Female perpetrators either believed that the victim had brought shame and dishonour upon the family or their community, or they were forced to cooperate with the perpetrators. These murderers would be considered as heroes and would not be prosecuted for their crimes. There was no system to protect the victims. This meant families and the community were free to deal with such issues as a personal matter.

When we went to the villages, we would talk about all these types of marriages and explain they were a bad practice and tradition. People, and in particular women, should be free to make their own decisions about marriage. We also discussed female genital mutilation, which happened in some villages.

Our talks led to many girls opening up their hearts to us about their experiences with forced marriage. There was so much unhappiness.

However, these women were trapped.

In Iran, there is a saying: 'You go to your husband's house in a white bridal dress and you leave in a white shroud.'

Only death could bring a woman out of a marriage. Many unhappy and beaten wives stayed for the sake of the children and for honour. While a husband could easily divorce his wife – simply by saying 'I divorce you' three times – a woman could not seek the same in an unhappy marriage. If she divorced, she would be dishonoured and the children would always be given to the father rather than the mother. She wouldn't be allowed to see her children any more without her husband's permission.

Polygamy was also a normal practice, as Islam allowed it. There were many men with several wives.

'This all needs to change,' I said. 'Women should be safe and protected and be able to marry the person that they love.'

I thought of my own unhappiness with Azad. We Peshmerga girls knew in our hearts that it was not right that our own marriages should also be arranged. We talked to each other about how wrong it was and that we shouldn't be controlled in this way.

Yet at the same time, my heart and mind belonged to the party. It was difficult to question our own situations with the Central Committee.

After I had been in Sardarabad for around six months, I was sitting working in the department when I got a message that my father was there to visit me. It was a lovely surprise. He had contacted Baneh's regional committee to find out where Shaesta and I were located and he had travelled to Bukan and on to Sardarabad to find us, risking his own safety to do so.

I hadn't seen him since the day I had left home. As soon as I set eyes on him, we both burst out crying. We arranged immediately for Shaesta to come and join us from Elmabad. My father was so popular with the Peshmerga that he was quickly surrounded by them all, asking for news of Baneh. It was difficult for me and Shaesta to get any time alone with him, but it was still wonderful to see him.

'Our home is so empty without you girls,' he held us close to him. 'Our life has changed completely. We all miss you so much.'

He started to joke: 'Your mother will not cook any of the foods that you used to love. We've not had homemade hamburgers since you left! She says she will not make these dishes without you two in the house. She is crying all the time.'

I knew that the loss of us both had hit my parents hard. It was like another bereavement for my mother. They were also under pressure from the regime. My father continued to be questioned a lot by the pasdaran about our whereabouts. Each time he was arrested, he told them he had no idea where we were. My little brother had not been allowed to continue at school because we were a Peshmerga family.

It was the beginning of summer when my father came, and he brought a lamb and a few boxes of sweet and sour cherries that are so popular in the region. There were enough cherries for everyone. We feasted on the lamb until late afternoon when my father had to leave.

'Be careful,' he told us as he hugged Shaesta and me goodbye. 'Make me proud of you.'

I learned sometime later that my father was arrested on his return to Baneh and kept for three days for question ing. He was beaten by the pasdaran.

'Tell your daughters to come home,' he was told repeatedly.

'I cannot do that, they are Peshmerga now,' he replied. 'But if you can go and get them we will be happy to have them home.'

During my time in Sardarabad, Komala grew in strength throughout Kurdistan, with many people joining the Peshmerga or becoming activists or supporters. Our manifesto proved popular with Kurdish people, fed up with suppression under the Shah and now further oppression under the Islamic regime.

Komala didn't want any compromise with the government, unlike the Democrat Party, which was regularly in discussion with the regime.

In the early 1980s, Komala had been contacted by Etihad

e Mobarezan Comounist, the Union of Communist Militants, which was based mainly in Tehran but followed broadly the same politics and ideals as Komala. Our two parties began talks on how we could work together. Members of the Union of Communist Militants came to Kurdistan for secret discussions.

In 1982, as the crackdown on opposition groups in Tehran and other cities became ever more violent, many of the Union of Communist Militants' members were executed. Those that were able to escape Tehran fled to Kurdistan, including the party's leader, Mansoor Hekmat. Our parties began talks about joining together to become one national party, the Communist Party of Iran.

During this period, Komala ran lots of programmes, meetings and seminars to ensure that everyone understood the direction that we were moving in. They organised meetings in north Kurdistan known as the North Seminars, where the future of the party and its politics were the main agenda. The two parties were united in wanting to continue a socialist revolution and to rid Iran of the Islamic Republic. Other leftwing organisations joined the discussions.

Mansoor had lived in Europe for a long time. He had studied for his masters in economics in the UK, breaking from a doctoral thesis to return to Iran when the revolution started. He was highly intelligent and progressive. He was open-minded and familiar with issues of discrimination. He was extremely charismatic and had all of the qualities needed to lead an effective party.

Mansoor could see clearly how Komala operated, and the mistakes we were making. He criticised Komala's approach to the revolution, saying that it was populist and not communist. When I heard him speak for the first time, it made me realise how Komala had been simply repeating what we saw. The party used to say: 'The people are poor so we should live like the poor,' but Mansoor said poverty was unacceptable for all people, including its leaders. We should be a progressive and modern model for the people rather than simply copying them.

In one meeting, Mansoor said that women should be decision makers and should be in the Central Committee.

At his words, I stood up.

'This is all very well to say, but here we have to work so much harder than men to prove that we have a right to our place,' I said.

'The party needs to give women the opportunity to grow, to show their potential and have a proper role,' he replied. 'Women need to be part of the Central Committee and have a role in management.'

Hearing his words was a huge relief for me. This was something completely different from what we had heard from Komala.

The Communist Party of Iran would be announced later in 1983, with Komala becoming the Kurdish branch. This would signal a massive change within the party. It would be a strong movement and would work all over the country, uniting the workers and activists for a socialist revolution. It was thrilling to think of such a future for the party and for Iran.

Despite my excitement and happiness about the direction of the party, I was still suffering terribly from the loss of Azad. I thought it would be good for me to talk about my private life with Mansoor. I felt that he might understand what I was going through.

In the end, I worried that Mansoor would agree with what the others had said about me, that I was shameless and dishonourable. That would have been devastating. I decided to deal with it myself. I thought with the passing of time it would be less painful for me. When I got to know Mansoor much later on, I realised how open-minded and fair he was, and I believe he could have been a great support for me at that time.

I had faith in the party and its communist ideology, but I also knew that it had to make changes in the way it treated women. We had so many long discussions about women, and their position and responsibilities within the party. Influenced by Mansoor, Komala started to talk about women becoming armed Peshmerga but with limited power and military actions. The first Peshmerga unit of women with guns was established in the Hajji Kand area, with around eleven volunteers. This was the start of a revolution in the position of women and in the minds of millions of people around the country.

I didn't volunteer for this group. At that time, I thought it was just symbolic. Although these women would be armed, they would not be going into battle alongside the men. Their tasks would be limited to going to villages to talk about joining the Peshmerga. I didn't believe that the party could yet have true equality. Just look at the way I had been treated.

Another reason for my not volunteering was that I had lost some of my confidence through everything that had happened with Azad and all the talk about me ever since. I had started to doubt myself.

Alongside the discussion about the future of women in the party, there was also a general debate about how the party should be run. I and six members of the publishing department suggested that instead of the Central Committee making all of the key decisions, there should first be a discussion between members and supporters, the outcome of which should be put forward to the Central Committee. The party didn't like this idea. They saw it as a rebellion. To punish us for daring to go up against the party, they took away our pre-membership, the precious thing that we had worked so hard to gain.

Ebrahim Alizade, the leader of Komala at that time, criticised this attitude from the party. He said Komala needed to be more open to different points of view. His intervention led to everyone getting their pre-membership back, except for me.

I couldn't understand why. I talked to the publishing department manager and he said that he was not aware of the reason. He had got a letter from the Central Committee asking him to inform everyone else they had got their pre-membership back. He advised me to talk to the operations manager in the Central Committee. I asked Shaesta to come with me to a big meeting in Hajji Kand so that I could see one of the operational team leaders. I went to him after a seminar.

'Can I talk to you for a moment?' I asked. I explained the discussion in the publishing department and asked: 'Why didn't I get back my membership?'

'You know, lady, your approach to marriage is romantic and it's for this reason we didn't give back your membership,' he told me.

What? I couldn't say anything at first. Did I hear correctly?

'Is it really just because of that?' I asked quietly.

'Yes, it is because of that. This is a serious matter. You put yourself and your desires before the party. Goodbye.'

He left Shaesta and me in a state of shock. I burst into tears. I felt without hope.

I believed so much in this organisation. I had put my life and my family's lives at risk. I had just about managed to escape from execution. I was prepared to die for Komala. Yet for such a thing they would take away my pre-membership.

I was furious, but I tried to control myself and not say anything more to stir up trouble. The party's ruling was still like the word of God for me. I also didn't believe it was worth talking to them. Nobody seemed to want to listen to my opinion. I strongly believed they were wrong, but I felt I had no energy to challenge it at that point in time.

Shaesta tried to calm me down. All the way from Hajji Kand to Sardarabad, she talked about how great I was. I loved my little sister dearly. I was sorry that my problems were upsetting her.

Shaesta had to return to Elmabad. I went back to the publishing department. All the girls came to me and hugged me, and I explained what had happened. Mehri and Galavezh H were a great support for me, but everything was getting too difficult. I wanted to show the party that I was more than a hopeless romantic. Galavezh H and I decided that the solution was for us to return to the Baneh region and take up arms.

'Staying in the publishing department means staying always in the background,' I said. 'This should not be the role of Peshmerga women. I can't bear this anymore.'

I knew the best place for me would be Baneh, where I was well known and respected. It was time for me to prove myself.

Chapter 17

The Right to Bear Arms

It was autumn. Everywhere I looked was yellow, gold, bronze and red, from the leaves on the trees to the fields of wheat. Bright yellow quinces and deep red pomegranates hung ripe on the trees. Even the dust on the roads had a golden sheen. I was excited about my return to Baneh.

Galavezh H and I discussed our wishes with the publishing department manager and our friends. We got permission from Babak and Baqi in the Baneh Regional Committee, and they arranged for us to leave the publishing department. Shaesta, and some of her friends from Baneh who also worked at the hospital, decided to return with us.

The day before we left Sardarabad, they held a galta o gapp goodbye party for us. We had a feast of chicken and rice and everyone sang and told jokes. We danced late into the night.

We set off by car, going from village to village. In some areas it was too dangerous to drive and we had to get out and walk. The government had military bases all over the area. It had total control of some villages and cities, with checkpoints on all of the major roads. The Peshmerga of both Komala and the Democrat Party, as well as other small parties, also had bases and a number of safe houses that Peshmerga could rest in. It took about four days for us to arrive back in the Baneh area.

We were warmly greeted by Baqi and Babak, along with Massoud, an old classmate of mine from Baneh, and Jamal, who had been recently elected to the Baneh Regional Committee.

I congratulated Baqi on his recent marriage to Babak's sister.

Time had passed since I had rejected his proposal and I hoped this could now all be forgotten. Above all, it was good to see my old friends and to be closer to home.

There were two large Komala bases in the villages near to Baneh: one at Blakeh and the other at Banwan. The base in Banwan was inside a beautiful large building perched on a mountaintop with a clear view all the way down to Blakeh, in the middle of the valley. This was the headquarters of the Baneh Regional Committee at that time, as well as of the Baneh Company, the main fighting force for the Peshmerga in the region. The Baneh Company did not stay in one place. It was always on tour.

In each base, between fifty to seventy Peshmerga were stationed. They were split into smaller platoons of thirty or thirty-five, which were divided again into squads of twelve and fifteen and finally into smaller eight-person fire teams. Each base and platoon had both a military commander and a political commander.

Galavezh H was given the responsibility for procuring and distributing food and clothes for both Blakeh and Banwan, while Baneh's regional committee invited me to be the political manager for Blakeh base. The base had an overall manager called Raof. As base political manager, I came under his direct command, as did the military commander. The Peshmerga guards were organised by the military commander, but all of the meetings for the Peshmerga and in the villages were organised by me as political manager.

I was the first woman in this area to reach such a high position with such responsibility. I felt honoured. The appointment of a female manager was good for all the women. However, a part of me wished I had more responsibility.

Komala organised a team to go regularly to the village of Blakeh, which was one of the main business centres for all of the items smuggled in from Iraq. Smugglers brought in food and arms, as well as whisky and cassettes and video tapes, as alcohol and music were now forbidden in Iran. Komala stationed a Peshmerga team at Blakeh to take a customs tax from the smugglers. Those smuggling alcohol would have the highest taxes.

Shaesta was also located at Blakeh in a community team, which meant I was able to see her regularly. She had had a difficult time with the Peshmerga. The discussion on arming women had begun after she had been in Elmabad for several months. Some military training was organised for the hospital personnel so that they could defend themselves in case of attack. There was no proper department for training at this time and it was all rather ad hoc.

On the first day, a group of young male recruits gathered with the girls from the hospital. They were told how to clean a gun, take it apart and reassemble it. On the second day, they went outside to shoot. Shaesta's group was told to run while the men fired bullets.

Instead of shooting elsewhere, the men shot in front of the trainees. Shaesta could see bullets everywhere around her. She saw the others running forward but she was unable to move. She sat down suddenly and saw blood running from her legs. A bullet had gone through the back of her thigh and right through her leg. Shaesta was rushed into the hospital for surgery and spent several months in recovery. She was lucky the bullet had missed the bone.

I had been to visit Shaesta and had walked in just as Doctor Darnish was cleaning the wound. I took one look and fainted.

The wound was deep and became infected; it took a long time for Shaesta to recover. The recovery time was extended even further because Shaesta was allergic to almost all of the medicine she could be treated with.

The team leader who had organised the training was mortified by what had happened and came to apologise to Shaesta.

'If you had died, I would never have forgiven myself,' he said.

The Peshmerga who had shot her, however, never came to say sorry.

After this experience, Shaesta had left the hospital and joined a community team, as I had done previously, going from village to village to talk about our manifesto and women's rights and equality. She had become disillusioned with the atmosphere around women in the Peshmerga.

'I am a revolutionary, but the situation for women is hard to bear,' she told me.

At seventeen, my sister was extremely beautiful and many of the Peshmerga men wanted to marry her. A number of them had proposed but, not being in love with any of them, Shaesta had refused them all. Whenever a boy was refused by a girl, he would bad mouth her and say she was cheap. The men held all the power. They would even refuse to talk to girls who had rejected them and ban them from certain activities.

'I am really getting tired with all this talk about me,' Shaesta said. 'I will marry the next person who asks.'

Many of my female comrades from Baneh had also joined community teams. They were given guns as part of the gradual arming of women across Kurdistan. As more Peshmerga women were given guns, more men threatened to quit. Leave then, I thought. There are thousands of women who are ready to come and take your place. We needed people in Komala to really believe in the party and what it stood for: liberty and equality for all. If the men were sexist and couldn't accept women on the front line, this party wasn't the right place for them.

The Peshmerga women were supportive of me as political manager, but the men were more difficult to win over. However, Raof and the Baneh Regional Committee stood behind me, so the men had to accept it.

This didn't stop them going out of their way to annoy me and the other women and to try and hinder the work we were doing. They made jokes. They were constantly undermining me. They tried to make our work look insignificant.

One day I organised a half day meeting so that we could listen to some recorded speeches from a conference from the Komala Central Committee. Midway through, one Peshmerga called me out for a talk. When I came back another had changed the cassette. When I pressed play, music came out.

They would not have dared play such a joke on a male commander. I was furious. However, I tried to remain calm. It was important not to lose it. When I asked the group who it was that had changed the cassette, they all laughed. They thought that I would run away and cry. I stood there and put the meeting cassette back in. Before pressing play, I said: 'If anyone does not wish to listen to this conference speech, feel free to leave the room.'

No one moved. They saw that I was taking this seriously. I had a good idea who might have been responsible for changing the cassette. There was one Peshmerga in particular who was always making fun of women. I assumed it was him. After the meeting, I had my suspicions confirmed by some of the other Peshmerga. I made a complaint to the Baneh Regional Committee and also to Raof. They punished the joker by taking his gun away for a week. After this he apologised to me. I was treated with a bit more respect by the others after that.

I'd been in Blakeh for about a month or so when a Peshmerga team arrested a woman called Altun. Altun's husband was known to have been a violent man who regularly beat his wife. He had died, and some of the villagers believed that Altun had poisoned him. She was accused of being a murderer and a loose woman. Some of the villagers called for her to be executed.

Altun had been arrested by the Peshmerga simply because the villagers had complained about her. She was imprisoned while we decided what to do. This became a huge debate throughout the village and the Peshmerga bases.

I went to talk to Altun on several occasions. She told me that she had been forced to marry her husband at around the age of thirteen or fourteen and she bore him five children. He had been abusive throughout their marriage and had suddenly become ill and died. There was no way that she would have killed her husband and left her children without a father, she said. We couldn't prove it either way.

The Peshmerga women didn't believe that Altun should be executed. We all felt sorry for her. There was no evidence that she had killed her husband. However, some of the Peshmerga men were angry with Altun because of the rumours that she had been unfaithful.

'We have to punish her,' they said. 'She has not been loyal to her husband.'

'But she cannot be executed for being unfaithful to her husband,' I said.

It was so unfair. Altun had been a victim of forced marriage, child marriage and abuse. She was held in prison for two months. During this time, her eldest daughter looked after her four siblings. On the days they came to visit their mother, everyone cried.

Eventually, the Baneh Regional Committee decided that, due to a lack of evidence, Altun would be freed. When Altun heard the news, she started crying and making blessings to God. However, the villagers were angry about the decision. This meant that we couldn't just release her into the community, as this would have put her in danger. Many still believed she was guilty and deserved to die.

We explained the situation to the Komala Central Committee and one member, Dr Jafar Shafie, said he would be happy to talk to the villagers on the satellite phone.

I invited everyone to the mosque. This was the first time we had held such a controversial meeting in the mosque in Blakeh. Some villagers said that Altun didn't deserve to come to the mosque as she was not clean. The Peshmerga had to protect her.

During the meeting I spoke about forced marriage and the issue of honour, and explained that there was no evidence against Altun.

'In two months, no one has proved anything,' I said. 'This was simply an allegation.'

Dr Jafar made a powerful speech about 'honour' killings, women's rights and explained all of this in the context of Altun's situation with great passion on the satellite phone. His speech was vital in changing the minds of the villagers.

The meeting lasted two hours and by the end everyone was calm. Altun was freed and the villagers went home.

Saving Altun had been a great success. This incident gave the Peshmerga women more respect and power in the community, and many more women came to us to talk about their husbands' violence.

After this episode, I felt strongly that the girls in Baneh needed to become true Peshmerga. Just being in the bases did not make us full Peshmerga. I and the other girls started a long debate in Baneh about women being armed at all times. I talked to the other girls about joining the company. Some were hesitant. They wanted more time but Galavezh H and I decided we would leave the base and join the Baneh Company.

We had to get permission from the Baneh Regional Committee and also the company commander. Nobody was happy with our decision, but they said they would let us try. I think they all thought that we would not last long. Although the men were armed with Kalashnikovs, Galavezh H and I were given a long, heavy rifle each, which took a lot of our strength just to carry. All the men made jokes at our expense but we didn't mind. We would show them.

Armed with our rifles, we went to meet the company in another village. By the time we arrived we had a message waiting for us. My sister was to be married the next day. Shaesta had received another proposal, this time from Rajab, a deputy member of the regional committee. She wasn't sure what to do. She didn't love him but, worried about her reputation, she had agreed to the marriage. Rajab insisted on the wedding happening quickly, before Shaesta had a chance to change her mind.

Galavezh H and I had to go back to the base for the wedding the next day. When we arrived, the men all laughed at us for our short stay with the company.

'Our Peshmerga have already left the company and have come back instead to buy nice clothes for a wedding.'

I glared at them. They all immediately went quiet.

It was heartbreaking to see my sister so unhappy. She felt forced to accept this marriage without any love for this man. I didn't know Rajab well. He was about twenty four; Shaesta would always be my little sister and I felt this was too old for her.

'I don't agree with this decision, but I wish you all the best,' I told her.

After a simple ceremony, the wedding party began. The dancing lasted late into the night. Not long after we had all gone to bed, at around 3 a.m. we were woken by gunfire. The Blakeh base and village were completely surrounded by government forces.

Rockets rained down on the village and all around it. Our Peshmerga men immediately jumped up to defend us. During the fighting, Shaesta, the other girls and I stayed away from the front line, as was the usual practice. We told the villagers to head for safety in the valley. We helped the villagers prepare sandwiches for the Peshmerga, which we took turns in taking to the front line. When it was my turn, I bent over and ran as fast as I could through the alleys in the village. All the time I could hear the bullets whizzing past my ears along with screams of Allahu Akbar, 'God is the greatest', from the regime soldiers. They were ready to sacrifice themselves for God. The Peshmerga were shouting 'Long live socialism'. I felt empowered as I ran, proud to be doing something useful.

The Democrat Party Peshmerga were nearby and joined Komala in the battle. The Baneh Company also came to the village as reinforcements. In several hours, the Peshmerga managed to push the regime soldiers back without any major injuries on our side.

We arrested a number of soldiers who claimed they had been told that they were fighting the Iraqis.

'We didn't know you were Kurdish and Iranian people,' one said.

Another said he had been told that the Kurds wanted to divide Iran.

One of the prisoners came from Baneh but he had betrayed Komala and supported the government. In these early years, Komala executed its prisoners.

In the morning, while it was still dark, one of the commanders came into the girls' room to wake me up.

He asked me to follow him. He went out of the village and I walked behind him, wondering where he was going. We joined two more Peshmerga.

'You can execute him,' one of them told me.

I looked down and saw the Baneh prisoner leaning on a rock. He was blindfolded and in handcuffs.

'No, I cannot do it,' I said, shocked. I quickly walked away without looking back. I could hear the commander laughing at me. A moment later, a few shots were fired. I shivered as I heard the sound. I was distressed and angry at being asked. I was worried that they might think I was not strong enough to be a Peshmerga, but I didn't care anymore. I believed that execution was wrong, though I couldn't articulate my reasons why. Execution was later banned by the Central Committee.

After this battle was over, I knew that it was time for me to go back with the Baneh Company. I was concerned about leaving Shaesta in this unhappy marriage, but I knew there was little I could do for her. I discussed my decision with my sister and she wished me good luck. I told Galavezh H it was time for us to go, but she had changed her mind and did not want to return to Baneh with me. She enjoyed her job in procurement and wanted to go back to that.

I would go on my own to the front line.

Chapter 18

Girl with a Gun

In autumn 1982, I became the first woman to join the Baneh Company. As we left the base for one of the villages, I struggled at first to carry my heavy rifle along with my ammunition belt, which was weighted down with six extra rounds of ammunition and a grenade. I was of slim build and I was now having to carry an extra fifteen kilos.

We arrived at a beautiful village called Spidareh, which was on the top of a mountain, close to Najneh and Manijalan, and overlooking the Kokhan Valley. Around thirty or forty families lived there. It was late afternoon and I could see the other villages down in the valley under the shadow that the mountains cast during sunset. Spidareh still had some sunlight. Two Peshmerga remained on guard on the mountain while the rest of us were divided into groups of two and three to visit different villagers' homes for dinner.

I wondered what they would make of me, as the first armed female Peshmerga in the region. By now, they were used to seeing women from the bases dressed in the masculine style khaki clothing of the Peshmerga, but not armed and travelling with a company. The villagers were excited and curious. I spent time with some of the women in one of their homes explaining that we needed to have more female Peshmerga. They asked so many questions. Was I scared? Could I walk beside the men? Could I sleep comfortably? I tried to answer them all as best as I could. After we had eaten, we went to the mosque where all of the Peshmerga would sleep. One of the team leaders came to me and asked me to disassemble my rifle and reassemble it, which I did quickly.

The rest of the Peshmerga surrounded me to watch. When I finished, they all yelled, 'Hooray!'

The team leader asked me whether I could use the rifle.

'Yes, I can,' I replied.

When it was time for most of us to sleep, I asked to be put on night guard. The others were a bit reluctant at first but after a bit of persuasion, they agreed to give me the first night shift, which began at 10 p.m.

I went outside and got into position. The full moon was giving off a bright light. I could see clearly into the oak trees all over the mountains.

A group of Peshmerga reported to me that they were off on a mission and I watched them leave.

Sometime later I heard footsteps. I got my rifle out ready to shoot.

'Who are you?' I shouted loudly. 'Don't shoot, don't shoot!' I heard.

'Give me the night password,' I said, still holding my gun ready.

One of them gave the password. As they moved closer, I saw that it was the same group who had gone out on a mission a short while earlier.

One came running over to me, laughing.

'Our mission was to test you to see if you were capable of being a guard,' he said. 'None of the men can sleep tonight in the mosque. They're frightened you might run away!'

I was annoyed that the men hadn't trusted me, but I was also proud of myself. I knew that I wasn't an experienced Peshmerga but I was brave enough to defend them. I had passed my first test.

The next guard came to take over from me and I went back to the mosque. The men had given me a corner in the main room, slightly separate from them. Before this night, I had only slept in rooms with other girls and now I was sleeping amidst fifty Peshmerga.

It was strange at first and I struggled to get to sleep. It was not that I was frightened. I trusted the men. However, I didn't even know the names of some of them and yet I had to sleep in a large room next to them. I was preoccupied with what the villagers might say. People liked to joke that communists shared their women as well as everything else. It was also unusual for women to sleep in a mosque. While I was thinking all these thoughts, I must have fallen fast asleep. Before I knew it, it was morning.

When we got up, the boys were all so respectful that my worries went away. We split up to go to different villagers' homes for breakfast.

Later that morning, a group from the company took me to a mountain to show me how to prepare for war. My military training consisted of learning in much more detail how to shoot my rifle. I was also taught how to move around in different positions, how to sit when in a trench, and what you need to do to keep safe in different circumstances. They also showed me how to use a rocket propelled grenade (RPG) launcher, although it generally wouldn't be my role to use one.

I stayed with the Baneh Company for several months. The men quickly got used to having a woman with them. Little by little they accepted me.

It was not safe for the company to stay in the same place for long, due to a constant threat of attack by the government. We moved from village to village in the area to the west of Baneh. This was a green, mountainous region with villages sitting among the valleys. Thick oak trees sprawled all over the hillsides and were good for taking cover behind.

West of Baneh, at Kokhan, was a large government military base. The company moved frequently among the villages between Kokhan and Baneh. One of the company's key missions was to locate and attack other smaller government bases. In the early days the men tried to not involve me too directly in the close range fighting. At first, when there was a large operation, they didn't ask me to join in. Gradually, though, they began to include me in their hit and run operations on the regime bases.

In these operations we would be in teams of less than ten Peshmerga. The purpose was not to begin a battle, but to attack quickly and withdraw. During my first hit and run, I sat down next to a large stone with my fellow Peshmerga. I was scared about being injured or even dying. I thought about my mother and father and how they would feel to hear sad news. I began feeling really sorry for them but I had to pull myself back to reality. This was no time to be scared. I had to show I was brave and reliable. One of the Peshmerga launched the RPG. The rest of us fired several shots before running away as fast as we could, as the regime began to fire rockets back. As soon as the first shot was fired, my fear left me. It was exhilarating. It was the government who should be afraid.

Hit and runs were our most frequent operation. In one year alone, we carried out fifty-one in the Baneh region.

Each time we had a successful hit and run, I felt more confident as a Peshmerga. It was thrilling to feel that we were attacking the enemy. This was our land and country that had been invaded and occupied and they should have to run for their lives. I was furious whenever I thought about how we had no possibility of a normal life with our parents, relatives and within our communities.

One day, I was invited to a meeting with the Baneh Company commanders and about twenty other Peshmerga. The commanders were examining a map on the floor which showed several villages, roads, the mountains and the government's military bases.

They were planning a hit and run operation on all three military bases around Baneh at the same time. We were organised into three teams of seven Peshmerga to attack each military base, and we were to start the attack at midnight.

We set off after dinner and had a long walk in the fading light, through valleys and over mountains, crossing rivers and roads. We finally arrived at the spot where the teams would separate. It was nearly dark when my team arrived in a graveyard near a village, close to our target, but we were a little early and we had to wait a while to ensure that the pasdaran and soldiers in the military base were asleep and the other Peshmerga were in position.

Our team leader told us that we could go and rest in the graveyard until it was time to get ready for the attack, so I looked among the graves for a comfortable place to sleep. Salam, a male Peshmerga, aged about sixteen or seventeen years old, started to repeat 'Besme Allah' which means in the name of God and he appeared to be reading the Koran. He was clearly distressed.

'What is the problem?' I asked him.

'Aren't you scared?' he said.

'Scared of what?'

'Of the spirits of the dead and ghosts.'

'No, I'm not scared of them. I don't believe in ghosts and spirits. You aren't religious. How can you be frightened of something that doesn't exist?'

'But I can't sleep. What if they do exist?'

I pointed at two large graves.

'I'm going to sleep between those two graves, Salam. They are high and will protect me from the wind. Try and find a good spot and get some rest before we set off. We don't have much time.'

'Do you mind if I sleep between the next two graves, close to you?' asked Salam, moving near me.

'Sure, sleep well.'

As usual, I put my ammunition belt under my head as a pillow, then I lay down and went to sleep immediately. Two hours later, the guard woke us up one by one so we could prepare to move.

We approached the military base quietly and made our surprise attack at the same time as our comrades were hitting the other bases. After fifteen minutes of heavy gunfire, it was time for us to move back to join the rest of the company.

Salam came and thanked me the next day for supporting him during the night.

Whenever we arrived at a new village, all the villagers would rush out to see me. A teenage girl with a gun was an unusual sight for them. Everyone was proud of me as the first armed Komala woman in the region.

After a couple of months, four other women joined the company. We began to go together to the villages to talk about socialism and our fight with the government. The party still believed that the government was a temporary regime, but personally, I had come to realise that our revolution had been oppressed. Now all we could do was fight against the regime and hope to move them out of Kurdistan and continue our fight for equal rights for men and women and financial equality for all, with the dream of a socialist regime in Iran one day.

We invited the villagers to come to the mosques to talk. Women were reluctant at first. They had a perception that the mosque was only for men and it was a big step for women to enter there. However, little by little, they ventured out to join us.

Women started to bring their complaints to us and they would talk about family matters and problems with their relationships. As Komala was respected in the area, we had some power to intervene and try to prevent traditional practices – such as child marriage, forced marriage, bridal exchanges and honour killings, as well as domestic violence – from happening.

After several months of such activities within the company, the Baneh Regional Committee invited me to join an armed team of four working in the community. There were two community teams for the Baneh region: one covering the north and east, and my team, which covered the west and south.

I was the only woman in my team. Jalal, the youngest at about sixteen or seventeen, had the job of operating our satellite phone. He was our main contact with the company and the Baneh Regional Committee. Shaesta's husband Rajab was put on my team as leader for a month in order to help us set up. Omar, who had been a postgraduate student, also joined us. His role was to focus on our work with the villagers.

Even though Rajab was my brother-in-law, I didn't feel particularly close to him. He was loud and bold but conservative towards women. He felt more like a stranger.

The team's role was to go alone to villages to talk about Komala's manifesto and our fight for socialism. In the evening, I had to organise large meetings inviting all of the villagers to take part. I also organised women into groups in villagers' homes to talk about politics, women's rights, domestic violence and forced marriage.

Most of the women were illiterate and this was all new for them. They were extremely excited to have the opportunity to talk about their lives. Many of them faced discrimination and inequality, with some suffering from domestic abuse on a daily basis. They thought that this was the women's role: to obey the men in their lives, to cook and clean, to bear children, to take care of the elderly and disabled, to work in the field, as well as do all of the housework. Domestic violence and rape within marriage was so normalised and accepted, they felt they had to just put up with it, even though they knew in their hearts it was unjust.

When we spoke about violence, we were talking about their lives. By talking about these issues, we enabled them to give expression to their feelings of frustration. We were suggesting a different path for them and letting them know that they shouldn't accept this as a normal part of married life. We gave the women confidence to come to us and be part of our activities. They tried to engage with what we were doing and be part of Komala's underground organisation.

I enjoyed my work with this team immensely, as I had direct contact with the people I cared about so much once more. The villagers trusted us. Our work was of value. We were an armed team, ready to defend ourselves and be responsible for our own safety. I felt confident and powerful.

As we were a small unit, we were constantly targeted by the government. During the day, we would hide ourselves in the mountains and at night move closer to the government military bases. We had to take turns on guard every two hours throughout the night. The rota went 11 p.m. to 1 a.m., 1 to 3 a.m., 3 to 5 a.m. and 5 to 7 a.m., when it was usually light everywhere. The worst time to be on guard was between 3 and 5 a.m., as if the regime attacked, they would then have the daytime to fight in, which would be to their advantage.

The government regularly tried to ambush us. They would sit in silence somewhere they believed that the Peshmerga would pass, so they could shoot us when we went by, but we were always extremely careful. We usually identified them and managed to avoid these ambushes by going around them.

One night in spring 1983, we were in Manijalan, a village in a valley close to Upper Najneh. I was on the 3 to 5 a.m. guard shift and was standing on the roof of a house on the edge of the village. It was just before dawn and the weather was fresh and beautiful.

The next person to guard was Aso, from the Baneh Company. Aso, who was older and more experienced than me, had joined us for the evening. He had given his clothes to be washed the night before to the villagers, and he was wearing one of the villagers' outfits, dark in colour and much more easily seen than the usual khaki uniform of the Peshmerga. I called him to come and start his guard duty. While waiting for Aso, I stared into the horizon. The mountains were dark. I felt there were some movements between the oak trees but couldn't be sure. I had a sense that we were surrounded by government forces.

As Aso climbed onto the roof, I pointed out the movement.

'We must go and wake the others,' I said.

'Come on, you're imagining things,' he laughed at me. 'I am not imagining things,' I said. 'I can see movement. There is definitely something there. I will get down but I am not going to sleep again. Something is not right.'

Just as I climbed down from the roof, bullets started to rain down on Aso. He leaped down from the roof and ran to the room where Omar and Rajab were sleeping. They quickly got up to get their stuff. We all ran in the direction of the mosque, which was in the middle of the village, by a stream flowing down from the mountain, swollen with melted snow.

The villagers woke up with the shooting. One woman grabbed me.

'We will hide you – please don't go,' she said. 'You can take some of my clothes. Pretend you are my daughter.'

For the first time, when faced with this life and death situation, I decided that I would fight with the men.

We made our way quickly along the stream toward the top of the mountain. We knew we had to get up there somehow. As we started to ascend, we saw a group of Jash. This means 'baby donkey', and was the name we gave to Kurdish people who cooperated with the government. The Jash jumped up to try and stop us from getting past them. They wanted to arrest or kill us. The regime forces mistook them for Peshmerga and shot at them, giving us the chance to continue to ascend. The stream was the only way to escape to safety, and we had to climb up through it using our hands and feet.

We managed to get to the top of the mountain. From there, we could see the soldiers and the military cars and tanks clearly. There were hundreds of them and four of us. We were completely surrounded. On the other side of the mountains, in Upper Najneh, was our company. We heard gunshots from both sides. The company was engaged in a battle.

Chapter 19

On the Battlefield

What could we do? There was nowhere to hide. Our best chance of survival was to fight. We had to defend ourselves. We hid behind large rocks and began to fire back.

There was no time for me to think about this being my first time on the front line of a large scale gun battle. No time to be scared. All we could do was shoot and try to get to safety.

The regime soldiers were some distance away. This meant that my rifle, which could shoot at long range, was more effective than the Kalashnikovs carried by the men. I could see the enemy's guns reflecting in the sunshine and instinctively that is what I shot at. I couldn't tell from where I stood whether we had hit the soldiers or not, but it was not long before we could see that we were forcing them back. My rifle was proving effective at the longer distance. As we got closer in range, the Kalashnikovs were faster and more useful.

A group of Peshmerga from the Democrat Party happened to be close by. They joined us in the fight against the regime forces. One of the Democrat Party Peshmerga asked for my gun. Rajab also asked for it.

For a brief moment, I thought about handing it over. They might have more experience than me, but if I handed over my gun, they would talk about this later and say I was scared or couldn't use my gun and that I was useless.

'No, I won't give up my gun,' I said. 'I can shoot as well as you. What do you think I am doing now?'

The Democrat Party Peshmerga had never seen a woman shooting in the middle of a battle before. They started to comment on how brave I was.

It was a warm day. By the time we had made it all the way down the mountain to Lower Najneh, we were hot, tired and sweaty. My mouth was bone dry. I had not had a second to stop to take a drop of water from the springs that were everywhere in the mountains.

At Lower Najneh, the shootout had turned into a major gun battle with the Baneh Company. My team joined in the fight.

All the sounds you would usually hear in the mountains, of water running and birds singing, disappeared. All I could hear was the shouts of the fighters, screams of 'Allahu Akbar' and 'Long live socialism', and the noise from explosions and guns.

At first it was hard to breathe because of all the gun powder and smoke but I got used to it.

I saw Massoud, my old classmate who was now the political leader for the company and the deputy on Baneh's Central Committee.

'Where are all the girls?' I asked.

'We told them to wear women's clothes and to stay in the village, to pretend they are with their families. They agreed to do that.'

Although this was not the time to argue, I was angry and upset about it. Just like me, the other women should have the chance to fight shoulder to shoulder with the Peshmerga men. I promised myself that this was the last time this would happen unless it was an absolute necessity. We managed to push the government back to their large military base at Kokhan. Their vehicles seemed to fly back to the base, away from our gunfire.

It was dark and quietening down. Nobody had been killed or injured from the Peshmerga side, but quite a few of the regime soldiers had lost their lives. We asked the villagers to take the bodies back to Kokhan.

I felt sad for the soldiers who had been killed, but this had been a battle. They had attacked us. It was kill or be killed. My main concern was for my comrades and for the villagers.

That evening we asked the villagers to come to the mosque to discuss the battle and the villagers' safety. It was an opportunity for us to talk about the regime and to explain that the government would not tolerate any opposition.

Aso, who had earlier told me that I had been imagining things when I spotted the movement among the oak trees, came and found me. He admitted that I had done a good job in identifying the soldiers.

'You have to open your eyes a bit wider,' I said.

The villagers started to fight over me. They all wanted 'the brave Peshmerga girl' to go and have dinner with them. With Massoud I went to the home of a farmer for a specially prepared meal of chicken. When the villagers offer you chicken or lamb it is a mark of great respect.

The villagers told us that the pasdaran had come looking for me everywhere. They had even looked in the tandoor ovens for me. They had assumed that I would not stay in the battle for long and would instead be hidden away by the villagers.

One of the villagers had written poems about me, romanticised versions of what he had seen. In the poems, he talked about how strong I was as I ran with the gun, shooting the enemy, how my pale hair was blowing in the wind. This battle was a turning point. The villagers had wanted to hide me, but I had chosen to fight. I was proud of myself for making this important decision. I was grateful that they wanted to help me, but I had to prove that women could behave differently on the battlefield. For the first time I was able to see that fighting ability was not limited to men. I felt powerful with the knowledge that I could defend myself, my team and the community. The next day, Komala wanted to show its strength by moving closer towards the regime's base in Baneh, instead of retreating. We walked to the village of Sad Bar, behind the Baneh mountains, and asked the people to come to the mosque for a meeting to discuss our party's manifesto, the battle and what we were fighting for. All of the villagers had heard about the battle and about my actions.

My community team later had a meeting with the Baneh Company. I'd made a significant decision that day, I told them.

'We missed an opportunity to make the girls feel equal and confident that they can fight,' I said. 'You put them back and made them act like normal people in the village. It is not good for our movement. This must be the last time it happens. Women need to be in this fight as equals. You need to accept us as equals.'

All of the women were in agreement with me. Although some of the men were moaning under their breath, none of them opposed this openly. They wouldn't have dared.

I returned to my community work, but this time Rajab left us to join Shaesta. He was replaced by Bahram, who was five or six years older than me, but always treated me as his equal. Both Bahram and Omar were calm in temperament – we made a good team. My community team was separated from the company once more.

Word of my fighting spread. In the villages we visited, all of the girls crowded around me, excited to speak to me. They too wished to be Peshmerga, free from the culture of oppression in the villages.

There were no showers or hammams in the villages, so the girls would invite me to go to their homes to wash myself. They boiled water in a huge pot over a tandoor oven, and next to the oven they would put a large bath pan, which I would sit in to wash. I wanted to wash my clothes myself, but the girls didn't allow me to; they always insisted on doing it for me.

'It's normal for us to wash clothes for the Peshmerga,' they said, taking my dirty clothes from me. 'This is the least we can do to help you. You must eat and rest.'

They took extra care with my clothes and would put nice soap in between them to make them smell good. It was the same treatment everywhere. Whenever I came back from the villages, I had sweet smelling clothes.

It was not only the women. The men also respected me. When they went to the cities, they brought back presents for me. On good days I was treated to chicken or lamb stew and rice at villagers' homes, but often we had simple food like fried tomato or boiled potato with bread.

In summer it was hot, up to 40° or 45°C. My face burned in the sun and was quite painful. My nose was always peeling but I didn't pay any attention to this. What could I do to help it? Sometimes women would bring me yoghurt to cool my face and calm it down.

One hot day, I had my scarf wrapped around my head to protect it from the sun when a villager came up to me with a cap.

'Wear this so you have shade over your face,' he said.

This was a kind gesture. However, the heat from the earth was so hot that the cap made me even hotter, so I didn't wear it often. After a few days one of my fellow Peshmerga who was bald came and took it from my head. 'This is better for me, my head is always burning,' he smiled.

Everywhere my team went, we talked about freedom and equality and how we wanted a regime that allowed people to make decisions about how to rule the country. We discussed women's rights, the importance of creating a system to protect women, and how we must put an end to discriminatory practices.

The girls confided in me wherever I went. In one of the villages, a beautiful woman told me she had been married for twelve years but was still a virgin. Her husband, a kind and gentle man, couldn't perform. It was, of course, not possible for her to seek a divorce.

If the women spoke to me about domestic violence, I would go to their homes to talk to their husbands and tell them they must stop. Women were stuck in these violent situations. We worked hard to raise awareness and edu cate people that women were equal human beings, and used our standing in the community, our power and respect, to change people's minds.

Our work did reduce domestic violence, forced marriages and child marriages. Many villagers were frightened about their daughters joining up with the Peshmerga and being on the front line, so they started to accept their daughters' wishes to not get married so young, or to marry a person they chose or loved.

I became well known as a speaker in the area. Usually our meetings ended with me making a speech. In my speeches, I pointed out that the mothers and girls shouldered all of the hard work in the villages. As well as doing all of the housework, the women made a huge contribution financially, working alongside the men in the fields. The men did not even wash their own socks.

'You are speaking the truth,' the men would reply. 'We haven't really got any way to argue against this, but this is the way it has always been. It's our culture and way of life.'

I challenged this attitude. I strongly believed we needed to change the brutal inequality in the villages and not respect such customs as 'culture'. In many countries around the world they had changed their behaviour towards women, so why couldn't we?

I challenged the imams, particularly on the issues of polygamy and child marriage. Always, the villagers were hugely interested in such discussions. They were starting to question many issues that were the cultural norm.

'God has the answer to this,' said one imam when questioned about polygamy. 'It's acceptable for men to have four wives.'

'In that case, is it acceptable for women to have four husbands?' I asked.

GIRL WITH A GUN

'No, of course not – women are not allowed to have four husbands because the father of the children needs to be known,' the imam said. 'After many years of war, polygamy helps widows by allowing them to marry.'

'Iran is a rich country and the government should give financial help to everyone in need, including widows and single mothers, so women are not forced to marry men who are already married, becoming a second, third or fourth wife, just to be able to eat,' I said. 'I am sure no women would choose to marry a polygamous man if she was free to choose and financially secure.'

'Mohamed himself needs to come and explain this,' the imam replied.

A man who had four wives stepped forward to defend polygamy.

'Of course you would defend polygamy,' I said. 'Your wives are the victims of polygamy, so you are not allowed to give your opinion. You cannot speak on behalf of your wives. Let's allow your wives to come forward to talk about their lives in polygamy.'

Everyone laughed and clapped, and the man fell silent. Members of the Democrat Party used to come to our meetings, and I would openly challenge them. Komala did not feel that the Democrat Party represented the people's interests. When I went to their meetings they would say, only half joking, 'Galavezh is here so we might as well give up.'

Karim, the son of Shaesta's nursemaid when she was a baby, had joined the Democrat Party and had become a military commander. He had moved to their Baneh Company. He used to tell all of its members that I was his sister.

'We will give you a Kalashnikov if you come and make a tour of the villages with me,' he said.

I did have my own Kalashnikov by this time, but he was offering me a patterned one with a fold up handle that was easier to carry. Karim thought that if I went on tour with him, it would make the Democrats look good and he would gain more supporters for his party. The Democrats didn't yet have women on the front line.

'If I go with you on a tour of the villages, I will talk about Komala and socialism and communism, so it will be against all you stand for,' I said.

'I will accept that,' he said.

'I won't spend a minute with the Democrat Party,' I told him. 'It's not my party.'

In the Baneh area, the relationship between Komala and the Democrat Party remained civil. We both had a number of armed volunteers in the different villages representing our two parties. There was tension in the air, but we tried to avoid any clashes. We were all Peshmerga armed against the same enemy.

However, in other parts of Kurdistan our relationship was gradually breaking down.

One cold winter's evening, my team was in the village of Manijalan. The temperature was around 20° C. There was thick snow everywhere.

It was around 7 p.m., and we went to a villager's home for dinner and we were told about a poor girl who had a sick mother to care for. The girl had gone to the mountains to bring firewood to cook with, as there was no oil in the village. She had been out all day in the snow collecting the wood. She was seen carrying the wood home by the village landlord and he ordered her to take it back to the mountain. The villagers were furious with him. The Democrat Party, who had a certain amount of power and following in this village, sided with the landlord and said it was his right to order the wood back; it was his forest and his mountain. I thought this response was completely heartless.

My team went to one of the armed volunteer Democrat supporters in the village. He was angry with the Democrat Party over this issue. He wanted to give up his support for them and come and join us.

I was pleased. I went with Omar and Bahram to speak to the landlord.

'You have no right to order the girl to take the wood back,' I told him. 'This girl and her father have worked all their lives for you. There is no oil in the village and it's freezing cold. They deserve to have some wood to keep their home warm.'

'The land belongs to me and the Democrat Party support me on this matter.' The landlord wanted to dismiss us. 'Nobody has the right to take anything from my land.'

'You are wrong. The Democrat Party may be supporting you, but the Democrat volunteers in this village agree with us on this issue. It is her right to have wood. It is a life threateningly cold winter here. You must allow this family to have wood or we will bring it for them.'

Omar, Bahram and I organised a public meeting to discuss this. We invited all the villagers to come to the mosque. Support for the girl was unanimous. Everyone was angry with the landlord.

The villagers brought wood from their homes to this poor family to keep them warm that night, but the next day we took the girl back to the mountain to fetch two big bundles of wood. Shortly after, her family switched to supporting Komala, apart from her father, who remained a Democrat.

It was exactly this kind of issue that was beginning to create problems between the Democrats and Komala. Komala wanted a classless society, while the Democrats supported the landlords against the poor. They did not care about the people and their suffering. They wanted Kurdistan to be controlled by their party and under the Islamic regime, while Komala wanted regime change and freedom and equality for all in Iran and Kurdistan.

Not long after this incident, the Baneh Company managed to take over a government military base and bring back lots of guns and Kalashnikovs.

A number of Peshmerga came to find my team in Manijalan. They knew we had a good relationship with the villagers, and they asked us to find a safe place to hide the guns. We decided to go to the landlord of Manijalan. We had to grease the guns before burying them so that they would not corrode. His large house would be a good place to do this in.

We went to his home with a number of villagers that we had

enlisted to help us with the greasing. He was shocked to see us.

'You cannot come in here with those guns.' We could see the hatred in his face. 'You are going to make a complete mess in my home.'

We ignored him and set about laying down cloths in his front room so that we could oil the weapons on top of them. When it got dark, we went to the mountains to bury the guns.

Our action had been a show of force. It was a way of punishing the landlord for his attitude towards the young girl. It was also a way of making him accept our work. We wanted him to know that he must help the people.

I went with Bahram, Omar, Jalal and another comrade, Aziz, to a village close to Baneh to stay in a house which belonged to a well-known Jash.

Aziz was older than us and a great public speaker. He was hugely popular with both the villagers and the Peshmerga. He always had funny stories to tell. He often went to visit his family in the village of Spie Kamareh when we were close by.

It was late at night when we knocked at the Jash's home. As soon as the Jash opened the door he knew we were Komala. Only Komala had women Peshmerga with them. At first he thought we had come to arrest him. He looked scared. We assured him that we had just come to stay there for twenty-four hours.

'Our comrades know we are here,' Bahram told him. 'If anything happens to us, you and your family will be arrested by Komala.'

The Jash put us in his guest room and set about bringing us food for the night. A group of pasdaran would be arriving the next day for lunch, he told us. We didn't believe him, but we thought that if they did come, it would be safe for us, as the Jash wouldn't talk. If he did, he would be in danger, as there would be a battle within his home. We locked the door of the guest room after he left.

The next day we had to wait for the Central Committee to send us a message via the radio to give us our orders for our next location and mission. The committee received information from supporters and informers, and they would relay this information via numerical code and tell us whether we were meeting the company or whether we were in danger from the regime.

While we were waiting for the message, around eight or nine regime soldiers arrived to have lunch. One of them tried the door for the room we were in.

'Why is this door locked?' he asked.

'We have strong insecticide in there and we've locked the door so the children don't go inside,' the Jash answered. There was one thin wall between us and our enemies.

We could hear almost everything they were saying. We had to keep as quiet as possible knowing that if we were discovered we would be arrested and possibly executed on the spot. The Jash would be in as much trouble as we were.

I buried myself under about three or four blankets with a small torch and the satellite phone to try and get the message from the Central Committee. The blankets were heavy and it was hot and stuffy. I could barely hear, but eventually I managed to get the code.

It might have been the stress, but Aziz had a desperate urge to relieve himself. We could not open the door to let him out, so he had to wait in extreme discomfort.

We were worried that the Jash would give us up, but finally the pasdaran left.

We immediately opened the window to get some fresh air. We told the Jash to stop his support for the government. It would not end well for him and his family.

That evening we held a meeting for the whole village in the mosque. As usual, we spoke out against the government and about socialism and women's rights. We also discussed practical issues such as organising a council for the village, so that they could build a toilet for the women. At that time, the people in the village just used the bushes next to the river, which was unhygienic and led to the spread of disease.

After this meeting, we set off for another village, but when we arrived, we heard that the regime guards were close behind us. Someone from the previous village had reported us in the area.

We left immediately for another village much further away, where the soldiers wouldn't be able to reach us so easily. It was closer to the company so that we would be able to call on them for help if need be.

A few days later, a Peshmerga named Rahman, whom we all called Rahman Sad Bar because he came from the village of Sad Bar, joined us and asked me to go and visit his family and distribute fliers while we were there.

'I will come this afternoon,' I said. 'No problem.'

'See you later tonight,' Omar said. 'We will be on the mountain waiting for you.'

It was daylight when we set off and after walking for two or three hours in the mountains, we arrived in Sad Bar at around 4 p.m.

As we arrived at the entrance to the village, a number of villagers rushed out of their homes pretending to beat their rugs and shouted to us: 'Don't come in! Don't come in!'

The Islamic regime had a group made up of a hundred of the toughest Revolutionary Guards and commanders, called the Attack Company. It was always this group that you found on the front line in battles. They would make regular assaults on the Peshmerga and the villages and they would try to recruit spies. The Attack Company were hard on the Peshmerga and merciless on the villagers.

The Attack Company had heard that we were in the area and were waiting for us. I looked into the village and could see some of the pasdaran in the narrow alleys running alongside the houses.

Rahman and I took thirty seconds to decide whether to shoot back or run, but we knew we didn't want to start a suicidal gun battle. There were two of us and a hundred of them. We only had our Kalashnikovs, which could shoot at relatively short range. We had no choice but to run as fast as we could back to the mountain. We ran and hid from stone to stone, while gunfire raged all around us.

We only just managed to escape with our lives.

When we arrived at the top of the mountain, Omar and the others were relieved to see us alive. They had heard word from the company that we had to be on high alert for an imminent attack.

'We should not have allowed the two of you to go on your own,' Omar said.

'We are all right, don't worry,' I said.

Bahram, Omar, Jalal and I went on to another village without Rahman. It was not a completely safe place because the government Attack Company went there often during the daytime, although they didn't have a base there. But the regime soldiers were not there when we arrived.

We had just sat down to have breakfast in a villager's kitchen when a woman came running in to us to tell us that the village was surrounded by the Attack Company and a number of them had entered the village.

'This room is not safe; you must go into the cowshed and hide yourselves there,' she said.

We jumped up from where we had been eating on a large tablecloth spread on the floor, and ran into the cowshed, which housed around ten cows. We sat silently with our guns cocked, ready to fight.

We heard the soldiers enter the house. Death seemed very close. Time moved so slowly that I felt that it was frozen. For two hours I sat listening to every movement, watching the door, ready to shoot. I was looking at the cows thinking about what we should do if the soldiers came in. We would have to fight to our last bullets. We would not give up. If a shootout happened, all of the cows would be killed along with all of us.

Every now and then, the woman came into the cowshed to inform us what the Attack Company were doing and to tell us that it was not yet safe for us to come out.

At around noon, she came in once more.

'They left,' she burst out, laughing. I have never heard a laugh like that. She was so excited and relieved after all the tension of the morning.

'I haven't seen those soldiers for a long time,' she said. 'They noticed the breakfast things were out and I told them I had just got breakfast ready. They sat on the same tablecloths that you had sat on eating the same bread and cheese.' She laughed again. 'Let me cook lunch for you. You must not go straight away.'

We didn't want to linger there, however, so the woman packed up food for us to take. When we knew that the area surrounding the village was clear of soldiers, we headed into the mountains and stayed with some farmers until dark.

Chapter 20

Where is Galavezh?

Life in a team of four had become too dangerous. The regime was determined to track down my unit and execute us. There were always hundreds of government soldiers with cars, tanks and rockets wherever we went – we had only our guns. For our safety, the Baneh Regional Committee asked my team to base ourselves within the company. Omar, Jalal, Bahram and I would remain as a unit, working within the community, and we would continue to visit villages on our own, or with other Peshmerga for extra protection, but would return to the company regularly. We would always be close enough to the company that we could call quickly for backup. If the company were attacked, we would not be called to the front line unless there was an absolute need.

My father heard that I was back travelling with the company and was not too far away from home. One Friday afternoon, he rented a car with my mother and they came to find me. Friday was the only day of the week that they could travel, as it was the weekend and the one day my father closed the bakery. If they travelled any other day, the pasdaran would demand to know the reason why the bakery was shut. My parents called at half a dozen villages asking for news of the company's whereabouts. They finally found me in the village of Saysaram.

It had been many months since I had seen my parents and I was astonished to see them getting out of the car. My mother immediately burst out crying, and she held me for a long time. My father was so full of love and happiness to see me. My parents sent me parcels when they had news of where I might be travelling, which I always distributed among the other Peshmerga women. Now my father was carrying a big box of clothes for me and the others, along with dozens of sweets and biscuits. He also had a huge carton stuffed full of kebab and fresh sangak bread. Most of the other Peshmerga women did not have parents as supportive as mine. I knew that I was lucky.

It was a beautiful day. The Peshmerga gathered around my father as he stood and sliced the bread, adding fresh salad with the meat, with love and a smile for all of them. What a treat this was! I sat with my mum, who had brought some underwear and sanitary pads, which I gave out to the Peshmerga girls. She was so happy to be surrounded by young women. However, my parents had sad news for me. My cousin Eqbal, who was the son of my father's brother Ali, had been executed by the regime because of his political activities. He had been trying to cross the border into Iraq to join Peshmerga there and he was caught and executed on the spot. He was eighteen.

By evening, my parents had to go. As we parted, my father hugged me and gave me some money. I later shared this out with my friends.

We had been together for just a few hours and I missed them as soon as they left. I thought about my father's singing and his laughter and my kind, beautiful mother. My father had always had such high hopes for me and my education. My mother was concerned about Shaesta, who was also working in a community team, but in a different region, so they had not been able to see her on this occasion. We knew that her marriage was unhappy but we didn't know what we could do about it. I couldn't imagine what it was like for a parent to leave their children in such a situation, especially after hearing the news about Eqbal. Of course, they were now even more worried that Shaesta and I would share his fate.

For a brief moment, I wondered what it would be like if we could all have a normal life, a safe life for everyone, without war but with peace and freedom, but there was no time to think about such things. Perhaps it would happen for our children. I had to remain strong and focus on my duty.

Gradually I became more known by the government. Galavezh was a common name in my region, and the regime forces started to arrest girls called Galavezh in the villages. Whenever I returned to a village, there would always be one or two girls who told me they had been taken to the intelligence services.

'But then they realised we were not you and released us!' They laughed, as they were excited and proud to have the same name as me.

I had become a bogeyman for the government. In the regime's stories, I grew bigger and taller and more fearful than I really was.

The government also began to spread rumours that I had been killed in one of their attacks.

Several times different villagers told me that my parents had been informed of my death in battle. They had even held a memorial service for me. My parents were being emotionally and physically tortured by the regime and there was nothing I could do about it.

There were so many rumours that I had been killed that each time I arrived at a village, everyone would come out to hug me, shouting: 'It's Galavezh. She is alive!'

Children would run through the village to announce it before we all gathered in the mosque. The villagers would immediately send word to my parents that I was well.

One day, my team was in Manijalan when some villagers came to inform us that the government Attack Company had entered Najneh in the early morning and had arrested all of the men from the village. They had been ordered to walk to the military base in Kokhan. The villagers asked us to help them.

My team immediately called a meeting in Manijalan. We invited the remaining villagers from Najneh and the other villages in the valley. We decided that the villagers of Manijalan should show support and walk with the women and children of Najneh and those from other nearby villages to Kokhan to protest in front of the military base.

It was about 3 p.m. and close to the time that the farmers and shepherds come back home with their animals so that the cows could be milked and the lambs fed. Even so, almost everyone, around a hundred people, agreed to walk to Kokhan to demand the release of the men.

As soon as the government soldiers saw all the people walking to their base, they released the men and told them to return to the village.

I went immediately with Omar, Bahram and Jalal to the top of the mountain at nearby Spidareh. I looked down at all the rooftops below, glimmering in the sunshine.

Over the loudspeaker, I called the villagers to come to the mosque.

'Why did they arrest the men?' I asked, when they were all gathered.

The men laughed and explained that at around noon the soldiers had come to the village demanding to know where the Peshmerga were. The pasdaran had accused the villagers of supporting us.

'We didn't tell them anything,' one said. 'Because we stood strong, they took us.'

'They told us they will get Galavezh and kill her and put her in a carpet and chop her like a sausage,' another said. 'We laughed at them. They are not tough enough to take Galavezh and chop her. They must kill all the villagers first.'

It was funny to hear them talking about me in this way. I felt proud to be loved and respected by so many people. This was why I was wanted so much by the pasdaran.

I spoke once more through the loudspeaker. My voice echoed as far as Kokhan and to all the villages below.

'The government must stop behaving in this way or there will be consequences.'

In retaliation for the government's actions, Baqi and the rest of the Baneh Regional Committee decided that the company should attack the government base at Kokhan.

'We will give them a lesson they will never forget,' Baqi said.

One of our teams spent days monitoring the movement of the guards and the times when they changed over, in order to make effective hit and run attack plans.

I was to join a team of twenty Peshmerga for the operation while the rest of my comrades moved to the other side of a main road to wait for us. We would join them there after the attack. I hugged the women and shook the hands of the men before we left for Kokhan.

The operation began by several Peshmerga launching RPGs from different angles while the rest of us fired at the military base. We had taken the pasdaran by surprise, and at first they didn't react, but after a few moments, they started shooting back. It was a dark night and we could see the bullets all around us, glittering like sparks of fire. It would have been a beautiful sight if we didn't know how dangerous they were.

After we had been shooting for about half an hour, it was time to withdraw from our hit and run. We successfully managed to move towards the other side of the main road to join the rest of the company.

After a short rest, my team continued on tour with the company. We received a letter from the villagers of Mahmali Abad asking for our help. They were extremely angry because the government was using their mosque to store military equipment.

The regime wanted to stop the villagers from being able to meet with Peshmerga in the mosque and to prevent us from sleeping there. The villagers tried to negotiate with the regime to get them to remove their equipment, but the pasdaran ignored their wishes.

After receiving the letter, we decided to attack. We hit both the base and the mosque with grenades from an RPG, causing explosions in both with quite a lot of damage in the mosque.

My team remained at the rear during the fighting. The battle lasted about three hours, with bullets flying all over the place, until the pasdaran began to retreat. The company managed to take over the military base and capture all of the guns and ammunition.

We took four prisoners with us and moved to the mountain. It was dark and we had to walk single file on the narrow path. We continued for around six hours, passing through several villages in order to avoid being attacked by the regime military groups at daylight.

The next day the military went to Mahmali Abad and asked the villagers to fight against the Peshmerga. The Peshmerga had blown up their holy place of worship and they were told they should demonstrate against us.

However, the villagers were hostile to the pasdaran. They replied that the Peshmerga had only blown up the mosque because it was being used to store their military equipment. The villagers started to throw stones at the pasdaran and they were forced to leave.

During the day we rested on the mountain and had our guards on different strategic peaks. From the military base, the regime shot rockets towards us from time to time, but none of them reached us. Bahram and I were asked to talk to some of the prisoners. We had captured two nervous looking Iranian conscripts who had been fighting with the pasadaran. It was no longer Komala's policy to execute prisoners; they had decided it was wrong. Instead, we would talk to our prisoners about socialism and equality. Sometimes conscripts would change their minds and stay and fight with us.

However, the pasdaran were usually deeply religious, and they believed that if they were executed they would become martyrs. Some of them wore a key around their necks which they said was the key to heaven. They would tell us that we were disbelievers, bent on dividing Iran to sell Kurdistan to the Iraqi government.

We would usually try and exchange such prisoners. We didn't have enough food for the Peshmerga and it was difficult to keep prisoners, particularly those who would not switch sides.

The two soldiers started to open up and talk about their lives. They were cautious not to be disrespectful of the regime because of the two pasdaran with them who repeatedly asked us to kill them and allow them to go to heaven.

In the late afternoon, we moved to another village. We divided the Peshmerga into groups to go to different homes, and took the prisoners to the mosque, where villagers brought them food. We rested until five in the morning, when we had to return to the mountain. We all filled up our water flasks and carried bread from the villagers.

The Baneh Regional Committee decided to free the soldiers and send the two pasdaran to the central prison. The soldiers were overjoyed, but the pasdaran were disappointed that we had not sent them to heaven.

Everywhere we went after this, villagers talked about how we had overtaken Mahmali Abad's military base.

The area was no longer safe, so the company moved to the regions west of Kokhan base called Dasht e Tal and Siaoma. Instead of the familiar large and leafy oak trees that covered the mountains close to Najneh, this area was known for its gum trees. The villagers tapped the trees for gum to use in medicine and also in chewing gum. The area was less rocky and less mountainous, which meant there were not so many hiding places. It was harder for us to stay in one spot for long.

In Dasht e Tal and Siaoma, my team began the usual activities of organising meetings in the villages and talking about our work. Many men and women from this area wanted to join Komala. When we arrived in a new village I was greeted with: 'Are you Galavezh? We know all about you,' or, 'We heard about you speaking in the mosques and talking about how men shouldn't beat women. Are you going to have a meeting here?'

Whenever we arrived at a villager's home, we were greeted with a cup of doogh, which is a drink made from yoghurt and water shaken for several hours in leather containers. The doogh is flavoured with mint, dill or rose petals and sometimes a sprinkle of salt. It's really refreshing.

One day my community team was resting with the company on the top of a mountain close to a road. It was a beautiful sunny day and the bright green mountains were covered in different

DIANA NAMMI AND KAREN ATTWOOD

coloured flowers. There was a light wind blowing. The day watch reported that a military jeep was speeding towards us on the twisting dusty road. We wondered what they were doing. They were either overconfident or just didn't realise that there were Peshmerga on the mountain.

When the jeep got closer, we started shooting at it, but it was going so fast it looked as though it was hovering above the ground. Around two hours later, the day watch reported a group of four regime soldiers walking towards us. At first, we thought they were part of the government Attack Company coming to fight us, so we took position, but we could see that there were only four of them. This was strange. First the jeep and now a few soldiers. Fully alert, we allowed them to come near.

Raof shouted: 'Stop, don't move! You are surrounded by Komala.'

'We have left the government's service and wish to join the Peshmerga,' one of them said, looking overjoyed to see us.

'Put your guns down on the ground and put your hands up,' Raof shouted.

The men did as instructed.

My comrades, Hassan and Baqi, went towards them and took their guns away from them. Another Peshmerga searched their body for bombs.

'They are clear!' he said.

Up to that moment, we had all been waiting silently in position, ready to shoot. With the commanders declaring the situation to be under control, we began to relax.

We gathered around the soldiers and welcomed them by offering tea and bread with butter. They introduced themselves as Naser, Sadegh, Reza and Omid. They told us they were in the jeep that we had been shooting at earlier. They had wanted to join us then but couldn't stop because we had been shooting at them so fiercely.

This was not the first time that soldiers had joined us. Each time it happened, we would talk to them about our manifesto and hold meetings for them, but often they would go back to the city quite quickly. Some of those who returned to the city continued to work for Komala and would become members of our underground network.

Naser had been the commander of the government Attack Company. He was charismatic and easy to get on with. In the first few days he spent with us, he gave us lots of information. The government had told him that all Kurdish people were apostates and communists working against the regime and all it stood for; that all Kurdish people wanted Kurdistan to be separated from Iran. Naser realised, after being in the cities and talking to Kurds, that we were kind and hospitable. Many Kurds spoke to him about our oppression and our desire for socialism. Naser understood that the regime had lied to him and used him against his own people.

Naser was a brave man and rose through the Peshmerga ranks. We were in a number of battles together, and we became close friends. He was good with the RPG 7, a portable rocket propelled grenade launcher. Once we were attacking one of the government bases in a hit and run. Naser targeted a tiny window and managed to shoot a grenade straight through the middle.

Several months after Naser had joined us, we were visiting a village when his mother arrived. She had travelled from Tabriz to find him. She was deeply religious, and it was important to her that her son join the government against the Peshmerga. She asked Naser to return home with her.

'I will not come back,' he told her. 'I am staying with the Peshmerga.'

'Don't kill yourself for Kurdish people,' she cried. 'If you want to fight, fight for the Islamic regime.'

It was 1983 and the Iran–Iraq War continued to claim hundreds of thousands of lives on both sides. Many young men had been conscripted to join the military and forced to fight. Even young children were sent through fields full of landmines so they would be blown up instead of the soldiers, while many others chose to wear a suicide bomb belt to explode Iraqi tanks and cannons.

When Naser tried to leave, his mother held so tightly on to his legs that he couldn't move and he ended up staying to comfort her. She managed to take him back to Tabriz with her. A short while after this, we learned that Nasar had been captured on his return to the city and executed for being a traitor. I think his mother took him back trusting the regime. She did not think they would kill her son.

Conditions were tough for the company towards the end of 1983. The regime had taken control over most of the region and it was difficult for us to stay in the villages during the day. One autumn day it was raining heavily. We were on a mountain and had made a big fire, but it had been extinguished by the heavy rain.

I used to really suffer with my periods. The pain was so bad that I would vomit and I was not capable of doing much. We had a sleeping bag that we would take turns to go and sleep in. One of the Peshmerga, knowing that I was in pain that day, told me to go and sleep in the bag for one or two hours. When I got into the sleeping bag it was full of water, but it was hot water as people's bodies had warmed it up. I tried to sleep for an hour and when my turn was finished I got out for someone else. All through that night it was impossible to get my clothes dry.

We used to wear ponchos, which were supposed to be water-proof, but the rain was so heavy that they didn't help at all. Even my underwear would get soaked through. In the evening, when we went to the villages, I would go to the tap in the main square and put my head right under and wash all my clothes to try and get the mud off.

In the winter it was extremely cold and the mountains were full of snow. Over our usual clothes we wore white plastic trousers and raincoats so that we would not be easily seen by pasdaran from afar.

Trudging through the snow was tiring. Sometimes people fell asleep while walking. We were all exhausted from walking all the time. We couldn't have more than five minutes' rest. We couldn't allow anyone to sleep for longer. It was too dangerous. We had to walk all the time to keep ourselves warm and to wake up. We stayed in the villages at night as it was not safe to sleep in the mountains. Sometimes there were avalanches, which made huge, terrifying sounds, almost like an earthquake.

Usually during the winter, our routine changed. We attacked the government less and instead had lots of meetings in the villages. It was the best time for community activities as the villagers would not be working in the fields.

Morale remained high, even throughout all of this hardship.

Every time we got to the top of a mountain, we were all so happy that we would all dance and sing. Even in the snow or heavy rain, we never forgot to sing and dance at the top. It was such a good feeling. Some of my comrades had beautiful voices and others used pans as drums. After dancing, everyone would sit and rest with their equipment to one side. Some would read. I would get a notebook out and write down my thoughts, feelings and memories. We would somehow convince ourselves that this was our last mountain, but there was always another one. There are endless mountains in Kurdistan.

Chapter 21

Losses

In early 1984 the regional committee decided that the Baneh Company needed some support. Around thirty Peshmerga from the Divandareh Company came to join us. These thirty were called the Shahidan Chia (the Martyrs of the Mountain) and had had a lot of success in battle.

The Baneh Regional Committee discovered that the government Attack Company had planned a large scale assault. They decided to organise a pre-emptive strike on the soldiers as they made their way along the main road towards us.

We were arranged into different teams. I was put with a woman called Shahla Mohamadi, who had joined us from the Divandareh Company. She was aged around eighteen or nineteen, and had several Peshmerga brothers and sisters. She was kind-hearted and we got on well immediately.

I was also with Alireza, from the Baneh Company. Alireza often came with my community team to protect us when we spoke in the villages. Sometimes he was a team leader within the company. We had become good friends, as we had spent quite a bit of time together. He was always making me laugh.

My team's mission was to be a support to the main assault as lookouts on the top of a mountain. We would defend the Peshmerga if any soldiers came to attack the company from the rear. We stayed in a village for part of the night, and at around 3 a.m. we got ready to go up the mountain.

It was a full moon. I picked up my Kalashnikov. Shahla came to me with a chassis rifle and ammunition belt around her.

'Am I beautiful with my chassis rifle?' she said, standing there in the moonlight while turning around to show off the weapon.

A Kalashnikov could shoot thirty bullets at a time but the chassis rifle had a single lens binocular on the top and could only shoot one bullet at a time. It was designed for long range sniper shooting.

'Have you used one of these before?' I asked Shahla, worried about her ability to use it effectively, and wondering how useful it would be for defence.

'No, it is my first time,' she replied, smiling.

'Alireza, she shouldn't have this gun – she should change it for a Kalashnikov,' I said. However, Shahla insisted she would have the chassis rifle.

Alireza, Shahla, three other Peshmerga and I made our way carefully to the top of the mountain. As soon as we arrived, gunfire started. The government Attack Company had already taken a position at the top of the mountain, so our plan to act as lookouts went out of the window. We had to shoot back.

We all lay down on the ground. I managed to move several stones in front of me to protect my head. Shahla was next to a big oak tree and tried to use that as a shield. Her gun was not suitable for this close range shooting. It kept getting stuck and she would run to me to unjam the weapon. Two bullets were being released at the same time, so I had to release one to make the weapon work. Twice she came over for me to help her.

'Stop coming to me – it is not safe,' I told her. 'Just stay where you are. Release one bullet and it will work.'

She ignored me. As she came running to me a third time, she was shot in the head.

Time slowed down. Everything went silent. I could no longer hear the sound of gunfire and grenades. It was sunrise, and I could see everything around me with startling clarity. I saw Shahla collapse on her back onto the ground. She had a black scarf around her head and I could see her brain spilling onto her scarf. I ran quickly to hold her and carefully pushed her brain back into her head and tied the scarf hard around it.

'We must save her!' I screamed. 'We cannot leave her to be taken by the government.'

The soldiers that had been shooting at us heard my voice and realised who we were at that moment.

'Are you Komala? We are Khabat, don't shoot,' they shouted. Khabat was another Peshmerga group, but they were anti-regime and religious. We had mistaken each other for regime forces.

By this time, soldiers and pasdaran from the regime's Attack Company, on hearing all the shooting, had come up the side of the hill and had begun firing at both Peshmerga groups.

We could see from our position that a battle was taking place on the other side of the road. We would have to return the opposite way through the valley.

'I will carry Shahla,' Alireza said. I took Alireza's gun and another fighter took Shahla's gun. Alireza put Shahla onto his back.

A Khabat commander came towards us. 'We are leaving now. The government forces are coming through this way.'

'If you leave us now we will shoot you,' I shouted. 'We have an injured person. You have to defend us while we get her to safety.'

After a short discussion, they agreed to cover us while we moved back to the village with Shahla.

It took us more than an hour to get to the village as Shahla's unconscious body was extremely heavy. Alireza couldn't carry her on his own; I had to hold her body from the back. We were both dripping in sweat. As we walked the sound of the rockets was so loud that I couldn't hear anything else. I didn't think of anything, I just concentrated on getting Shahla to safety.

By the time we arrived back at Dasht e Tal, it was noon and all of the villagers ran out to help us. A group of them carried Shahla to a house where we had a first aid kit.

I had done a little training in stitching and injections back when we were in the city. The company's doctor was in the battle on the other side of the road. We managed to reach him by walkie talkie and explained the situation. He advised me on how to treat Shahla.

He instructed me to shave around the injured area, to use Betadine antiseptic on her head and to inject her with a pain-killer. Although Shahla was paralysed down her right side, she was drifting in and out of consciousness and her left side had tremendous strength.

She kept trying to scratch her head, shouting: 'My head, my head hurts.'

It took several men to tie her left arm down with rope to a strong wooden board so that we could get her still enough to shave her head.

As soon as the company came back from the battle, they made a stretcher out of wood, put Shahla's now unconscious body on it and tied it onto the back of a horse. A team of Peshmerga and vil-lagers took her to a hospital in Iraq. She died around forty-eight hours later.

I will never forget Shahla with her gorgeous face, smiling in the moonlight, saying: 'Do I look beautiful with my chassis rifle?'

We had no time to mourn. The Baneh Company had planned an operation to attack two regime military bases close to the village of Somaqan in the mountains. The bases were linked by a road with several checkpoints. Our plan was to attack the check-points early in the morning so that we would be there before the regime soldiers arrived. This would put us in a strong position to be able to attack the bases themselves.

Mamad, the military leader for the Divandareh Company, and Salah, the political leader for Divandareh, called a meeting with all the political and military teams to decide how best to attack the bases.

My role was to organise a small fire team of six Peshmerga. With another two teams, we were to make up the front line group and had to go to the top of the mountain ahead of the company. Our mission was to set up two ambushes on two different points of the road between the two bases.

Mamad was a handsome man. He was married and his wife and children remained in the village of Divandareh, but he was having an affair with his beautiful cousin Chiman. She had loved him since they were children and had followed him into the Peshmerga. It was clear Mamad had feelings for Chiman too and he was in conflict with himself.

Chiman, despite her heartache, always appeared cheerful. She was so sweet and energetic, and sociable with everyone.

A few days before our mission to take the checkpoints at Somaqan, Chiman confided in me about her situation. In Iran, marrying cousins was normal and she wanted to wed Mamad.

'Perhaps he doesn't want to choose you and to live with you because he is already married,' I said. 'Perhaps he just wants you for a while. It is better that you don't think of him in this way. What can you hope will happen? It is a difficult situation and any blame will fall on you as the woman.'

'But I love him so much that I can't think of a life without him,' Chiman said, with her lovely smile.

The day before the Somaqan mission I received some Kurdish clothes from my father, a kava and pantol that were darker brown than the usual khaki that we all wore. Seeing me in my new clothes, the family I was staying with in the village commented on how beautiful they were. The man asked me to swap them with their clothes, only half joking. I laughed and refused. I loved my new kava and pantol. I was not going to part with them.

It was a fresh spring morning on the day of the mission. Raof and Mahmood came and woke me and my team at around 5 a.m. We prepared ourselves and went out to meet the rest of the company before setting off for the checkpoints. It took more than an hour to get there and by this time we could see all around us. Our job was to survey the enemy and make the first move, but as soon as we arrived, someone started shooting at us.

The mountain was covered in wheat, and as we had moved along the wheat had betrayed our position, as it swayed with our bodies. We radioed back to the company leader, who told us we had to retreat back to our base.

By the time we got back to the base it was around noon. From this position we could see the top of the mountain clearly, and we watched as several government attack companies came together from other parts of the mountain. Instead of being able to attack a small number of soldiers at the checkpoints, we were now facing several hundred soldiers, all alert to the fact that we were there.

Despite this, Mamad insisted we continue with our original plan.

'We cannot just continue with this mission as it stands,' I argued, along with the rest of the military leaders. 'There are now hundreds of them there. Our plan was dependent on taking the checkpoints first. This is now too dangerous. It's important we stay safe, regroup and make a different plan.'

Another leader agreed with Mamad, and dismissed my concerns: 'We have to go on the attack. We cannot just give up on our mission.'

Under Mamad's orders, the company had to go back up the mountain. It was 4 p.m. by the time we got there, as we had to walk slowly and carefully. As soon as we arrived, all hell broke loose, rockets and grenades and machine gun fire poured down on us, making a noise like a sewing machine: nah, nah, nah, nah, nah, nah.

We had no choice but to withdraw back toward the base in the village. The journey took three hours. It was broad daylight, so our movements could be seen easily, and it was a life or death race with the regime forces following us.

On the way down the mountain, my comrades hid between stones and among trees to catch their breath before moving to the next hiding place. Most managed to reach the river at the foot of the mountain in this way. From there they could make their way to the village safely. However, wherever I hid myself, the soldiers continued to shoot at me. Everyone else had khaki outfits. My brand new brown clothes could be easily seen.

I had no time to shoot back. I just ran at full speed from one stone to another. Every stone I got behind was pelted with rockets, RPGs and revolvers. At one point, I jumped behind a large stone that had another stone in front. An RPG hit the stone in front and it exploded into hundreds of pieces, some of the fragments hitting me.

'Galavezh has been killed,' I could hear all around me.

Moments later, I jumped from behind the large stone to run towards the river. My comrades burst into applause.

It was springtime, which meant the river was deep and fast running. We had to be careful not to fall in, as we would have been swept away. Walking gingerly along the edge, while being shot at the whole time, we reached a large rock around a metre high. If we made it over the top we would be out of the range of the gunfire.

We had to take it in turns as it was a dangerous place to leap from. I took a deep breath and jumped.

Once I was on the other side, the sound of the gunshots, which had been so loud in my ears, seemed to be coming from far away. I realised that the girl in front of me, Shaheen, had been shot in the chest and had fallen in the water, while the Peshmerga who should have jumped after me, Kamal, had not made it over. He had also been shot and had fallen backwards.

I managed to grab Shaheen's clothes somehow and pull her out of the river.

The first aider with us, Iraj, was a tall man and he managed to wade through the water to bring Kamal to the bank of the river. By this time about twenty people had made it over. Together, we helped Iraj bring Kamal to safety. He had been shot in the bladder.

It was getting dark and the villagers came with horses to carry the injured.

Kamal died by the time we got to the village, but Shaheen was still alive. She was taken to hospital in Iraq where her life was saved.

Shattered, I went back to same house where I had stayed the night before, where the owners had asked me to exchange my outfit. I looked down at my clothes, which were now so badly damaged that I could never wear them again. They were destroyed but I was not seriously injured apart from my hands and knees. The skin had been torn right off both hands and they had small bits of stone and shrapnel embedded. After Iraj had finished with the rest of the wounded, he came to me and bandaged my hands and cleaned my injured knees. The next day, with the help of villagers, we buried Kamal.

I knew that Mamad's plan had been dangerous. He didn't have the wisdom or patience required to be a leader. He didn't allow an analysis meeting immediately after the mission but other military leaders explained to the Baneh Regional Committee what had happened.

A short while later, Mamad was called to the Komala Central Committee in Maluma, Iraq. Chiman went with him. I was pleased to hear that Mamad had been demoted. I was told later that Chiman had become pregnant.

Mamad refused to marry her, and in shame, and with no one to turn to, she shot herself with her Kalashnikov.

One of the leaders of Komala condemned the suicide and spoke publicly in support of her. However, his words came too late for Chiman.

I was shocked and saddened by Chiman's death. I couldn't stop thinking of her and her unborn child. She had trusted me to talk about her love for Mamad. He had broken her heart, and she hadn't had any other support. What society were we living in that she felt so lonely and isolated that she had no option but to commit suicide? She could not imagine raising her child without a proper marriage. The issue of honour was too heavy in our culture, whether you were from the city, a villager or a Peshmerga fighting for freedom.

I was exhausted and I told the Baneh Regional Committee that I wanted to go to our base in Kareza, in Iraq, to see my sister, who was several months pregnant. I accompanied some other people who were ill and needed taking to safety. We walked about two days to cross the border before taking a car to Kareza.

In 1982, during the Iran–Iraq War, the Iraqi government

had contacted all the Iranian opposition parties to offer various arrangements, and some of them had moved their bases to Iraq.

Forced out of much of Iran and pushed close to the Iraqi border by this time, Komala had opened diplomatic relations with the Iraqi government in order to get permission to set up camps for its Central Committee. Over time, the camps in Iraq housed Komala's publishing and printing departments, Radio Komala and Radio Communist Party, our hospitals, information department, telephone and communications department, secretary and a base for education and training of new Peshmerga.

At first, I was against this cooperation with Iraq, and I think many others felt the same. I considered the Iraqi government to be a dictatorship, and Saddam had brutally oppressed the Kurdish people. The reality was, however, that we had to take this opportunity and use it for the benefit of our movement and against the Iranian regime.

We knew that the Iraqi government was not to be trusted. They could turn against us at any time and we needed to be prepared for the worst case scenario.

Iraq imposed a number of conditions on us while we remained in the country: we were not allowed to do publicity or talk to the Iraqi people about our goals, policies or political activities, and we could not support the Iraqi Peshmerga.

It was many months since I had last seen my sister. She and her husband Rajab had decided to leave the Peshmerga, to try and have some kind of a normal life with their child. For some months they had lived in the villages around Baneh when they had still been under Peshmerga control. When these villages were taken over by the regime, Shaesta and Rajab had moved to Iraq.

I gasped when I saw my sister. She had short hair and was wearing a long, light pink and white dress. She was sweeping the stairs to her home when she saw me. She stood up straight and stared at me with a big smile. She dropped the broom so that she could greet me with open arms. I hugged her for a good while, kissed her and caressed her stomach to feel the new life growing inside. I felt she was one of the most beautiful pregnant women I had ever seen. I had missed her dearly.

We went into Shaesta's home, which was small but clean and well organised. I was so happy to see her. I stayed with her for a few days and we talked constantly. I asked her about her life with Rajab but she didn't say much about him. However, I could sense that she was not happy. It was lovely to spend time together but it went too quickly and soon I had to say goodbye to my dear sister.

I'd had stomach pains for a long time and not long after visiting my sister I was sent to the hospital in Sulaymaniyah to see if there was any treatment. To my surprise, after arriving at the base, I saw Mehri, my close friend from the publishing department. She was heavily pregnant and had come to Sulaymaniyah to give birth.

We had not seen each other in a long time and we warmly hugged each other. We sat down together and she told me that she had married Jalal, a fellow Peshmerga.

'After I heard that my friend married my ex, I was depressed for a while,' she said. 'But then I got close to Jalal. We married just over a year ago and now look!'

She laughed while pointing at her large belly and hugged me again.

'I have missed you so much, Galavezh. Things were not the same after you left. I wish you could have been at our wedding. Jalal is such a good man. You remember him, don't you? We are very happy together and I am over the past.'

'Congratulations, dear Mehri. I am very happy for you and Jalal. I remember him well as a really nice man.'

'But what about you? How about your love life?' She held my hands tightly.

'No, I don't have any love life. I am still suffering from the loss of Azad. I can't see any other man. Perhaps I need more time to learn to forget him.'

Mehri held me tight. 'Will you come with me when it's time for my delivery? The doctors say I am due any time now.'

'It would be my honour for you to trust me. Of course I will come.'

We continued to catch up about all of our friends and my experiences in Baneh.

On my second day in Sulaymaniyah, Mehri went into early stage labour and she came to find me. Jalal was on a mission and could not be with her for the birth. I quickly went to fetch the nurse and she arranged for a car to the hospital. We arrived at the maternity department of the children's hospital and after waiting a while we were led to a small room with only one bed. We were left alone.

Mehri was in a lot of pain and it was getting stronger and stronger. Her waters broke and I went to inform the nurses, but they didn't pay us any attention and simply told me to remain with Mehri. I could hear the nurses in the other rooms shouting at the pregnant women and calling them names. These poor women were scared of the nurses. It was unacceptable, but there was little that I could do. I had to focus on helping Mehri and the baby.

Time seemed to be passing slowly, but Mehri's labour became stronger and she was screaming in agony.

'I think the baby is coming!' She started to bleed.

I ran to get the medics, and a nurse and a midwife took Mehri to the delivery room. After a while, they came and handed me Mehri's son and told me that she was still in theatre.

The baby was beautiful. He started crying and moving his head toward my breast. He was hungry but what could I do?

I asked the other women what I should do and they were extremely helpful. One of them breastfed him while the others helped me get him dressed.

The women started to talk about the nurses and how harsh they were towards them.

'They look at us as if we are prostitutes and continually insult us,' one said.

'How is your friend?' another asked. 'Go and check on her. She might be on her own.'

I immediately left the baby with them and went to find Mehri. I asked one nurse where Mehri was and she pointed at a door to her side without looking at me.

I opened the big double door carefully and was shocked to see Mehri still on the delivery bed. The bed and the floor were soaked in blood. I called her name. Mehri slowly moved her head toward me and asked me to hold her before she lost consciousness.

I called her name but couldn't get a response. I ran to one of the nurses on the night shift, Khadijeh, and told her about Mehri.

She gave me a dirty look and told me: 'Your friend didn't think about this day when she was making love.'

I lost my patience. I pushed her to the wall and slapped her on the face as hard as I could.

'Go and ask a doctor to come! She is dying.'

Khadijeh ran to the doctor's room, not to ask for help for Mehri, but to complain about me. All of the women on the ward were watching closely to see what would happen.

The doctor came and told me off for being violent toward Khadijeh.

'She is a nurse, you have to respect her,' he said. I was furious.

'My friend is lying in a pool of blood half dead in the theatre room on her own and the nurses are rude and won't do anything,' I said.

The doctor immediately went to the theatre and called for blood for a transfusion and extra medics to come and assist.

These actions saved Mehri's life. She finally came round and was moved to a better room. All of the women in the hospital thanked me for standing up for Mehri and for them.

It was time for me to say goodbye to Mehri and her lovely baby. As I hugged her, I thought about Shaesta and wished that I could be with her when it was her time to give birth.

Chapter 22

War Between Peshmerga

I'd had a number of tests for my stomach pain and I was given medicine so I could return to my community team. We headed to the village of Shahinan, close to Najneh and as we arrived, a number of villagers came rushing up to us, shouting: 'Galavezh, we had been told that you had been killed!'

Another group of Peshmerga passing through Shahinan had a number of letters with them, including a tiny one for me, stuck together with Sellotape. It was from Galavezh H, who had returned to her work in the print department in Sardarabad.

I knew instinctively that this letter contained important news about Azad. I didn't want to open it in front of the other Peshmerga. I went to the river, even though I knew it was not safe to go on my own. I sat on a large stone overlooking the water. It was a beautiful day and I could hear the birds singing and the sound of the water running.

I began to shake. I opened the letter with my pen knife and read it quickly. Galavezh H had written to tell me that Azad had got married to a girl called Farah, a Peshmerga from the Sanandaj region.

I read the letter several times, quietly crying, before I ripped it into dozens of tiny pieces and scattered them in the river. Up until this moment, I had kept all of the letters that Azad had ever written to me in a packet close to my heart. I now took his letters, tore them to pieces and threw them after Galavezh's letter. Galavezh had written on pink paper, while Azad's letters were on white. I remained on the rock staring at the pink fragments mixing in with the white bits of paper, watching them move down the river until they had completely disappeared.

I had had other proposals in the previous six months but they had meant nothing to me. I had never been able to see a future with anyone other than Azad. Throughout my daily routine and my usual activities, I could not forget him, even for a second. Even in happier moments, he was always on my mind.

Any hope that I had kept alive evaporated with Galavezh H's letter. It was difficult for me to accept that the possibility of a life with Azad was impossible, but I knew I must deal with it and not think about him anymore. My heart would remain with him but I had to learn to live with that. My dreams were over.

I came back from the river to join Omar, Bahram and Jalal. We had to move on from Shahinan. Inside I was destroyed but I tried not to show it. I didn't want to make this into a Peshmerga issue. I had to be strong. In any case, I had little time to dwell on it.

We carried on with our usual work on tour, travelling from village to village and I continued to be one of the main speakers. We invited individuals to join our underground organisation. In each village, I tried to see as many women and girls as I could. Some of them came without permission from their families, and I would talk to them about their rights. It wasn't an easy task. The law, the entire system, was extremely hostile to women. However, we tried to give these women hope for a better future and they were always so excited to learn something new. I was proud of this work.

After a while, we met back up with the Baneh Company and a team from Bukan came to join us. They wanted our help taking a wounded Peshmerga to the border to hand him over to a team from the central hospital in Iraq. He had broken a leg and an arm and was being carried on a stretcher laid across a mule. I was assigned to this difficult task with seven others, including Mineh, a member of Bukan's regional committee.

It was not easy to transport our injured Peshmerga through the narrow paths we called goat tracks, over the mountain. Sometimes we had to take him off the mule and carry him ourselves on the stretcher.

At one point we were resting on top of a mountain, waiting to receive orders to move to the border, when we were surrounded by government military forces. They didn't make a land attack but they fired dozens of rockets. We had to stay in this one place for several days without any food, until the rockets stopped.

There was a small fountain nearby and Mineh said that he wanted to go there to wash. He went with a bodyguard but returned a short while later, walking with the help of a stick and being held up by the bodyguard.

Mineh had slipped and cut his foot on a sharp tree branch and it was bleeding profusely. For some reason none of us understood, we had a first aid rucksack with us, even though it was usually the medics that carried those.

'Can anyone use this?' I asked, but nobody had used the equipment before.

I believe that Mineh confused me with my sister, as he had most likely seen her work as a nurse in Elmabad, and he turned to me and said: 'I trust you to stitch the wound and dress it.'

'I've only ever seen doctors do this,' I said. 'I've not done it myself without supervision.'

'I trust you, Galavezh. Just do it.'

I was shivering with fear, but I knew there was no one else to do this and no time to call anybody else. The blood was coming fast. I had to get on with it and do my best.

I carefully opened the first aid rucksack and found everything I needed; a syringe, needles, anaesthetic and Betadine disinfectant. After cleaning the wound I applied the anaesthetic before taking a thick, curved needle and thread, which would later dissolve. I pushed the needle but it didn't go through the skin. Realising it was the wrong one, I tried a thin needle that I had assumed would be used for delicate skin, such as around the eyes, but to my surprise, this pierced the skin easily. I made about twelve stiches before administering Betadine again and dressing the wound.

We waited for a further twenty hours for a team from Bukan Company to come to take Mineh back with them. They also brought much needed supplies. We managed to complete our mission by taking the injured Peshmerga to the Iraqi border. We returned to Baneh the same night and joined our company.

Shortly after, a team from Sanandaj joined us. Azad's sister Leyla was among them, along with a woman I hadn't seen before. She had a beautiful smile. Leyla appeared happy and excited. As soon as she saw me, she came over.

'Galavezh, meet my brother's wife, Farah,' she said.

I shook hands with Farah and I welcomed her to Baneh. It was extremely difficult for me to do this, even though I knew none of it was her fault. Leyla was clearly thrilled to be with her new sister-in-law and she informed me that Farah was heading to the Central Committee in Iraq to join Azad.

Farah and Leyla went to dinner at a villager's home, but I had no appetite, neither for food nor for talk, so I decided to go to the mosque with some other comrades.

The team from Sanandaj left the next day.

Tensions between Komala and the Democrat Party began to ramp up. When our parties spoke about each other on the radio the language changed into threats.

Everyone in Iran used to listen to radio broadcasts from opposition movements and the government was always putting a block on the frequencies. We had to move them around regularly to make sure they could still be heard. Our radio base was in one of Komala's camps on the Iraqi border and a large number of people worked there. Radio Komala was on an FM frequency and it could be heard from anywhere in the country. It was crucial publicity and was an extremely popular station with the charming voices of Hama Kamali, Goli, Shahin and Naseh, well known names among Kurds. At lunchtime everyone listened and in the factories and fields they tuned in while they were working. Radio Communist Party was also popular. It was in Farsi and had its own staff and producers, and could be heard all over Iran and beyond.

The stations covered political discussions and news reports on battles with the government, along with the activities of the workers who were protesting against the regime. We also had a question time session. People would send in their questions and several members of the Central Committee would come on air to answer. The communications teams would give their news via their walkie talkies and this would be relayed on the radio. The radio was also used to give the companies and communications teams vital information via secret wire codes, and we would translate these into messages. We would find out about the movements of other Peshmerga groups in this way: where they were and whether we should join them. When teams heard news about the government forces' movements, they could warn us over the radio.

Over several months, relations between Komala and the Democrat Party continued to worsen, and whenever my platoon saw them, it was difficult between us. Before we would always have spoken together if we were in the same village, but now we started to steer clear of each other. Democrat Party supporters tried to avoid letting Komala Peshmerga into their homes. Instead they shouted at us whenever they saw us.

Komala wanted socialism, workers' power and women's rights. The Democrat Party was nationalist. They wanted Kurdish people to rule Kurdistan within the Islamic Republic of Iran. They defended the feudal system and the landlords. They didn't accept our desire to help the poor. By establishing the Communist Party of Iran, we had become even more popular and more powerful than them in many areas in Kurdistan. The Democrat Party saw Komala as a threat, growing stronger day by day. They wanted to destroy Komala and become the main party of power in Kurdistan.

Furthermore, the Islamic regime wanted the Democrats to finish off the communists in Kurdistan. They ordered the Democrat Party to see off the threat from any other political parties in the region; the Democrats had attacked a number of other smaller political parties to save the regime the job. 'The Democrat Party always wags their tail for the government,' we used to say.

Just a few months after I met Farah, I heard that she had left the Central Committee bases and gone to Hawraman. A short while later, the Democrat Party made a surprise overnight attack on the Hawraman base.

The Democrats killed twelve Peshmerga while they were sleeping in their tent. Farah was among them. Some of the girls' dead bodies had been assaulted before they were set on fire.

The news was horrifying. I cried for Farah and for the other Peshmerga. I had met her just the once but I could remember her face so vividly; so happy, smiling and full of laughter. I felt so sorry for her. She had lived such a short life, like so many Peshmerga.

Hawraman marked the start of a real war between Komala and the Democrat Party. Komala went into high alert and we had to change the way we had been working. The organisation decided to take all of the small teams back permanently into companies. Small units were too weak and insecure to function alone with both the Democrat Party and the government on the attack.

Omar, Bahram, Jalal and I joined back in with the Baneh Company, which had been combined with the thirty Peshmerga from the Divandareh Company some months before. The Democrat Party restructured their army, creating larger companies of Peshmerga. They had more Peshmerga than us and they assumed that they would finish off Komala quickly.

In the meantime, Komala tried to begin negotiations with the Democrat Party in order to bring to justice those who had ordered and carried out the attack on Komala in Hawraman but the Democrat Party refused to take part.

The Baneh and Divandareh Company remained in a few villages for the whole winter of 1984. There was barely enough food to feed the villagers, never mind 150 extra mouths. It was an extremely difficult time.

Komala retaliated against the Democrat Party in Hawraman, and managed to get the party out of the area, but this only served to escalate the war. Komala was forced to restructure. Four big battalions were created, with a few hundred Peshmerga in each.

I belonged to the Border Battalion, which was close to the border of Iraq and made up of the companies from Sardasht, Piranshahr, Baneh and the thirty Peshmerga from Divandareh Company.

The South Battalion was made of the companies from Sanandaj, Kamyaran, Hawraman and Mariwan and the rest of Divandareh; the Mockryan Battalion was the Bukan, Saqqez and Mahabad companies combined, while the North Battalion was the Rezaeieh, Margavar and Targavar companies.

When the Sardasht Company joined us, I was reunited with my good friend Mahmood. It had been a long time since we had seen each other. We hugged and immediately started to catch up on news about our families and mutual friends. We also talked about how we had fared over the years. I was so pleased to see him.

Every day, Mahmood and I made a point of finding each other to have a good discussion. We talked about politics but also about love. I felt as though I could talk to him about anything. I was even able to pour out my heart to him about Azad. In turn, Mahmood talked to me about the person he loved. He quickly became one of my closest friends.

Mahmood had been promoted to the position of political commander for the Border Battalion. We were initially based in Shanakhse, a village in Iraq that had been bombed and burned down by Iraqi president Saddam Hussein. Saddam had wanted to destroy the region to ensure that the Iraqi Kurdish Peshmerga, who had been fighting against him, had nowhere to eat, rest and hide. He ensured they would have no access to support from the people.

Saddam had ordered the demolition of all the villages and their lands up to 20 km from the border inside Kurdistan in Iraq. All the roads to the villages were demolished, but military roads were left as they were needed for the war with Iran.

All of the villagers were moved by force to newly built towns before the bombing. They were, of course, devastated by this, but no one could protest against Saddam. He would wipe out anyone who opposed him. The bombing campaign left many villages in the border region with half demolished buildings.

Here and there you could find one or two families of runaway soldiers living in those demolished villages. They would try to rebuild the houses, but living in that situation was extremely dangerous. It was a war zone; there was no food or any amenities. The surrounding fields were full of unexploded landmines, which led to many women, men and children being disabled.

One day, I was walking back into Iraq from Iran in this area, I went ahead of the others with two comrades, Hassan and Raof, into a small field of bushes. As we walked into the field we felt something catch around our ankles, and when I looked down I could see a tiny wire wrapped around our legs. We looked around and saw a large landmine, half buried in the ground with a ring attached to the wire around our legs. If we had walked a step further, we would all have been blown up.

'Stop! Stop! Don't come!' we shouted to our comrades. 'This is a minefield.'

We had only gone two metres into the minefield, but we had to walk back slowly, stepping only on the footprints that we had made on the way in. My heart was pumping the whole time. Everyone held their breath in total silence. As we stepped safely out of the minefield, we started to breathe again. Our comrades all began laughing and some came over to hug us. We had had a lucky escape.

Minefields were used by both sides throughout the Iran–Iraq War. The Iranian regime would send children crawling through these minefields, either by force, or they were brainwashed and they would volunteer to be blown up, in order to ensure the soldiers could come through the fields safely. The regime was good at using the media and the power of song to manipulate people during the war. Military anthems about taking care of the land, your wife and sister were played constantly on Iranian TV and radio.

In Shanakhse, the snow was a metre deep. We put a tent over the half standing walls and made a base for ourselves to sleep in. It was freezing cold and we had no food. We sent one team further inside Iraq and another to the villages in Iran to try and fetch something to eat. My friend Saeed, who was always ready to do hard work, said that he knew of a tandoor oven in the next village where we could go to bake bread if anyone was ready to go with him. My comrade Shirin and I volunteered to accompany him to make bread for the whole battalion.

It was about a twenty-minute walk to get to the tandoor and we had to carry flour and water with us. The snow was deep on the ground and we had to trudge through a heavy snowstorm. We held the large bread board (which we were going to use to flatten the dough on) above our heads in an attempt to keep the snow off. We could barely open our eyes.

We found the tandoor. It was built up on the floor about a metre deep and fifty centimetres wide. We gathered wood from the damaged houses to build the fire. We waited until the fire was smouldering but not so hot that it would burn the bread. We were there about three or four hours making the dough and baking bread for 200 people. Saeed was so full of energy and really determined to help.

By late afternoon, we called for help to carry the bread back. The other teams had brought cheese and meat from the villages and there was plenty to feed everyone.

We remained in Shanakhse in these conditions for several weeks. We started a bread making rota to ensure everyone took their turn helping out, and there were other teams to cook and to wash dishes. Despite the difficult circumstances, everyone was helpful, and spirits remained high.

One night, I was trying to sleep in a room with about fifty Peshmerga. I was on my period, which was so bad it was making me vomit and shiver. A number of Peshmerga were selfishly sleeping all around the wood burning stove and didn't allow me any space to get near.

'I am really freezing – let me get close to the heater,' I asked. One of the boys moved over a tiny bit but the rest seemed to be in deep sleep and didn't budge.

Mahmood and Hama Ali Waziri, another close friend, knew that I was freezing and ill and had no space to sleep. 'Let's go and find somewhere else,' said Mahmood. We went through the rubble in the village and found another house, which was half standing. The boys brought a number of large branches. They cut them and made a bed for me by laying the branches on shelves on the side walls. They found a metallic bowl and took some of the hot coals from the oven and put them under the makeshift bed. They found an old sleeping bag from within our equipment, which, strangely, was not being used by anyone that night, and put it over me so that I could sleep for a few hours.

I was so grateful to them both. They didn't sleep the whole night as they were on guard duty, instead they were busy discussing politics. The next day when we woke up, everywhere was covered in fresh snow.

It was no longer safe for the battalion to remain stationed in Shanakhse due to the ongoing Iran–Iraq War, and we started to move once more.

I was one of the communications officers in the Border Battalion, along with some other comrades who were good at translating the codes from the Democrats to try and find out their plans. I was responsible for the satellite phone. It was big and cumbersome but I had to carry it with me at all times. I also had a walkie talkie on me, and I would take messages from the Central Committee and from the different units within the battalion.

In the villages and cities, Komala's followers generally supported Komala and Democrat Party followers supported the Democrats, but all of them were completely against the war, between the two parties. They called for peace and unity.

'This is a war between brothers and you shouldn't allow this to happen at all,' we were often told when we went into the villages and cities at night to speak. To keep the support of the people, we had to appeal directly to the community and keep them informed about the conflict. The truth was the Democrat Party started the war. We told the people that Komala was ready for a ceasefire and negotiations, but the Democrat Party wanted to finish off Komala and didn't want a ceasefire.

As well as garnering support from the public, we also needed to motivate our own members and long time supporters to keep up their own efforts.

As usual, I was one of Komala's key speakers during this campaign. I made sure I got the message across that the Democrat Party were collaborating with the government and with the landlords, and they were compromising people's lives. Kurdistan needed Komala. Only Komala were on the side of the poor. Only Komala were calling for equality for all.

In early 1985 we received incredible news from Komala's South Battalion. They had managed to seize the central base of the Democrat Party, in Azhwan, and had captured all of their equipment.

The Border Battalion decided to move to the village of Salok, which was deep in a valley. We knew that the Democrat Party were not far from us but we didn't know their exact location. On a freezing cold winter day, with thick snow and ice everywhere, I was with Mahmood and some other Peshmerga in one of the villagers' homes. We were resting after eating lunch when we heard gunshots coming from the public toilet. It was the Democrat Party. They were shooting directly into the houses.

We jumped to attention, took our guns and ran out to respond to the gunfire. We started to fire at the toilets and the surrounding area, but it seemed they had a great spot and the Kalashnikovs were not effective, so Mahmood took an RPG. He aimed it at the public toilet and managed to blow it up. For a few moments, the

Democrats didn't react and this gave us the opportunity to take different positions and get closer to them.

A fierce gun battle broke out, lasting about an hour. Some of the Democrat Party soldiers were injured so they started to draw back. One of our Peshmerga was killed.

With no time to reflect on our latest loss, we moved on from Salok to Kandal, a nearby village on the top of the mountain. We walked for about an hour, arriving in Kandal around 4 p.m. We distributed Peshmerga in different homes in the village but we couldn't relax. We remained on high alert.

I was on guard duty at the bottom of the village. Another guard was on the other side while two more guards patrolled. It was dark and difficult to see if there was any movement.

A Peshmerga came to relieve me after an hour. I went back to a villager's home and just as I was about to try and dry out my frozen clothes, gunshots started. There was no time to rest. The Democrat Party was close to the village.

We always tried to take our battles out of the villages as quickly as possible to minimise harm to the villagers. We moved swiftly to the top of the mountain and the Democrats came after us. This was another heavy battle lasting several hours. The Democrat Peshmerga were further down the mountain and they could easily see our movements on the horizon, making us clear targets.

As the Democrat Party was in negotiations with the government, the regime did not attack the Democrats, and when the Democrats were in battle with us the government would join in and would attack Komala.

From our position on the mountain, we could identify a government army column from Baneh on the other side of the mountain to the Democrats, moving towards us from the main road. They started to fire rockets at us. We were right in the middle of two armies.

I lay down and began shooting alongside another Galavezh, known as Galavezh Sardasht after the city she was from. Her husband was a few metres away. Also with me was a young

Peshmerga, Rebwar Ahmadi, who I looked upon as my little brother. He was one of the youngest Peshmerga. He had blue eyes and blondish hair, and was about seventeen or eighteen.

It was cold and dark. After we had been shooting for about two or three hours and had several injured I heard some Peshmerga ask for bullets and others replied that we didn't have many. I had to make sure I didn't use up all of mine. I didn't want to shoot at random.

Suddenly Galavezh Sardasht stood up and started shooting. It was as if she just got fed up with lying on the ground firing bullets with no end in sight. I tried to ask her to lie down, but it was too late.

She was shot in her heart with a single shot.

Galavezh fell down on the snow. I could see the blood coming up around her neck and onto her scarf and the snow. I tried to talk to Galavezh, but she couldn't say anything. She took just a few gasping breaths before she died. Tears streamed down my face, but again there was no time to grieve. I still think of her pale, beautiful face and black scarf lying on the snow, turning red from the blood. When I hear the story of Snow White, it reminds me of her.

Galavezh's husband Bahram came over to us and started crying. He held onto his wife's body and tried to carry it a few steps.

'I am so sorry,' I said. I left him to mourn for several moments.

Another Peshmerga tried to hug Bahram but we had no time to do anything with Galavezh's body. We had to continue shooting over her as she lay there.

I informed the battalion commander over the walkie talkie that Galavezh had been killed. I could hear his distress. I realised that he thought it was me who had been killed – as I was from Baneh, I was much better known to him than Galavezh Sardasht. I tried to explain to him that it was not me, but he couldn't hear me because of the sound of the bullets raining down on us, but also because he was so upset.

A few minutes later, I heard Rebwar screaming: 'I am burning! I am burning!'

I went immediately to him. He had been shot in the bladder and was begging for me to take his weapons off him and open his ammunition belt.

I opened the belt and put his head on my lap and told him: 'You will be OK.

Rebwar begged me to open his peshtwen, which is the long Kurdish belt we all wore wrapped tightly around our waists, made from around two metres of material. I assume he felt this would have made it easier for him to breathe.

'Don't open his peshtwen,' the first aider, Iraj, said. 'He has just minutes to live. The bullet has hit him in a bad place. If you keep it fastened tight, it will give him a few minutes more.'

Rebwar continued to beg. I looked into his blue eyes and I told him: 'It's OK, I will open it.'

I pretended to open the peshtwen.

'Galavezh, you are an angel,' Rebwar said. 'If you open my peshtwen I will be OK.'

'Rebwar, dearest, I will do it,' I told him. He closed his eyes, and his arms and legs flopped open as he died.

Time stood still. I could no longer hear the sound of the bullets. Two people had been killed right next to me. I could not control my tears.

We were exhausted. The Border Battalion military commander decided we must go to another village, called Zarwaw, which was in the control of the government army. Our commander believed that the regime would think we would move to a village further away from them, not closer.

In total, eight of our Peshmerga died in this battle, and many more were injured. We had to leave the dead bodies behind; we could only carry our injured. One of them bled to death on the way to Zarwaw while Mahmood was carrying him.

I had just one pack of bullets left; many of the others had no bullets at all. We had to contact the Mockryan Battalion and ask them to urgently send us ammunition. They were two or three cities away from us and we needed it immediately. They sent bullets to us via the villagers and we had them by the next evening.

In Zarwaw we ate and rested a bit and managed to dry our clothes. However, we were on a main road and it wasn't safe to stay, so at night time we marched to another village.

It was a long night. It was snowing the whole time and our clothes were frozen. Even our eyelashes were frozen, and the boys had ice hanging from their moustaches.

On arrival, the villagers informed us that the Democrat Party had been there before us. They had asked the villagers to collect the bodies of the dead Peshmerga from Kandal.

Morale was low after we lost all these comrades. For the next two weeks, in an exhausted state, we continued moving from village to village, avoiding both Democrat and government forces.

We couldn't carry more than one round of ammunition each, so all of the bullets we had received from Mockryan we had to put onto horses. At one point, we had to cross a river that was wild and high over a wooden bridge one by one, but it was too rickety for the horses, so they had to come through the water. However, the river was too powerful for the horses and they were swept 200 metres downstream. They managed to get back to us but we had lost all of our spare bullets once more. We later learned that they had turned up in a village far away.

In the next village we arrived at, I discovered that my mother had walked from Baneh in the freezing cold weather to come to see me, but she had left by the time we arrived. At the next village after that, we heard that she was in the next village along. She also heard that we were close by, so she tried to come back and find us, but we kept moving and she was always a village away.

I decided to ask the villagers to bring my mother to us by horse. She arrived an hour or so later, frozen solid and crying, praying for me and the rest of the Peshmerga. She had some biscuits and food and some clothes for the Peshmerga women. It was good to see her but it was also heartbreaking. We had just one evening together as we had to move out quickly. I had to say goodbye once more.

My battalion decided to travel back close to the border of Iraq, around Somaqan, so that we could take our injured to the hospital in Iraq. We had to walk many hours to get there and try to ensure that we were not engaged in other battles, as our Peshmerga had no strength left.

On the way, we heard the news that the Mockryan Battalion had been involved in a large battle with the Democrat Party and needed our help.

The Border Central Committee decided to send fifty-seven Peshmerga men from Baneh – known as the Gordan 57 Zarbat, or 57 Attack Platoon – to Mockryan for this battle with the Democrat Party. This was an entire platoon, so it weakened us further.

The Border Battalion was left with around 200 Peshmerga. Another thirty had to take the injured to the hospital in Iraq. Our battalion was becoming smaller and smaller.

When finally, we arrived in Somaqan, on the Iranian side of the mountain, we distributed Peshmerga among the villagers' homes. On one side of the river Peshmerga from the south were resting, and those of us from Baneh were on the other.

We had just started to eat dinner when we heard an RPG explosion. The Democrat Party had ambushed us. Peshmerga on both sides of the river were completely surrounded. There was only a wooden bridge over the river and the Democrat Party quickly took control of it.

A heavy battle started. The Peshmerga on the other side of the river did not respond to any of our calls. There were far more of them than us and we were already feeling shattered. Taking shelter in different houses, we ended up in a shootout that lasted for several hours, until the military commander ordered us to go up to the mountain and towards Iraq.

The group from the other side of the river were eventually able to join us.

Aziz, whom I had worked with when I was in the community team, had managed to come to the bridge and somehow cross the river. He found us after a few hours.

'They were coming after me and they jumped into the water and they shot into the water, but I hid myself among the reeds and trees,' he told us.

Twenty-three of our Peshmerga were killed that night in Somaqan, including several women. One of them had got engaged just a few months before.

Chapter 23

Promotion

Despite my many years of service, I had still not risen up the ranks, unlike all the men I had known and served alongside, many of whom had the same experience as me, or often even less. In the Baneh Company, the leaders had never given women opportunities, and also we ourselves lacked confidence.

For quite some time, a team from the Sardasht Company, now joined with Baneh Company on the Border Battalion, had been discussing with me the possibility of becoming a military commander for a squad of ten to fifteen Peshmerga in their company. They had observed my achievements on the battlefield, and my rapport and popularity with the community and among the Peshmerga.

This would be an excellent opportunity for me to show what I was really capable of. I was tempted, but I wouldn't move to their company without the approval of Baneh Regional Committee. However, when Jamal, Mahmood and Rahmat on the committee heard about this offer, they were determined to keep me.

'We cannot give Galavezh to another city – we need her here,' Jamal said.

'Then you need to let her grow in her work, as she is capable of being a leader,' said Haji Tavani, the political leader for the Sardasht Company.

After a long discussion, I was promoted to be military commander for a squad within the Baneh Company. I would be in charge of twelve Peshmerga: ten men and two women.

Most of the squad were supportive, but some of the men were

unhappy and they tried to reject me. When it was their turn to guard, they would insist it was my turn to go first. It was difficult for them to accept a woman as their military commander, so they tried to discourage me so that I would give up.

One Peshmerga in my squad, Hassan, a sweet young man with a beautiful smile, laughed at me: 'No woman can do this kind of work. It's not a woman's place to be a commander. She would be scared and run away.'

When he saw how annoyed I was, he said that he was joking, but for me it was a serious matter, not something to joke about. I talked to him and to the others at length, but he would not change his mind. It was only much later, when he had seen me in battle many times, that he accepted that I was as capable as any man.

Komala had been severely weakened by the Democrat Party in Baneh and the party started a discussion on what we should do to reverse this situation. Too many Peshmerga had been killed from the Border Battalion. Our morale was low. We wanted to go and rest at our bases in Iraq, but the Central Committee decided we had to restructure once more. We were sent to join forces with the South Battalion in Mariwan in southern Kurdistan. We would become a regiment of over 500 Peshmerga.

My battalion had to trek for several days to get to Mariwan. It was winter and we had to walk from village to village, crossing many rivers and main roads, hiking up and down the mountains, and trudging through endless fields. Some nights we had to sleep on the snow and ice and we spent days living on raisins. We heard that the government was following us, but in our debilitated state we tried not to engage in any battles. We wanted any fighting with the government to be on our terms, when we had planned and prepared for it.

The South Battalion came to welcome us at a point in the journey close to their bases in the border of Iraq and Iran, in an area called Narmalas, which is next to a huge snow covered mountain. Narmalas had been the Democrat Party's main base before Komala's South Battalion had seized it.

The Democrats had built a number of houses with roofs and four walls, which were warm and cosy. We were no longer accustomed to such luxury after living in our bombed out buildings. We were given good meat, rice and naan to eat, and gradually got some energy back.

We were extremely tired and our confidence was greatly diminished. It was uncomfortable for us to see the way that some of the South Battalion looked upon us with pity, as though we had not been a match for the Democrats. In the south, Komala had the upper hand. As well as Narmalas, the South Battalion had managed to capture quite a few other bases from the Democrat Party. They had also been in several battles with the government and had been successful at taking over their military bases or defeating them. We had been so crushed by the Democrats along the border that we thought the South Battalion would be feeling as dispirited as us. It was strange to find them in such a good mood.

Joining the South Battalion was clearly a strategic decision. The Komala Central Committee wanted to save us from further losses and give us time to regain our strength. We were allowed to rest for a few days, and then the South Battalion started to involve us in the planning for a large operation. We joined their meetings and activities and began eating and working together.

The South Battalion leaders told us we needn't fear the Democrats. The Democrat Party had to accept that we existed and accept that there were other political parties that needed free movement and freedom of speech and expression in Kurdistan. I felt stronger, safer and much more confident being with a larger group in such high spirits.

I was put into a team to go on an overnight mission to investigate the Democrat bases, which were on the other side of a big, wide valley. It was pitch black, so we wore cameras with night vision. Everywhere there was ice and rocks, and the snow came up to our waists. It was difficult to climb and took us about three hours to get there. We watched the base carefully for two hours.

We had to study the guards' patterns and changeover times, and discover any weak leaks. We had to map out the bases so that we could work out the best way to attack. We counted how many trenches they had, and how they had been organised. At around 3 a.m., we headed back to give a report to the regiment leaders.

The commanders drew up detailed attack plans. We needed some Peshmerga to defend our bases in case the government or Democrat Party attacked. Our main telecommunications expert provided a comprehensive report and translated all of the Democrats' codes from their walkie talkies and telecommunications.

The next evening, all commanders and team leaders were invited to attend a top secret meeting. We were informed that the operation would go ahead. We were to attack the Democrats' military bases in Bayer and Bordama. Habibolah was the commander of this operation. He was realistic about our enemies and knew them well. His plans were always successful. This gave us more faith, particularly those of us from the Border Battalion.

I felt confident, but I was also frightened. We were going to war with the Democrats again. Just a few nights before, I had been at their bases, so close to their trenches that I could hear them speaking clearly. We will surprise them, I thought. I was determined that I would not be captured.

After dinner, we were all given raisins, pistachios, almonds and dates in small plastic bags. Just after midnight we were ready to depart for a long march in the snow and rocks of the valleys. We had to cross rivers and pyawein on the mountains (pyawein is the Kurdish word for making a path through the snow). It is exhausting to walk in untouched snow. All the while, we were thinking that we were heading to an operation that could be a matter of life and death for any one of us.

We came close to their base. We had to remain silent, as noise travels faster and louder in the night and cool weather. We got to our position and we started out firing the RPG before shooting with our Kalashnikovs. The Democrats hit back and the real battle began.

Any fears I had disappeared as soon as we started to shoot. I was fully conscious of the threat around me, but at the same time knew that we were fighting strategically. We managed to take over their bases and they retreated to other side of the valley.

The Border Battalion had had so many unsuccessful operations that to find ourselves winning a battle completely changed our mood. The next day we returned to our base tired but successful. I had mixed feelings, however. I wished that there had never been a war with the Democrat Party. We had been forced into this situation by them.

Despite these thoughts, I enjoyed my time in Narmalas. We became close friends with the South Battalion. We had study teams together and continued our social activities, such as our galta o gapp evenings.

Little by little the snow started to melt and spring came, bringing first saffron crocuses, then yellow and white daffodils covering the mountains all around our base. The air was fresh with the scent of flowers. Vegetables grew everywhere. My favourite was wild rhubarb, which I would eat with either sugar or salt. One day, I bent down to gather a large bunch of rhubarb. As I parted its wide leaves, a large snake slithered out. I jumped out of the way quickly and allowed it to pass me. Each time we went for a walk, we would return to the base with huge bags of rhubarb, mushrooms and many other wild edible vegetables that we cooked with egg and ate with fresh bread. On such beautiful days I felt as though I could live like that for ever.

The communications team continued to listen 24/7 to the Democrats' walkie talkie messages. We needed to know the Democrats' plans and movements in detail as well as information about their equipment, the number of Peshmerga, even their state of mind and what food they had available.

The communications team didn't rest until they managed to break the Democrats' codes. They found out that the Democrats were planning a huge revenge attack and had gathered Peshmerga from all over the region for the assault. They wanted to take back Narmalas.

However, due to our clever code breakers we knew their plans in such detail that we were able to make a powerful ambush for them. We built trenches out of rocks all around the base and down into the valley. To do this, we would find one large rock and build a wall of smaller stones around it, this would provide us with protection against the bullets. Each of these trenches was about a square metre in size and could fit two people in each one.

Ahead of the planned assault, around 700 Komala Peshmerga sat all over the mountain, in pairs, waiting. I was with my comrade Hama Ali Waziri. Hama Ali was married to one of my old boarding school friends, Aziza, and they had a daughter who lived with Hama Ali's family. For a while she had been in the base with them in Iraq, but it became unsafe, so she was sent to her grandparents.

While we waited Hama Ali and I shared memories about our friends who had lost their lives. We talked about our families and how much we missed them. We discussed politics and wondered what would happen in this war with the Democrats.

We stayed awake for forty-eight hours, not moving except to relieve ourselves. Peshmerga teams brought us sandwiches and tea. I don't know how our hands could hold the guns for this long, but we were wide awake from the fear and adrenaline.

At one moment, I fell asleep for just a second and my head fell and hit a stone. I immediately woke up. I looked across at Hama Ali and I could see him continuing to watch carefully in the dark.

The Democrats attacked us at 5 a.m., just as it was getting light.

We were ready.

They began their assault from one corner at the top of the mountain. We allowed them to come close.

They didn't attack us from the side where I was waiting. I watched the start of the battle as the Democrats fired off rockets and the RPG before trying to take over our trenches. This led to fierce face to face fighting.

Over the walkie talkie Komala ordered the Peshmerga on my

side of the mountain to get closer to the front line. We left our trenches to go to the trenches on the other side. As I made my way into the heart of the battle to help my comrades, I continued to shoot the whole time.

For several hours this battle continued in the dark and into daylight. All I could see around me were grenades exploding and bullets whizzing past my ears.

Komala managed to push the Democrats back and regain the trenches. We had defended our bases so well that the Democrats started to retreat. By early afternoon, we could see hundreds of them running back down the mountain. We fired in their direction to make sure that they continued to run and didn't attack us again. A few of them fell down. We could have shot them in the back as they ran away, but our commander ordered: 'Don't shoot! Let them go!'

I was relieved by this decision. For me, it was enough: to see them running away. It showed that they were broken mentally. They had failed in their carefully planned attempt to take revenge on Komala.

We had lost twelve Peshmerga in this battle, but the Democrats had so many casualties that they had to leave their dead and injured behind. We later told them to come unarmed and take their injured Peshmerga back with them. We would not shoot them while they did this.

With this operation, we had taught the Democrats a lesson.

The South Battalion had become so strong that the Border Battalion also lost all fear of the Democrat Party. The South Battalion had the full support of the villagers, who gave them regular food supplies and other necessities.

Despite our successes over the Democrat Party, they still refused a ceasefire. The South Battalion decided that we needed to go and do a tour in the villages to inform the people that we wanted peace. The Peshmerga from the south, who were known in the villages, led these talks but I would often accompany them. We remained on high alert at all times.

We wanted the Democrats to hear that we wanted a ceasefire and for the people to put them under pressure to accept peace. All we were doing was harming each other. The only people to benefit were the regime leaders. The Democrats knew that they couldn't attack us much more. They had to accept that they had lost their way. They needed to allow Komala and other political parties freedom to undertake their own activities. We had both paid too heavy a price in Peshmerga.

In the south, even the government forces were no match for us. They gathered their soldiers in villages all around us, so in teams we went to investigate their bases, so that we knew how many rockets they had, and how many soldiers. We gradually managed to take over many of the government bases in the area.

One day we were in the village of Nashkash, at the end of a valley. It was a warm day and the Peshmerga were resting. My squadron was tired, so I volunteered to go on watch with two others to the top of the mountain. The farms and valleys all the way to Mariwan were visible.

We could see Peshmerga washing in the river. Many were cleaning their clothes in hot water in a big vat collected from the villagers. The two Peshmerga I was with were exhausted and wanted to sleep, but I had to stay awake, watching the main road from the city with a pair of binoculars. The road was dusty, not asphalt, and I thought I could see mirrors flashing in the sunshine on a line of cars travelling through the dust.

I woke up the other two.

'Can you see the same thing as me?' I asked.

'It looks like a whole army regiment coming towards us from Mariwan!'

I continued to watch through the binoculars. At the same time, I frantically tried to contact all of the other military commanders by walkie talkie, but no one responded to any of my calls.

It was getting to the point where I would have to tell one of the boys to go down the mountain to warn everyone to get ready for an attack.

'I don't want to go down,' one of them said, although the other volunteered to go.

I could see that the cars had stopped by this time. The soldiers were walking towards the entrance of the village. I was deciding who to send down to the village when someone responded on the walkie talkie. It was one of the top military leaders of the regiment.

'Any news?' he said.

'What are you doing?' I replied. 'I called you about an hour ago. Regime forces are quite close. They are about a mile away from the village. The tanks and cannons have stopped and those walking seem to be tired and sitting. It looks as though they are organising themselves for an attack. You need to act quickly.'

He passed a message to the other military commanders that everyone needed to follow my orders.

One of them came on the walkie talkie.

'Lady Galavezh, what do you want from us?' He was laughing.

Even at such a time, they wanted to make jokes about women telling them what to do.

'There is no time for discussion,' I replied. 'The government are coming to attack us. Listen to me. You must arrange a squad and a platoon and I will tell you where to go so that you can ambush them. Go to the second corner on the road and be ready for them.'

From my vantage point, I could see exactly where the government soldiers were coming from, over the river and around the side.

I set up the teams and gave them all the information they needed.

One brave squad went and ambushed the regime forces while they were resting. Within a matter of ten minutes, they had hit their cars with RPGs and had arrested all of the group, including a few Jash. This marked the start of a battle that lasted for several hours, while I continued to give commands from the mountaintop.

Finally, the regime soldiers retreated back to the cities. We managed to take about five or six cars from them, which had been left behind. Some Peshmerga came back to the village in the military cars. The villagers started to run to hide themselves and asked the Peshmerga to leave, as they thought it was the government military, but when they realised it was us, they cheered.

We had captured thirteen soldiers, including three Jash. It had been a successful operation. We went down to join the rest of the battalion.

Omar from the Komala Central Committee came and hugged me: 'Well done. You have saved the whole regiment. You should be applauded for the great work you have done.'

But another said: 'She did her communist duties well. There is no need to applaud her.'

If I had been a man I would certainly have been promoted or given a place on the Central Committee, but I didn't even get a better gun.

I listened to the radio report about the operation, explaining how successful it had been. They didn't mention our team and the part we had played. Usually those responsible for the decisions would be commended in such reports.

It was infuriating. All the time women were trying so hard, but we were not seen.

After this battle in Nashkash, we were ordered to move out to another village as it was not safe for us to stay. We went to Gawn Abad, still in the Mariwan area.

The next day, Mahmood was on watch with two other Peshmerga. They were laughing and talking and not paying great attention when two men dressed in Kurdish clothes walked past them saying, 'Good morning.'

I was sitting in the village when I suddenly heard gun fire. I jumped to my feet immediately to join the rest. We were ordered to the mountain. We realised we were surrounded by an entire battalion of government soldiers and Jash.

The two men that had walked past Mahmood and the others on guard had been two Jash, but our guards had mistaken them for Peshmerga and had waved them through. They had only realised they weren't Peshmerga when they saw they were followed by several soldiers, and Mahmood and the others started to shoot.

From the bottom of the mountain, the rest of the Peshmerga worked their way up to the top shooting the whole time. The battle lasted about three hours until we broke the government forces once more.

Sadly, we had several injured Peshmerga. One was Rahman Sad Bar, who had sometimes joined my community team, he had been shot in the stomach. Dr Ahmad and Dr Darvish, along with our other medics, had to do an emergency operation on him in the mountains. We made a bed for him with stones and wood and some of our scarves, and used tree branches to hold the drip. The operation was successful. The doctors also treated several other injured, and all of them recovered well, including Rahman. Though for several weeks, everywhere we went, we had to carry him on a stretcher from village to village. The day after we left Gawn Abad, we walked down into a valley along a narrow road to get to another village. On the way, we saw an old woman who was sitting under a tree holding her knees.

'Why are you sitting alone here?' we asked her.

'I want to see your Komala doctors,' she said. 'I'm ill.'

'How did you know we were coming this way?'

'We knew that you had been in a battle with the government in Gawn Abad and you would be coming this way,' she said. 'My village is ready to welcome you.'

The doctors laughed and hugged her and said they would help her. We strolled with her down into the village.

During these two battles, although we had injured Peshmerga, no one from our side had died. The Border Battalion felt much stronger. We had got back the confidence that we had lost through our war with the Democrats. We decided we should return to Baneh.

Our goodbye to our friends in the south was emotional. We had been in intense battles together, and now we were becoming a smaller team once more.

It was much quicker to go back to Baneh than it had been to come to the south. It was sunny and we were all feeling much happier. We walked back village by village, giving speeches wherever we stopped. In each one, we repeated our desire for a ceasefire but the villagers told us the Democrats were about to attack us. We knew we had to make the first move. We would show them we were back.

Chapter 24

Marriage

When they heard that I had returned to the Baneh region, my mother and father came to find me.

They brought with them one of my second cousins, who was at that time living in Europe but had come back to Iran to visit the family. My father wanted me to marry this cousin and leave the Peshmerga for Europe.

'I'm not asking you to stop being a Peshmerga and give up your political activities so that you can come and give yourself up to the government,' he said. 'I want you to go to Europe and live a safe life. This is the best chance you will have of doing that.'

I knew that my father was thinking only of my safety, but I was surprised he would ask this of me.

I looked at my mum, who was leaving the talking to my father. I understood that he was saying these words out of desperation. I didn't look at my second cousin. I was not interested in him at all. I didn't need time to think about this.

'We are in the middle of a war and every single Peshmerga has an important role to play,' I said. 'How can I leave all my friends and comrades here and go and live a safe life in Europe? I can't even think about this. Mum, Dad, forgive me – I have to refuse this suggestion.'

Over time, more women joined the Peshmerga. A number joined Komala with the top leaders of a small left wing organisation called Artashe Rahai Bakhsh. They thought their party was too isolated and didn't work enough with the community, and they liked our aims and strategy. I had become good friends with a number of them, particularly another Galavezh, known as Galavezh Kermanshah because of the city she hailed from. As there were already two Galavezhs stationed in and around Baneh, we asked her to take a different name, but she refused.

Galavezh Kermanshah came with me often to speak to the villagers and she made many friends. She was hugely popular within the community and was a big help to me in spreading our message on equality to more women in the villages. We were in agreement on most issues and we criticised the party for its treatment of girls. Galavezh Kermanshah's first language was Farsi. She spoke a different Kurdish dialect to our Sorani dialect, but she made efforts to learn Sorani quickly.

In terms of theory and information, Galavezh Kermanshah knew a lot, but when it concerned the practical day to day stuff, she struggled. She was always leaving her belongings behind.

Once on the way to a village, we lost her. We sent a team to look for her. Eventually, we found her sitting next to a waterfall.

'We lost you – what have you been doing?' I said.

'No, the company was lost, not me,' she said, closing her eyes as she talked with such a sweet voice. She had just gone off on her own. She hadn't waited for the company.

On our return to Baneh, Azad joined the Border Battalion, and became the military commander. He had not remarried since Farah had been killed. He did try and talk to me, but I went out of my way to avoid him.

My brother Asad came from the city to visit me and Azad stuck close with him the whole time, hoping to speak to me. I didn't chat to either of them during the visit. I didn't even go with them when they went to dinner at a villager's home.

Galavezh Kermanshah came to me and said: 'Azad loves you still. Come and speak to him.'

But I was still too angry.

I was exhausted. It had been battle after battle after battle. I had been living on adrenaline for months. I needed some proper rest. I also wanted to escape my feelings for Azad. I spoke to

Mahmood and the Baneh Regional Committee and told them I wanted to leave for a rest in Iraq. I wanted to go to Kareza to see my sister, who by now had a baby daughter. I wanted to visit her with my brother and take a break.

Plans were made for me to go with my brother. We accompanied some other Peshmerga who were ill and needed taking to safety. I left with the group taking the injured soldiers, including Rahman, to our hospital there. Seeing Shaesta with her baby daughter, Lena, for the first time was wonderful. Lena was six months old and very sweet. Shaesta had had an extremely difficult birth. I felt terrible that I had not been there for her.

She had gone into labour during our war with the Democrats. It was winter time, cold and snowy. The only hospital nearby belonged to the Democrat Party and Shaesta had no doctors or trained midwife with her, just the traditional midwife. These were women who had never studied to become a midwife, but had gained experience by helping during many births. In a normal and easy delivery they can be helpful, but in a complicated birth, they can be rather dangerous for the mother and the baby. Shaesta's baby was breech, with the legs coming first. The traditional midwife tried to turn the baby to the right position by hand, but pushed so hard that Shaesta began to haemorrhage. She was bleeding so badly she kept slipping in and out of consciousness. All the while she was surrounded by people from the neighbourhood.

Eventually somebody took her by car to the Democrats' hospital. They had to pretend that Shaesta was not from Komala so she could be admitted. Shaesta thought she was going to die, all alone without her family close by and with a husband who did not love or support her, but the doctors saved both Shaesta's and the baby's life.

It took Shaesta a long time to recover from the birth, but her neighbours rallied round to assist her.

I was crying as she told me what had happened. How sad to have to give birth in a foreign country without your family close by and without doctors and midwives. This was the fault of the Islamic regime tearing apart all our families. How lonely and helpless Shaesta must have felt. Asad and I hugged her tight.

After one week, my brother went back to his job with my father at the bakery. If he stayed any longer, he could be prosecuted for not being in the city.

Once Asad had left, Shaesta admitted to me that she was fighting with her husband, who had no patience with Lena. Whenever the baby cried, he shouted at her, 'Stop crying!' and even put his hand over her mouth.

I was shocked. 'How could he do that?' I said. 'Why do you accept it?'

'But what can I do? Where could I go? How can I bring up my baby without any money?'

'What if I talk with him about it?' I asked.

'He doesn't listen to anyone. I asked his family to talk to him, but that made him even angrier with me. He is scared of you because he thinks you are the only one that would help me no matter what.'

She admitted he had even bitten Lena.

'Has he bitten you too?' I asked.

Shaesta burst into tears. 'Yes, several times. The way he treats me and the baby is unbearable. I try to keep everything calm and do everything that he wants, just to keep us safe.'

I held her close and hugged her.

'My beautiful little sister, he doesn't deserve to have you. He is a violent man, taking you and the baby for granted. I have to do something about this. I will. Let me think about it – you think about it too. I will not let you go through this and suffer in silence, I promise.'

I knew we would have to think carefully and come up with a good plan to ensure that both Shaesta and her baby were safe.

Rajab usually came home in the afternoon with his cousins, who also lived in Iraq. They would bring several boxes of beer with them and drink till late at night. Like a maid, Shaesta had to do all the housework and prepare all the food. During these drinking sessions, she had to feed the men constantly with fried chicken breast, nuts and fruits.

She was so unhappy; it broke my heart. I could bear my own problems but I couldn't tolerate what was happening to her.

I stayed with Shaesta another week before saying goodbye to go to our base in Maluma. It felt as though I had left my heart behind with her. I had to do something to help but she didn't want me to talk to anyone about it. Separation was shameful and she didn't want anyone to know what was happening.

In Maluma I was informed that the Border Battalion were going to be allowed to have a month's rest at our base in Iraq. There had been one final big battle between the Democrats and the Border Battalion while I had been with my sister. I think the Democrats thought that we were the same as before when they crushed us mentally and killed so many of us. But they underestimated us. This time we were stronger than them. We won the battle and the Democrat Party in Baneh were defeated.

The Democrats still thought they could finish off Komala, but it was impossible. Neither the Democrats nor the government could end Komala because we were rooted strongly within the community. We had thousands of members and supporters in Kurdistan and all over Iran. They had underestimated our power and ability.

Komala demanded a ceasefire but still the Democrats didn't accept it. Instead, Komala announced a unilateral ceasefire.

After ten difficult months, the war with the Democrats was over. Komala could continue to operate freely in Kurdistan. However, we would still need to be careful when the Democrats were around.

I was relieved but I was also deeply sorry for what had happened. So many lives had been taken and the government had enjoyed watching us killing each other. The Democrat Party had lost the most Peshmerga.

The whole battalion came to Maluma and I joined them there.

In the base there were lots of small rooms and tents and my company was given one large room, about ten by five metres, where we had all our meetings, ate and the men slept. The women slept in a tent separate from the rest of the company, while married couples had their own tents. At first, we did nothing but rest, but after a week, we had to join in regular activities, like cooking, guard duty, and getting petrol for the whole camp.

Maluma was surrounded by tall mountains, including one called Gapilon, which towered over the whole base. On the other side, it overlooked all the roads into Iran and the Iraqi border cities.

Fifteen of us were given the job to protect the camp. We had to remain on the top of Gapilon the whole time, living in a tent and taking turns on guard. We had no water up there, so either Peshmerga would bring us water from the base via donkeys every day or we would walk down and bring it back for ourselves.

Mahmood was by now the political leader for the battalion as well as being a member on the Baneh Regional Committee. We still continued to talk to each other as fondly as always, sharing our opinions on politics and love.

One day I came down the mountain to bring food and water back up to the tent when I saw Mahmood.

'We are getting really tired stuck up there,' I told him. 'It's cold and we've not had any chance to rest. We are always on alert. We have been there for two weeks and can't even have a proper shower. If we come down for a shower, we get covered with dust again when we walk back up.'

'What can we do?' Mahmood replied. 'The rest of the battalion are doing similar work down in the base too. Those who have partners have to be kept down in the base together.'

'It's not fair on single people! We are the only ones working hard here.'

'OK, then you need to get married and you will have a tent for yourself.'

We both burst out laughing.

A few days later, Mahmood came up to visit us on the top of the mountain to talk about our situation and to see if we could come up with a better way of organising the rota.

It was good to see him. I was feeling relaxed that day on the mountain and we enjoyed laughing together. He told us that the Baneh Regional Committee wanted us to stay there a little while longer. We couldn't object as we knew we had to do our duty as Peshmerga.

'Can I talk to you, Galavezh?' Mahmood motioned to me to move away from the others. This took me by surprise, as we usually carried on our chatter and jokes in front of everyone.

I followed him a short while and he turned to me and said: 'I want to propose to you. I love you.'

He was confident as he said this, but I was shocked. I had never had a hint of such feelings from him.

'What kind of love is this? Just a short while ago you were in love with Nasrin. This is not a good idea for us. I don't have romantic feelings for you. We have a strong friendship. Let's leave it that way.'

Mahmood looked disappointed. He left without saying anything more.

I told Galavezh Kermanshah about Mahmood's proposal.

'But do you love him?'

'Not in that way, but I care about him a lot. We are great friends. We have lots in common and maybe that is enough. Is this a good reason to marry him?'

After about two weeks, I felt that I must make a decision. I still loved Azad, but the situation seemed hopeless. I decided to tell Mahmood I had changed my mind.

I went down the mountain with Galavezh Kermanshah to talk to him. He was with a group from Baneh's regional committee.

'Is it good news or bad news?' he said, moving away from the others. 'I hope it is good news.'

'Yes, it is good news. I will marry you.' His face broke into a big smile.

'See, I am cleverer than you,' he said. 'I knew this was a good idea and now you have changed your mind.'

We set the wedding for the following week and went to inform the secretariat.

'Congratulations,' they said. 'We will give you a tent.'

I went back to guard duty on Gapilon for another week. I thought a lot about my feelings for Mahmood. I hoped in time our friendship would develop into love.

My wedding day was in May 1985. In the morning I was sent to exchange four political prisoners that we had captured from the Democrat Party for four of our own. Now the ceasefire was in place, we could make these exchanges. One of our Democrat prisoners was Karim, Shaesta's milk brother. I had been visiting him regularly in Komala's prison. On the way to make the exchange we talked about our families and we laughed about our memories of when we were growing up together. We talked about the war between Komala and the Democrats. Neither of us had ever wanted to fight each other.

It was a hot sunny day and we had to walk with the prisoners for several hours to make the exchange. It was late afternoon by the time we got back, and we still had to take our Peshmerga to the Central Committee, another half hour walk from the base.

When I came back to our base, I saw that everywhere was looking clean and smart. My sister was there, and Mahmood's sister Behjat, along with so many Peshmerga from different platoons, all dancing and drinking lemonade made from water, lemon juice and lots of sugar. We drank this on special occasions.

When they saw me from afar they said: 'Hooray! The bride is coming!'

However, all my clothes were full of dust. You couldn't even see my face and hair. I was annoyed that I had been sent to exchange prisoners on my wedding day.

'You have to go and shower and get changed!' Shaesta said in horror. Mahmood had called for her to come to the wedding, but Rajab had stayed at home.

I didn't have any spare clothes. I was wearing all that I had. I quickly went to have a shower.

Mahmood's auntie Ashraf was visiting him at that time. She had complained about his choice of bride and told him: 'She is very skinny. She is not beautiful. Why are you marrying this woman? Could you not get anyone better?'

Mahmood had told me this and I had laughed.

This aunt found out that I was going to have a shower and insisted on coming with me. I didn't feel comfortable being naked around her but we couldn't stop her. Looking at my body, she said: 'Oh, you are not that bad!'

Shaesta and Behjat quickly washed all of my clothes and hung them in the sun. They used a heater to try and dry them but they were still damp when I had to put them on hurriedly. I rushed back to the wedding ceremony.

Somebody gave me the sarchopi to lead everyone in the dance and I joined in with gusto.

Seeing that I was not playing the role of the modest, shy bride, sitting quietly while everyone else enjoyed her wedding, one of the Peshmerga said: 'Oh, you are so bold.'

This is my wedding, I will dance if I want to, I thought.

Although I appeared to the world joyful and excited, in my heart I was having doubts.

Mahmood was handsome and such a good friend but I didn't love him in the right way yet. I hoped that we would come to care deeply for one another. I needed to be loved, and I believed that this could develop in my heart.

We were given a dirty old tent with many holes in it to live in after the wedding, but I tried to avoid it and went back to the girls' room after the dancing had finished. I still had no idea about virginity and marital relations and felt too shy to ask anyone.

A few days later, Mahmood suggested that we go to Kareza for the day. We took Shaesta and her baby and Galavezh Kermanshah with us. We had lunch together in a good kebab restaurant and went to a photo shop to take a few portraits. We had not been to the city for a long time and it was good to stroll around. We looked at the shops for a while, but it felt strange to us. We were so used to living with Komala in the mountains that we didn't need anything, not even clothes, kitchenware or anything like that. Instead, we bought some cake, biscuits and bananas. It was odd because Mahmood was walking a few steps in front of me and it seemed as though he expected me to walk behind. He had never done this once during our friendship, when we had very much been equals, but this was the first time we had walked down the street together. My relationship with him somehow felt changed in a way I couldn't quite fathom. Although our marriage should have brought us closer together, I felt as though a distance had opened up between us.

Chapter 25

Spies and Ambushes

Around a week after my wedding, the Border Battalion was sent back to the Baneh region. It took us five days to get there. We had been resting for a month and it was difficult to hike all day, every day up and down the mountains. I just had to concentrate on putting one foot in front of the other. All we could see in the distance was mountains.

It was about 4 a.m. when we arrived in the village of Ghoolatrer, where we joined up with the Mockryan Battalion, who had been patrolling in the region during our absence. On arrival, I immediately went to the girls' room to find somewhere to sleep. Zahra, one of the Mockryan Battalion's Peshmerga, was getting ready to go on night patrol. She pointed at the thin mattress on the floor where she had been sleeping.

'Go and take my place,' she said. 'It's nice and warm now.'

I hugged Zahra before she went up to the mountain with two other guards. Taking my ammunition belt to use as a pillow, I settled into her warmth in the handmade blankets. As I fell asleep, I thought about Zahra and her fiancé Salah, who was on the Central Committee. Zahra was a beautiful girl with light skin, green eyes, striking dark eyelashes and short dark hair. The pair made a handsome couple. They were obvious in their love for each other and so sweet together.

I was so exhausted I fell asleep quickly, but I was soon woken by the sound of gunfire, grenades from an RPG and rockets. I had been in such a deep sleep that I thought the sound was from far away at first, but I soon realised that it was right next to me. We were completely surrounded. I and the other Peshmerga women in the room got up quickly, took our guns and went outside. It was still dark, but we could see movements around us. We joined the others and organised ourselves into teams to fight back and break the enemy.

Rockets were hitting the village, and we could see the fire from the explosions lighting up the sky, while shrapnel, stone and soil fell all over us. We could hear nothing but the sound of explosions and bullets.

Some villagers went to safe rooms, while others volunteered to bring us food and water.

The job of my team was to try and force a gap in the circle of soldiers surrounding the village, so that my comrades could move through the gap and up the mountain, giving us the advantage.

My team managed to do this successfully. Afterwards, we were sitting and resting near the stream in the valley when we were informed via walkie talkie that Zahra and the other two guards had been shot dead by the government attack group, when they first went to the top of the mountain to go on watch. Zahra and I had hugged just a few hours ago. I could still feel the warmth from her body from when I slept in her place on the floor.

I wanted to scream loudly, but I kept all my anger in my heart. Instead I cried quietly for her.

I was feeling distraught when I saw a number of government soldiers. For a second I thought they were coming after us. I got ready to shoot them, but Mahmood quickly held my hand. He told me that these soldiers had been captured and they were our prisoners.

'Don't you see the Peshmerga with them,' he asked.

I hadn't seen the Peshmerga. I shivered from the shock of almost shooting at my comrades. I was relieved that I hadn't fired on them and I thanked Mahmood.

The battle on the other side of the village continued and was intense, but we had been told to stay alert in our positions. A team would bring all the injured and dead to us, as well as the captured. Our side was also a protected corridor for the rest of the Peshmerga to withdraw down when the battle finished.

The battle took several hours but we managed to defeat the government forces and they retreated. Three of our Peshmerga had been killed and four injured.

The villagers came to help us bury our dead. We sang the Communist Party's anthem 'The Internationale' at the funeral for our comrades.

The villagers made wooden stretchers for the injured and offered their horses and men to come with us to the next village where it was safer and from where we could send those with serious injuries to our hospital in Iraq.

We had captured a number of prisoners from the regime. We would have to take them to our central prison, where they would be educated about human rights and Kurdish people. They would later either be set free or exchanged for our political prisoners.

I could still hear the sound of explosions around the village, but luckily no villagers had been injured. We had been about 300 Peshmerga and they numbered over 1,000, with heavy equipment, yet we had still managed to defeat them.

We started our routine tour in the villages and began to speak to the people again about what we were trying to achieve. This was always the best part of being a Peshmerga. The kindness shown toward us was incredible. The villagers supported us with everything they could. They were our family. We attended their weddings, their funerals and shared in their happiness and sorrow.

While moving from village to village, we continued to attack government bases on the way, using hit and run guerrilla tactics. Sometimes we launched bigger attacks and took over their bases. We would leave shortly after, as they would always come back the next day with a greater number of soldiers. The purpose of these tactics was to create an atmosphere of fear among the government forces. We wanted to exhaust them. We wanted to tell the government: You must have the fear of Peshmerga always. We are here around you. You are not safe.

We arrived in the village of Haft Ash, which means 'seven mills'. Haft Ash was high in the mountains with a spectacular view of the plains below it. There was no government base in Haft Ash, so we started to relax a little. We put several people on guard and split up into different people's homes. The men went to the river to wash while I went with the women to villagers' homes to clean our clothes and ourselves.

I was feeling rested. I'd had a bath and my clothes were drying so I changed and decided to go and visit Rana, one of the villagers who was heavily pregnant. Rana was a strong woman, in charge of her household. She had three children and they seemed to be a happy family. I stayed with her and the children for about an hour. Her children were hanging onto my legs as I got up to go. They wanted me to stay and play with them, but I had to leave. Rana wrapped me up a naan sandwich made with organic butter and mountain honey and also brought some dried fruit and nuts. She gave it to me to have on the way as we left the village. I always tried to have some food on me as our lives were so unpredictable. I said goodbye, hugged and kissed them and left to join Mahmood.

At around 3 p.m., after a short team meeting, an announcement came across the walkie talkie. The regime forces were close to the village.

Immediately we grabbed our equipment and gathered with the commanders, who organised the teams into position. The mood among the Peshmerga was positive. Our plan was to defeat the regime on the road and move slowly toward the mountain. Every team volunteered to go to the road where the military cars would arrive. My squad was sent to the top of the hill on the east side of the village. The villagers came to us with bread and dried fruit and asked if they could help. The commanders told them to find safety and take care of their families.

We went to the middle of the mountain and waited for the regime forces to come closer. On the main road, the battle started. As usual, the regime started to send rockets around the village and also to the top of the hill where we were waiting for them.

We had to take shelter under any large rocks that we could find. However, we knew that if the rockets hit the rocks, this was even more dangerous, as it would send thousands of sharp stones flying all around us. We had to be extra cautious and try not to move around.

The battle in the road was heavy and soon our Peshmerga to the west were also engaged as the soldiers tried to surround us.

Whenever we were surrounded in a village, we knew we had to get to the highest place and take the battle with us. One team had to break the enemy line by shooting their way through and running all the way to the mountain. At the top of the mountain, they would continue to shoot while the other teams tried to escape. My squad remained on the top of the mountain. From the bottom of the valley, there was a platoon of Peshmerga engaged in a close battle. We were joined on the mountain by those with guns for long range shooting. After a while, they went up to the top of the mountain and we stayed where we were.

I hadn't seen Mahmood during the battle. I had a walkie talkie with me and I contacted the Peshmerga at the top to see if Mahmood was with them.

'Where is he? I can't see him anywhere.'

'Don't worry, he is fighting on the other side,' one Peshmerga told me.

I was worried because I didn't hear anything more about Mahmood. I asked several Peshmerga about him but they didn't seem to want to respond. I was frantic with worry that something had happened to him. I tried to convince myself to stay positive. Why should I think that something bad had happened to him?

By 6 p.m., the battle was over. Lots of the regime soldiers had been killed. The government troops left the village and we took it over once more. The regime continued to send rockets to the village and one of the villagers was hit and killed.

When I came back into the village, I saw Mahmood with our comrade Rahim.

'Where have you been?' I said, running over to them. 'I couldn't see you.'

He explained that two Peshmerga had been left in the village. Mahmood and Rahim had gone back into the heat of the battle to get the two men out and had been encircled. Although the two other Peshmerga had been able to shoot their way out with the help of Mahmood and Rahim, Rahim had been hit in the leg and Mahmood had stayed with him. They had hidden themselves behind a large rock. The regime guards had tried to find them but had been unable to do so.

The commanders had thought the pair had been killed but didn't want to tell me during the battle. It was so good to see Mahmood safe. My strong feelings of warmth towards him returned.

Komala was in a difficult financial situation by this time and we needed to raise some money in order to take pressure off the villages.

I was one of ten people chosen by the Baneh Regional Committee to write letters to all the rich people in the cities and villages asking for donations.

Some of the wealthy folk we targeted tried to make excuses. They said that the government would arrest them if they were seen to be helping the Peshmerga.

However, we told them that we would arrest them if they didn't pay up. In the end, they had no choice but to give us money.

One of the government's tactics against Komala was to try and get the villagers to stop supporting us. We encouraged the villages to run their own councils to organise their affairs, yet the government set up 'yellow councils', run by landlords and mullahs.

Many dervishes were on the yellow councils. Dervishes were Muslims belonging to a sect that had taken a vow of poverty. The men grew their hair long. They would go into trances and cut themselves with daggers. They hated communists and socialists, so it was easy for the government to turn them against us.

In one of the villages, a dervish priest incited the villagers to attack Komala.

'This is a communist party,' he told them. 'They are against religion. Men and women work alongside each other.'

One morning, while we were all sleeping in the mosque, the night guard woke us. We found ourselves completely surrounded by around sixty dervishes from the nearby villages wielding daggers.

We didn't know what action to take. We were armed but we didn't want to fight a group of religious people.

Some of my comrades said we should fight.

'We cannot stand for this,' one said. 'If they do this against us, they will do this to the villagers.'

Mineh, the military leader I had stitched up when he was injured, ordered everyone to defend themselves.

'We cannot allow them to have the upper hand over the people,' he said. 'They surrounded us and we must surround them.'

We quickly had the dervishes encircled. For several hours we didn't allow them to move at all.

Finally, we let them go and called a meeting with the villagers. Some of the villagers thought our actions were correct. The dervishes were going to attack us. Others said that they were religious people, so we should have left them alone and in peace.

'But they didn't leave the Peshmerga in peace,' another said.

We told ten of the leaders that we were arresting them. We contacted the yellow council of this village, which was run by the dervishes and landlords, and told them we were shutting down the council and replacing it with a people's council.

In the village of Kandhsoora, we learned that the mullah was a government spy. A team of Peshmerga went there and arrested him and sent him to prison in Maluma. After a while, the villagers asked us to excuse the mullah and said he would stop working with the government. We released him after a few months and gave him to the people's council. As soon as we released him, he moved to the city and openly cooperated with the government.

Mahmood had been on a special mission and we had been apart for three months when I heard he would be in the village of Klaval at the same time as me. I had missed him during our time apart. As soon as he arrived in Klaval, I went to find him.

'Come and join me in my house,' I said.

'I'll wait until they tell us where to go.'

'No, you must come with me.'

I took his gun from him, and leaving both my gun and his at a villager's house, I led him to my home, which was on the other side of the stream to the mosque.

It was late afternoon and around sunset. We were just talking with a group of villagers at the square in front of the mosque when gunfire started. We were surrounded by a hundred soldiers. It was the government Attack Company.

The soldiers had mixed themselves in with animals, lambs and cows, walking to the village so that the Peshmerga on guard duty didn't notice until they were close enough to the village to start shooting. I was angry with myself that I had taken Mahmood's gun. We were the only two unarmed Peshmerga. Instead of going to help in the battle, we had to go and fetch our guns. It was fifteen minutes back to where we had left them, so we had to run while being shot at the whole way. It was a tense fifteen minutes.

Finally, we joined our comrades in the battle. We managed to push the government Attack Company back and they retreated.

I knew that I had done the wrong thing, but I had not been expecting an attack at sunset. Government assaults usually took place during the daytime as a night time attack would give the Peshmerga the advantage.

Chapter 26

Chemical Bomb Attack

In 1986, I moved to our military academy in Zergwez, Iraq, to work in training Komala's Peshmerga. I also became the political manager for a platoon of new Peshmerga. I remained in the military academy for a year and a half while Mahmood stayed with the Baneh Regional Committee.

I worked closely with the information team at Zergwez, whose main mission was to look for government spies among the new recruits. The government tried many times to send their spies to infiltrate our Peshmerga, so this team was vital. The government would teach the spies how to behave like Peshmerga. We usually managed to identify them in interviews and also by observing them closely. We learned through experience to spot the right signs.

There were three Komala bases in Zergwez: one on the main road at the start of the valley, one in the middle and one at the back of the valley. This final base was where the Central Committee lived along with a first aid team, the information centre, publishing team, communication team and the committee's bodyguards. It also housed the party's academy for its most dedicated and senior members, where they mainly studied Marxism.

The middle base housed the military academy for new Peshmerga. The new recruits would spend six months training in military techniques, and take classes in politics, Komala's manifesto and in working with the general public.

We had our hospital there, with nine doctors and about fifty devoted nurses working to help injured Pesh merga and the villagers. Our hospital personnel were well known in the region and people would come to us from afar for treatment. On a few occasions we hosted medics from Doctors Without Borders, a charity that sends medical teams into conflict zones and disaster areas.

Radio Komala and Radio Communist were broadcast from the base on the main road. The Peshmerga defence force was also based there. From there they would go into the mountains to be the watch for the whole area.

The three bases were served by a large kitchen and self service area where all Peshmerga of every rank worked on rotation. There was also a tent for visitors, who had to be vetted before being allowed entry.

During the winter we stayed in tents with four or five women in each. We put extra plastic over the tents to protect them from the snow and rain. It dropped to 30°C. During the summer months, when the daytime temperature soared to 45°C, we would make our beds from wood from the forest and sleep out in the open air with a small net around us to keep the mosquitoes away.

Compared to the daytime heat, it was so cool and fresh at night. Whenever it was a full moon, it was magical to fall asleep with the trees and the mountains all around us. The men would also sleep close by. We would all stay up late, chatting to each other from our open air beds, watching the sky and counting the shooting stars.

After the years of intense fighting, this was a far less stressful period of my life. It was safer and we had a routine. During the day I was extremely busy with one to one interviews, political educational classes and military training. I also had management meetings and many decisions to make. I had great friends and comrades and I was satisfied with my job. However, I often thought about my marriage. Mahmood and I hardly saw each other and I began to question our relationship. I looked at other couples I knew in Zergwez. Most of them seemed happy, they were living together or at least visited each other regularly.

Before Mahmood and I were married, we had talked all the time about everything, but this closeness had seemed to disappear. On the rare occasions we did meet, our conversation consisted of pleasantries. This was not the partnership of equals that I had wished for and dreamed of.

We were both busy with our jobs and we often went three or even six months at a time without seeing each other. During my time at the academy, I went just once to visit Mahmood at the Baneh Regional Committee, when they had a base in Chwarta, Iraq. I had a week's leave to stay with him, but our strained relationship made me so uncomfortable that I left after three days.

A month or so later, Mahmood and a few of our friends came for a meeting with the Komala Central Committee. They had to travel through my base to get there. The friends came to visit me but Mahmood didn't. I was really hurt by this.

I was invited to go and work in Radio Komala. Before starting, I decided to go and visit my sister who I missed dearly. Baby Lena could now walk without any support. It was so lovely to see her.

While Rajab was at work, Shaesta made us both tea and I had the opportunity to ask her about her relationship. The situation had not improved and Rajab continued to be violent towards Shaesta and their daughter.

'I don't know what to do,' Shaesta said in despair.

'I know what you need to do,' I said. 'Let's pack your stuff. You and your daughter are coming with me to the base.'

'What about Rajab? He will get angry.'

'Isn't he already angry with you and your daughter? You have my support. I will be there to help you get through this. I will explain it to our family if I get to see them.'

In less than half an hour, Shaesta had packed luggage full of the baby's clothes. We left, never to return.

We rented a car with a driver to take us to Zergwez and went straight to the visitors' tent. They welcomed Shaesta and asked her to stay there until she and Lena could be permitted to enter the base. The pair were given food and were able to rest. Meanwhile, I went into the base to talk to Behjat, my sister-in-law, about them. Behjat decided to bring them both to her tent. I was so grateful to her.

When he saw that his wife had left him, Rajab followed Shaesta to the base, but she refused to speak to him.

Rajab's options were limited at this time and he asked to rejoin the Peshmerga. He was immediately accepted back in and given a role in the South Battalion. It was not long before he was made political manager for a squad.

With nowhere else to go, Shaesta also applied to return to the Peshmerga. However, the Central Committee told Shaesta that she would only be permitted to come back in if she sent Lena back to Iran and if she started her training from scratch at the Peshmerga training base. Shaesta was extremely upset at this discrimination. It had been her husband's idea to leave the Peshmerga, yet he was allowed back in and given responsibility.

However, it was true that it was no longer safe to keep Lena at the base. The Iranian government had begun bombing the bases, and we were on high alert all the time. We had to run to our shelter several times a day, which was extremely hard on the children. Komala decided that due to the increased danger from the bombing campaign, all children had to be sent back to grandparents or other relatives in Iran. Behjat's own daughter, Kvesty, had been sent back to stay with her grandmother some months before. We had all watched as the minibus pulled away. Kvesty ran from window to window, screaming and crying for her mother. Everyone there cried for those devastated children and their parents.

My sister had no choice but to send Lena back to my mother. However, my mother had recently given birth to her own baby girl and she could not cope with looking after two young babies at the same time. Instead, Lena was sent to Shaesta's mother-in-law and sister-in-law to be brought up. This was painful for Shaesta. She went to the training base to start again from the bottom.

I had to say goodbye to my friends to move to Maluma to work for Radio Komala. At Radio Komala, I worked on a new issues based programme called 'Our Listeners and Us'. Members of the public from the cities and villages would write in with questions and we prepared each programme based on their questions. I also worked some of the time in a team that monitored and analysed the news from the different Farsi and Kurdish radio stations, including the government controlled stations.

The bombing from the Iranian government continued daily and many Peshmerga were killed or injured in the attacks. Life had become extremely precarious once more.

In late 1987, Mahmood was transferred to the city of Sulaymaniyah to work in diplomatic relations with the Iraqi government. He was put in charge of all diplomatic issues, such as getting permission for Peshmerga to come over the border to live in Iraq and also for visitors who wanted to come in and out of Iraq. Komala also had diplomatic bases in Kirkuk and Baghdad, and we had a procurement centre in Sulaymaniyah through which all food and provisions would be allocated to our three different bases.

Mahmood came to visit me in Maluma to ask me to move to Sulaymaniyah with him. There would be a job for me in the communications department and we would be able to spend time together. I told him that I would think about it. I enjoyed my work at the radio station. More importantly, I was worried about our relationship. Yet perhaps this was the time to give our relationship a chance. We had never lived together properly. I wondered if it was the time apart and our difficult life circumstances that had caused our problems. We both agreed we should try to make it work, and I moved to Sulaymaniyah in 1988.

My job in the telecommunications department was straight-forward. I worked closely with one other girl, Fakhri, usually in shifts but sometimes together. We had to contact Baghdad and Europe by telephone and our other bases in Iraq via walkie talkie. By this time, many of my comrades had moved to Europe, especially those who were badly injured or suffered long term ill health. Half of the Central Committee were living in Europe and I would connect their telephone meetings to our bases in Iraq.

We also had to give reports to the Central Committee about our relationship with Iran and our position in Kurdistan, and reports about anyone arrested. Teams of Peshmerga would do tours in Iran before coming back into Iraq. Sometimes our Peshmerga were arrested on the border by Iraqi guards and we had to sort this out. We had two phone lines to operate and they were nearly always busy.

There were between seventy and eighty Peshmerga living in Sulaymaniyah, including those in the procurement and passport departments. Everyone took shifts to do guard duty, including the night shift. Mahmood was the exception, and did not do the guard shift due to his position in diplomatic relations. However, he did take turns with cooking shifts like everyone else.

Under orders from Iraq, we were not allowed to talk to the Iraqi people in Sulaymaniyah, so we mainly stayed in our bases. Everyone knew that we were Komala's Peshmerga. Although we had guns and guards in the bases, we were not allowed to have guns when going out.

Shaesta finished her training in six months and took part in a ceremony along with another fifty new Peshmerga in which she was given a gun. After this she was put in charge of looking after the families of Peshmergas who were unarmed and living in cities in Iraq. She was responsible for looking after the family's safety, education for the children, food and housing. She arranged regular meetings with them to ensure they were included and updated about the latest party news and anything about the political situation that might affect them directly. Sometime later, she joined the Mohabad Company within the Mockryan Battalion. She spent some months on tour inside Iran with the battalion before being posted to Bote, a village in Iraq, to guard technical equipment that was based there, as well as Radio Communist and one section of Radio Komala.

On 16 March 1988, towards the end of the Iran–Iraq War, Iraqi aircraft were seen above the Iraqi city of Halabja, ten miles from the Iranian border. Halabja had been taken over by Iranian regime forces fighting with Iraqi Peshmerga against the Iraqi regime. After the Iraqi army fired artillery shells into Halabja, the air force began to drop chemical bombs containing mustard gas on the city. The Iranian regime military had been wearing masks and protective clothing, so the chemical bombs did not affect them as much as ordinary Kurds.

Eyewitnesses described clouds of white, black and yellow smoke billowing into the air. Some people died instantly, but many had prolonged, agonising deaths. There were reports of eyes turning red from the gas, and people vomiting a green liquid. Up to 5,000 Kurds, mostly unarmed citizens, died in this attack, with thousands more severely injured. Three quarters of the victims were reported to be women and children.

Komala's Showan Company, named after its commander, were stationed in Sirwan, a town close to Halabja, when the chemical bombs fell. Although the Showan Company Peshmerga didn't die immediately from the attack, they all partially lost their eyesight and control of their bodies. They needed to find a way to get to safety. Komala tried to rescue them by renting boats to take them over the Sirwan River, but the Showan Company couldn't find the boats. Their judgement had been too badly affected by the chemical bombs.

Iranian soldiers seized this opportunity to surround the Showan Company on three sides, and they managed to push them back to the river. The Peshmerga fought until the last bullet. Sixty-five Peshmerga were killed in this battle – only three survived. Among the dead were my good friend Hama Ali Waziri and his wife Aziza.

Komala openly criticised Saddam's actions in Halabja and the destruction of the Showan Company on the radio.

In August 1988, Shaesta was having a shower in Bote when there was a warning that planes were overhead. She ran to the shelter under a bridge so quickly her clothes were half unbuttoned. She waited for the usual sound of dropping bombs, but this time the planes were silent. The group waited for fifteen minutes until one of the Peshmerga shouted: 'Come quickly! This is a chemical attack.' The Peshmerga had been trained to run to the mountain in case of a chemical attack, but the mountain was being bombed. Shaesta ran with twelve comrades to the river, where they sank into the water. They moved up the river to try and reach safety, keeping their bodies completely immersed, with just their eyes above so they could see the way.

When they got out, they started walking down a road to what they believed was a safe place when they saw Ismael, one of our comrades, driving a bulldozer.

'Don't go that way! It's a chemical bomb!'

Ismael took them in the blade of the bulldozer to Ranya, a small town where other Peshmerga were living.

Shaesta and her comrades showered thoroughly and rested there overnight before they were taken to Sulaymaniyah, where they were to remain in quarantine for a month. Komala urgently contacted the Iraqi government to restart negotiations.

Shaesta and her comrades were not allowed back to Bote. All of Shaesta's possessions had been burned in the attack, including her notebook, diary and photos.

On the day of the Bote attack, I was walking along the road with several comrades. A number of villagers joined us and asked for the latest news. As we chatted, we heard the sound of aircraft overhead and could see a number of planes in the sky above Bote.

The villagers immediately shouted: 'They are chemical bombs! Chemical bomb attack!'

As they ran to their homes, they told us to put wet blankets over the windows and doors to stop the chemicals from getting inside. As Peshmerga, it was not possible for us to go and hide ourselves. We had to go and help.

I felt as though I was a bird in a cage with a fire lit beneath it.

We were put on red alert and organised into different teams.

The first aid team was sent ahead with masks and clothing to try and protect them from the chemicals, which were being spread by the wind.

I was organised into a team to go to Bote. We were all given masks with small oxygen capsules, which were really uncomfortable to wear. My team didn't get far before we were asked to go to Golan instead to help the injured and poisoned. Another team continued into Bote, helping many Peshmerga on the way and taking them to the hospital in Golan. In the morning, we heard devastating news of the massacre. Twenty-four Peshmerga from Shaesta's company and eight Peshmerga from the radio departments and other units were killed in the attack on Bote. Seventy-five more were poisoned and suffered from the effects for the rest of their lives.

Chapter 27

New Life

The Iran–Iraq War ended in August 1988 and Iranian aeroplanes were no longer constantly flying overhead. The region became less volatile. Mahmood and I were busy with stable jobs in Komala. Mahmood's family and my father regularly sent us money. We were no longer carrying guns all the time and we didn't need to be on high alert. For the next year or two, I experienced a calmer kind of life, certainly the most 'normal' for me since I had left my parents at the age of seventeen.

My relationship with Mahmood had also improved considerably and it felt like the right time for us to have a child. It was something that we both really wanted. Over the years, when Peshmerga couples had children, if they hadn't sent them back to grandparents in Iran, the children would be cared for in a twenty-four-hour facility in Kirkuk or Sulaymaniyah. Neither solution was ideal. I had seen the fear in children's faces when they were taken away and the pain this had caused Shaesta, Behjat and other mothers. I didn't want to have a child for him or her to be ripped from me. I couldn't bear any more losses. Although we were in a safer situation now, I knew this could change at any moment. The fire was still smouldering under the ashes. However, I thought it was the right time to take this risk.

I became pregnant in mid-1990 but I didn't realise for three months, even though my periods had stopped. The first sign was a mad craving for unripe pears. The neighbouring house to our base had many pear trees. I put myself on 3 a.m. guard duty just so that I could go to the roof and take four or five pears. I didn't tell anyone about this. For a week I had delicious pears every day. After that week, I went in the early morning to grab some more, but to my disappointment all the pears from the garden had gone. It was hot and the neighbours had been sleeping on the roof, so perhaps they had seen me stealing their fruit. After this I went and bought pears from the market, but they didn't taste as good. I realised I needed to go and see the doctor.

Mahmood was overjoyed about the baby and at first the pregnancy brought us closer. I needed him more. The quality of the food in the base was poor and there never seemed to be enough. Once a week we might have chicken, otherwise it was lots of potatoes and rice with soups. Mahmood tried to get healthy food for me, he brought me lots of fish.

However, after a few months of this warm behaviour, Mahmood became busy at work again and began to spend a lot of his time at the diplomatic base. He often didn't come home until 1 or 2 a.m.

My pregnancy coincided with Saddam Hussein's invasion of Kuwait in August 1990. The Americans thought that the Iraqis would also attack Saudi Arabia, which would give Saddam control of much of the world's oil supply.

Half a million US troops gathered in Saudi. When Saddam refused to withdraw from Kuwait by January 1991, the US and coalition forces bombed Iraq for a month, destroying much of the infrastructure of the country.

This led to violent rebellions all across the country, which the Iraqi government tried to suppress with bombs and military action on the ground. Within a couple of months, 2 million Iraqis, the majority of them Kurds, fled the battle-torn cities to escape to the mountains and cross the border into Turkey and Iran, into Mariwan, Sardasht and Baneh. Many fled into our base at Maluma.

In Sulaymaniyah, Iraqi Peshmerga belonging to the Patriotic Union of Kurdistan (PUK) took over the city with ferocious fighting. In retaliation, the Iraqi government bombed the mountains all around the city.

During this battle in March 1991, I was driven back to Maluma in one of the diplomatic cars. It was cold and raining. The usual thirty-minute journey took about seven hours, as the roads were packed with people trying to flee the fighting in the city. We took as many people as we could with us in the car. Everywhere I looked, there were children crying, and pregnant women walking with just the clothes they were wearing. I was sorry we couldn't take any more people with us. We invited many of those fleeing to come and stay in our tents in the mountains.

The situation was incredibly tense and unpredictable once more. I worried about what would happen to me and the baby. I knew that I had been taking a chance by choosing to have a baby in this environment, but I wanted this child so much. I had lost so many friends. I couldn't see my family. There was a distance between me and my husband that we didn't seem to be able to bridge. I needed to have someone in my life who I could love unconditionally and who would love me unconditionally in return.

I knew that my baby would be a girl even though I had not been told this. I could tell from the reaction from both the nurse and midwife after a scan. They both turned their backs to me and whispered to each other before looking at me and telling me that the baby was healthy. I asked to know the gender but they told me it was their policy to not announce it. I knew that if the baby was a boy, they would immediately let the parents know. Having a boy was honourable, but a girl was worthless. They didn't want to give me bad news. Perhaps they were worried about my well being. Many husbands would divorce the mother or force the woman to have an abortion if the baby was a girl. Some families would make their daughter's life hell for giving birth to a girl.

With difficulties in my marriage once more, it was stressful to be around Mahmood. I decided to stay in Maluma. Mahmood didn't object, which made me wonder whether he cared about me at all.

I was given a small room in a concrete block at the west edge of the base, near to a stream running down the valley alongside the forest. There were several similar rooms with other Peshmerga families living there, one woman with her baby daughter and three other couples. Some of the Central Committee's tents and rooms and their guards were in the north of the base, while the defence company was on the east side and there was a square in the middle. Every morning all the Peshmerga used to gather in the middle of this square to sing 'The Internationale' before the duties of the day were announced, such as who would be on guard duty, the chefs of the day, the self service team, the library team, and the guest room team. I was exempt from daytime activities.

The dining room was next to a rather large meeting room. We used to gather in this meeting room almost every night for political activities and different entertainments such as games, watching films, or having galta o gapp evenings or friends would visit each other in their tents.

I would stay up late, often until past 1 a.m., watching TV with my neighbours. One morning we woke to find the TV had gone missing, along with a number of Kalashnikovs from various tents. A day or so later, we discovered that booby traps had been set in the trees. Someone had put down grenades attached to a tripwire which would set off the grenade if someone stepped over it. Fortunately, we discovered the trap before anyone was injured. These incidents created an atmosphere of mistrust, which was different from what we had known among the Peshmerga all these years. We all became extra vigilant. Was there someone within the Peshmerga sent by the government to harm us?

Every morning for several weeks there seemed to be another incident. We doubled the number of night guards at the base but I still didn't feel safe. I knew I had other responsibilities now and needed to protect my baby. I felt on high alert once more, as if I were back on the battlefield.

One night, I went to bed late but I was shivering and couldn't get warm, so I got out of bed to switch the heater on. It didn't help much. I heard some voices out of the window in the direction of the forest. I looked out and couldn't see anything, but the noise sounded quite close. I grew really scared. I imagined that the Iranian government had sent a team to attack us. I waited for about an hour, but the noise continued. I couldn't sleep.

'This noise is killing me,' I said to myself. 'I have to go out and face it.'

I took my gun and put my ammunition belt over my shoulders, as I couldn't tie it around my large belly. I went to the back of the house.

There was a full moon, but I couldn't see anything. I sat under a tree with my gun ready to shoot. I didn't move for two hours. At around 5 a.m. I decided to go back to bed.

'Why am I living all alone like this?' I asked myself.

I spoke to Mahmood to explain what had happened and to ask him to come and be with me at night. He said that the road was not safe to travel every day due to all the terrorist groups in the area. He could only come for meetings. I understood the situation. He was right, the road wasn't safe, but still I hoped that he would take a few weeks off and be with me. The gap between us was getting wider and wider, making me lose any hope that our relationship could get better.

I realised I'd have to start thinking about how I could take care of the baby on my own. I needed to be prepared for her, no matter what happened between me and Mahmood.

I spoke to one of my friends and she agreed to come and sleep with me. I could give birth at any time.

The party arrested a number of new Peshmerga recruits, who were aged about twenty-three. A number were Iranian Kurds, while a few were from Tehran. We had so many Persian people with us that this was not unusual. They were extremely ideological and spoke about God and how fantastic the Islamic government was. The men confessed that they had been sent by the Iranian government to terrorise the Peshmerga and to create an atmosphere of fear across the camp. They had been successful in creating a fearful atmosphere, but they had not killed any Peshmerga.

GIRL WITH A GUN

I was angry but also scared. Not just one but several men had managed to get through the training base interviews and become Peshmerga. We had trusted them and they had terrorised us.

For the first time in years, the party executed two of the spies, the pair who were responsible for the grenade trap. I was horrified by this decision. The executions created a division in the party, as we had been against capital punishment for a number of years. Many Peshmerga criticised the Central Committee, while some members of the Central Committee were also angry it had happened. It had to remain one of our principles not to execute prisoners. We had to stand against capital punishment in all circumstances.

It got closer to my due date and I decided to return to Sulaymaniyah to be with Mahmood before the birth. The Iraqi Peshmerga belonging to the Patriotic Union of Kurdistan were now in complete control of the city and the fighting was over. Iraqis were gradually returning to their homes.

One of my friends from Baneh, Fatemah, was living in Sulaymaniyah. I told her that I was worried that my baby was overdue and she took me to see a well-known medic, Dr Parvin, to have an ultrasound in her surgery, but when we arrived we were told that she was working at the hospital. The hospital was not fully operating due to the exodus from the city, and there were only a few doctors, nurses and midwives. The building didn't have electricity, so the staff were using a generator which could only work for short periods. At the hospital I couldn't find the doctor I had seen before, as he had fled. Instead, I found Dr Parvin and another medic, Dr Feraz. They checked me and told me that my baby was around seven and a half months, as she was small. I assured them that I was overdue and insisted on having an ultrasound. I ended up having three. The final ultrasound showed that I was overdue. The doctors told me I needed to stay in the hospital but I wanted to have a shower first and pack the baby's clothes to bring with me. They agreed and I promised to return to the hospital the next day.

251

Mahmood sent a message to Shaesta to come to Sulaymaniyah to be with me for the birth. Shaesta had recently married a Peshmerga called Majid, who was a member of the Komala Central Committee. I knew Majid from my time with the South Battalion, as he had been on the regional committee for Mariwan. He was kind and well-liked and I knew that he would look after Shaesta.

Mahmood's sister Nosrat also came to help take care of me. She had spent three years in prison because of her political activities, but she was married by this time with a child of her own.

The next day Fatemah, Shaesta, Mahmood and I went to the hospital. I took some clothes and some medical equipment from Komala's hospital in Maluma, in case the hospital in Sulaymaniyah didn't have it.

I had another ultrasound. This one revealed that the placenta was dry and was not giving enough nutrients to the baby. The situation was becoming dangerous. The doctor decided it was time for the baby to come and asked me to go to the labour ward, a large room in the basement, with water leaking from the roof where the hospital had been hit and damaged by rockets. Inside, there were eight beds and about thirty women in labour. Some women were in a critical situation while others had lost their babies.

The doctor gave me Syntocinon, the drip, to induce labour. I was told that it should bring about labour almost immediately but instead I fell asleep.

'You're supposed to give birth,' Shaesta said, shaking me gently. 'You cannot be sleeping.'

I remained in the delivery room being injected with Syntocinon, but I couldn't keep awake. After four days, the doctor brought a psychiatrist to see me.

'We haven't experienced anything like this before with Syntocinon,' she said. 'I believe that you are not allowing the child to be born because of the war. You believe that it is safer inside you. Am I right?'

I realised what she was saying was true and I started to cry. I thought about her words for a long time. I reflected on all the things that I had seen since I was sixteen. I'd seen young mothers killed in the war while still holding their babies, children who became orphans, and families who had lost their children. It was true that I didn't want my daughter to come out into this world. She was safer in my womb.

The decision was finally taken out of my hands. The baby's heart rate dropped and the doctors had to perform an emergency caesarean section.

During the caesarean, although I had general anaesthetic, I could hear people talking and saying I was giving birth to a baby girl. However, I was in a dreamlike state and I fell asleep before I could hold her.

When I woke up, I could see shadows and a strong light. I realised that it was the sunshine coming through a corner of the roof that had been hit by a big rocket.

There were a lot of Peshmerga friends and family around me. They were laughing and joking. For a few seconds, I didn't know where I was but then I saw Mahmood sitting by my side. The others were standing around, but I couldn't identify them yet.

'Where is my daughter? Is she all right?'

'Don't worry, she is fine and safe,' Mahmood said, smiling. 'The nurses told me to take her back to our room in Sulaymaniyah as it is not hygienic here. I don't want her here in this hospital. It's safer for her to be at home.'

I didn't believe him. I thought there must be something wrong with my daughter and that was why they had taken her away.

'Please bring her to me,' I said.

'You will see her soon,' said Mahmood. 'Don't worry.'

The next day they all came back to visit me but they didn't bring my baby. When the doctor came, I told her that I didn't have my baby and I hadn't even seen her yet.

'You have to go and bring her now,' she told Mahmood. 'The baby needs her mother's milk.'

'But I have been advised by the nurse to take her home as the hospital is not clean; she may get ill from germs here.'

The doctor firmly asked Mahmood to bring her back and when he returned with my daughter, I immediately fell in love. She was perfect. Finally, I had everything I needed.

Mahmood brought chocolates, sweets and flowers to the hospital to thank the doctors and the nurses. Those who didn't know us congratulated us on having a baby boy, as it was still unusual to celebrate the birth of a girl in such a way. However, just as my father had done with me, Mahmood told everyone we had a baby girl and we were as happy as could be.

Chapter 28

Separation

Mahmood and I decided together on a name for our daughter. We had a list with suggestions from family and friends, and settled on Tara, it means 'a bride's veil' in Kurdish, which we thought was a beautiful name.

After three days in the hospital, we took Tara back to our home in Sulaymaniyah where we had everything ready for her. Shaesta and Nosrat stayed with us for a month to help. We didn't have any nappies; we had to use material, which Mahmood washed by hand every day. Mahmood tried to find good food, such as kebabs and fish for us all, but everything was in short supply after the war. I craved a glass of milk. We knew a family with cows, so Mahmood went to them and asked to buy milk, but he came back empty-handed.

For two months, I breastfed Tara. She cried a lot – so much that it seemed as though she was in severe pain. We took her to the doctor, who said she had colic and gave us some medicine to ease the discomfort and to help her sleep.

Sometimes I pondered over my relationship with Mahmood, but it became of secondary importance to me. I was completely besotted with Tara.

One sunny day, Tara was peacefully sleeping when the Iraqi government tried to take over Sulaymaniyah once more. They sent rockets to the city and one of them hit our yard. It exploded with a great noise on the tiled garden next to the wall where Tara was sleeping in her cot. I ran to her and covered her with my body before taking her and holding her tight. I sat without moving in the corner of the room, listening to the explosions and gunshots. Tara opened her eyes for just a moment and fell asleep again, but with every explosion she frowned.

Mahmood was in the diplomatic building a five-minute walk from our home. There were many Peshmerga working in the building and I was worried about their safety. I was deep in thought when the door opened. Mahmood and two comrades entered the garden. They came quickly into the room where I was still sat in the corner.

'Are you OK?' Mahmood asked, concern all over his face.

'We are fine!' I replied.

The three of them came and sat next to us, talking animatedly about the Patriotic Union of Kurdistan (PUK) and discussing whether it was possible that the Iraqi government would take back Sulaymaniyah.

'No, it's not possible,' one said. 'Saddam is too weak now after the attack by the Americans.'

The sound of the rockets seemed to be moving further and further away. The PUK had pushed the Iraqi soldiers back to their bases, and remained in control.

Slowly, the Iraqi people returned to the city. They tried to clean up the streets and the rubble and debris. Shops reopened and Sulaymaniyah started to return to normal life.

However, the city was no longer safe for Iranian Peshmerga and opponents of the Iranian regime. The PUK had a good relationship with the Iranian government. After the PUK took control of the city, many Iranian pasdaran moved there; one of their bases was quite close to our home. We had no guards for our home, and everywhere we went we could hear Farsi spoken by men in the street. We did not feel safe.

Komala asked Mahmood and I to go to Kirkuk for a while and we accepted. It was a more stable situation there. There were no battles taking place and the Iraqi government was in control.

We had a comfortable home based in an Arabic neighbourhood

in Kirkuk. It was hot and Tara and I couldn't go out much. We usually stayed at home during the day; I tended to go out in the late afternoon, close to sunset when it became cooler, and I met some of the women of the neighbourhood. It was difficult at the beginning as I couldn't speak Arabic, but I soon managed to pick it up. I began to remember what I had learned in Arabic lessons at school.

My sister and Nosrat came to stay with us in Kirkuk and my mum was also able to visit me for a week. This was the first time I had seen my mother for several years. It was such a joyful reunion. My mother cooked my favourite dishes and added the pomegranate puree that Mahmood had made. We ate the traditional Iranian dish fesenjoon, which is pomegranate juice mixed with crushed walnuts, served with chicken and rice.

My mother helped me with Tara. I bathed her for the first time under her supervision. I'd been worried about doing it on my own and Mahmood, my sister, Nosrat and other friends had been showering her. It was a big step for me to feel confident enough to do it and Tara really enjoyed it. My mother shared many of her experiences in bringing up babies.

It was lovely weather in a beautiful city; we couldn't hear any bombs. Shaesta and I hadn't had proper time with my mother since leaving Baneh. When we had met while we were moving with the Peshmerga, it had always been stressful and too brief. This was the first time we could be together in a peaceful city. Mahmood got on well with my mum and he was always making her laugh and telling funny stories. It was such a wonderful week.

I still wasn't sure about my relationship with Mahmood but I didn't tell Mum anything about it. I didn't want to worry her. I think she sensed something, but I told her: 'Don't worry, our relationship is good.'

She admitted that the whole family had changed after we left. Our beloved father had become depressed and aggressive. He was cross with my brothers. For a long time, my mother hadn't cooked any of the food that we liked. My father always used to sing songs every evening and play with us when we were little, but he no longer wanted to play with the younger children.

'He is angry with me,' my mother said. 'The happiness from our home has gone. All the time we have been worried about you two and your comrades. So many times the Islamic Revolutionary Guards came to our home and told us that you were dead. When we heard that Shaesta was no longer an active Peshmerga we were relieved, but we were always worried about you, Galavezh. Your father has always been thinking about you and trying to find a way to take you out of the Peshmerga.'

My mother was of course concerned about my father. Many times he had been questioned and imprisoned for days, with the government always making the same request that he bring me and Shaesta back home.

Always he told them, 'You are the powerful government with all the military and you cannot bring them back! How can I bring them back? I am their father. They don't listen to me.'

'I am so sorry I have to leave you all alone again with the baby, but I am confident that you can do it yourself,' said my mother. 'But I will miss you. You are our eldest daughter. I so wish we lived together and could spend the rest of our lives together.'

We accompanied her to Sulaymaniyah by car and found someone to take her back to Iran. It was not an easy route, but it was much safer than before, as the battles had stopped in the area.

Mahmood, Tara and I only stayed for a few months in Kirkuk before we were posted back to Sulaymaniyah. I returned to my job in communications with Fakhri. It suited me well as I was able to take Tara with me to the communications room.

On 1 May 1991, on International Workers' Day, there was a huge demonstration in Sulaymaniyah with thousands of workers in the streets. I took Tara to her first demonstration in a pushchair. All the parties on the left from Iraq and Iran were there and there were many speeches. I was elated to see so many comrades.

After the end of the Gulf War there had been a lot of discussions within Komala about our role and our future. Since the uprisings in Iraq, the Iraqi Peshmerga belonging to both the PUK and the Kurdistan Democratic Party (KDP) had full control of the whole of the Kurdistan region in Iraq. They had the support of the US and Europe. Kurdistan was now a no fly zone.

There were discussions in Komala about whether we could do the same in Iran and take control of the Kurdish region. We no longer had any bases there, so our Peshmerga could go into Iran for a tour of the villages and for hit and run attacks on the government, but we would have to swiftly return to our bases in Iraq.

The Iranian government put pressure on the PUK to limit our activities in Iran, which meant everything we planned had to be approved by the PUK. The PUK's relationship with Iran was of great concern for us – we worried that one day they would give us up to the regime.

The leader of the Communist Party of Iran, Mansoor Hekmat criticised Komala for moving away from socialism and turning towards nationalism. He said he believed that Komala hoped the US would come to rescue the Kurdish people in Iran.

For these reasons Mansoor could no longer work with Komala. He resigned from the Communist party, saying: 'I'm taking only my pen.'

However, half of Komala's members, including me and Mahmood, wanted to leave with him, equally unhappy with the direction of the party. This was not an easy decision to make. For almost a year there were discussions within the party, while comrades tried to convince each other of our opposing views. There were so many different opinions.

Komala had lost its way. It was no longer leading a socialist revolution. We knew that the point of our armed struggle was not to end up in camps in Iraq with our only purpose being to defend those camps. We had wanted to organise a revolution in Iran. What was the purpose of staying in the camps just to defend them?

I didn't believe that the situation in Iran or Iraq would get any better for the Kurds with support from the US – in any country that the US and Europe invaded, the most fanatical religious groups took power. We believed that the Americans had their own agenda. Human rights, and equality and safety for the Iraqi and Kurdish people were not on it.

In Iraq, the situation deteriorated day by day. More and more extremist organisations were being established in the region.

Mansoor established the Worker Communist Party of Iran and Mahmood and I joined. The new party organised a temporary Central Committee across Europe with connections inside Iran and Kurdistan, which would enable the party to start up.

The Worker Communist Party decided we would no longer carry arms and we would not take part in hit and run activities in Iran. In any case, the PUK would not allow it. Our military activities had already been reduced to zero. Leaving Komala felt like leaving my own family again.

As Komala Party members pledged to leave without anything, we would be losing our home, our work, as well as a lot of our friends. It was a huge wrench. We didn't take our guns. We left everything for Komala.

The Worker Communist Party believed that workers inside Iran – in the cities, inside factories – should organise and fight for their rights. We could support this goal. Student movements within Iran in favour of freedom and equality were strong too, and we wanted to have a greater role in expanding and leading them.

Mansoor suggested that all Worker Communist Party members should be allowed and helped to seek asylum in safe countries in the West, where we could continue our political activities. Part of the negotiation and agreement between Komala and the Worker Communist Party was that Komala would support all members financially until they could arrive in a safe country. Komala still enjoyed great financial aid from the Iraqi government and from the public, and they agreed to support us, knowing that we had left everything we had with them.

Mansoor got permission to stay in the UK. The party decided that Shaesta's husband should go to Europe to organise matters there and he was sent to Sweden. Shaesta joined him about nine months later. It was wonderful to see her excited about her new life. I relaxed a little, knowing that she would be safe and in a happy marriage, but I would miss her dearly.

The situation in Iraq for the Iranian opposition became harder and harder. The Iranian pasdaran set up extremist Islamic groups across Kurdistan in order to terrorise any Peshmerga and other Iranian opposition. These terrorist groups particularly targeted women. A midwife in Sulaymaniyah was brutally killed. The terrorist left a note on her body, which stated that she deserved to die because she was working with a male doctor and had helped women with abortions. Although honour killings had been going on within families, this was the first open and politically motivated honour killing by Islamist extremists that I was aware of. A number of killings of high profile female political activists followed.

Kurdistan in Iraq was a tribal region and the tribes were becoming armed once more. Guns were cheap to buy. The society's structure had been destroyed. No one was prosecuted for terrorising women or for practising honour killings and other crimes. No woman felt safe, especially Peshmerga women.

The Worker Communist Party started to send more and more people to Europe. They prioritised those who were more in need, such as the disabled and injured Peshmerga, and families with children.

Mahmood and I no longer had jobs within the party and nowhere to live. We contacted friends in Sulaymaniyah to ask for their help. They welcomed us into their homes and we moved to a different family every few months. My father's cousin had been living in Iraq for some time and we also stayed with him for a short while. He was wealthy with a large family. Some of his family members were high rank ing in the PUK, which gave us some protection. Mahmood found a job as a taxi driver for a while, which was a great help and the party gave us some money to live on.

Our precarious situation affected my relationship with Mahmood. We were both mentally exhausted and at some point we stopped talking to each other altogether. I had expected the situation to make us closer but the opposite happened. I gave all my attention to Tara.

I thought about separating from Mahmood. I was extremely lonely and couldn't explain or share my feelings of desperation with him. I couldn't understand why he was cold towards me, even in this situation when we needed each other's kindness and attention more than ever.

I asked him to talk about our relationship. I started to explain what I thought had gone wrong but Mahmood didn't say anything in response.

'Listen to me!' I said. I listed various slights. 'We should be supporting each other, not tearing each other apart.'

We both started crying.

'Can we please give our relationship another chance?' Mahmood asked.

'Our lives are already too stressful,' I said. 'I can't do this anymore. I'd prefer us to return to the close friendship we had before we got married, if that is possible.'

The marriage was over for me and Mahmood moved out. Tara cried a lot at first and asked for her father. Mahmood also missed Tara. He came to visit us nearly every day. They would go to the shops together to buy cheese and bread. One day, Mahmood said Tara carried an egg all the way home in her hand. She hadn't allowed it to break.

For a few months I struggled. I thought about taking Mahmood back because of Tara. However, I knew that I had made the right decision. Tara would soon get used to the situation, and Mahmood and I would have a good friendship again. We would make sure that Tara's relationship with her father was always positive and supportive.

As my marriage collapsed, the Islamic government had identified all of the former Peshmerga in Sulaymaniyah. They started to terrorise us. They came to the homes of my comrades, rang the bell, and shot them when they came out. When would they would be coming for me and Mahmood?

Chapter 29

Europe

Towards the end of 1995, when Tara was four, I knew that we must leave Iraq and go to a safe country. I had to think of my daughter's future. I had made a choice to join the Peshmerga when I'd had to escape to Saqqez, but I couldn't inflict this way of living on my daughter. She couldn't attend school. We were constantly moving home. We had no rights in Iraq. An unsettled life on the run was not what I wanted for her.

It was extremely expensive to be smuggled out of Iraq and I didn't have any money. Komala could give us half the cash and Mahmood had also managed to save some money from his job as a taxi driver. We talked to family and friends in Iraq and they donated the rest to us.

At first Mahmood thought about going to the US, but he decided to come to wherever we were going so that he could continue to see Tara. He tried to persuade us to go to the US, but the smugglers told us it would be better to go to Europe. After a few months, we managed to pay smugglers, who got us to Turkey. We travelled by car to the border, along with a group of ten other friends from Sulaymaniyah who were also being smuggled.

We couldn't go through the border. We had to wait until nightfall and walk down the side of the border through cotton fields, which covered the whole area. The cotton was beautiful and glimmered in the moonlight, but it was extremely difficult to walk as the cotton buds were hard. It was a long distance and we were all shattered, but we knew that if the guards saw us they might shoot us or arrest us and deport us back to Iran. Other people trying to flee this way had been executed as soon as they were returned to the border in Iran. The smugglers had Kalashnikovs, but we had nothing with which to defend ourselves.

From the border, we had to wade across a fast moving river. It was night time in December and the river was cold and frightening. Mahmood carried Tara on his back. Once in Turkish Kurdistan, we had to hide ourselves for several weeks while the smugglers arranged Turkish residency permits so that we could travel by bus to Istanbul. We had to be careful and stay inside most of the time. We wore Kurdish traditional clothes so that the neighbours would think we were visiting family.

In Istanbul, our group was handed over to different smugglers, who were Turkish. Again, we had to stay in a safe house. We were told not to go out and show ourselves. The smugglers brought us food every day. One day we heard a noise. We thought it was the Turkish police. We were about to jump from the window when we heard the postman delivering letters to the house.

Tara and I were given forged passports, but Mahmood's documents did not arrive on time. He also needed to organise more money for us. This meant we would have to leave without him. I was scared at the prospect of going on alone without Mahmood, but knew that we couldn't wait. If the Turkish government found us we would be in serious trouble.

Our planned destination was the UK. At Istanbul airport the officials barely looked at our passports. Three smugglers came onto the plane with us and each one stayed with one group. We were all told not to talk to each other. Tara was bleeding with infected eczema and had a high temperature. For the whole of the four-hour flight, she kept asking me: 'Where are we going?'

I was terrified of the police. I didn't speak English. At school, I had done one hour a week and most of the time we had just laughed at the teacher. I had forgotten everything I had been taught. I didn't even look at the other people on the plane. I was so tense that I took no notice of anyone else.

However, I was also excited. I knew that if we were accepted into the country this would be the end of this terrifying stage of our lives. We would be safe. I told myself to think only of this, but I was carrying all of the stress in my body from years of war. It was impossible to get down from high alert.

When we arrived in the UK I would have to tell immigration officers that I was an asylum seeker. I tried to repeat the phrase in my mind: 'I am an asylum s . . .'

I kept stumbling at the phrase. When we got off the plane, the smuggler who had our passports disappeared with our documents. I guessed he would use them for someone else.

We got to passport control. I couldn't remember what I had to say.

'I am a refugee,' I said.

The three officers at passport control laughed. One shouted over to a colleague: 'You have a customer.'

We were taken to a room and given coffee and a juice for Tara. There were a number of asylum seekers, with one or two speaking Farsi. At some point, we got to see a doctor and he gave us medicine for Tara's eczema.

We had an interview with two police officers. They asked me lots of questions about why we had come and what we had done. I felt completely exhausted.

I needed to be somewhere quiet and not thinking about what we had been through. We needed a peaceful place. To not be worried about who was knocking on the door.

One of the police officers asked me whether I knew anyone in the UK.

'If you don't know anyone we can contact, we have to take you to prison,' he said.

They took us by police car for several hours and I heard one of the guards say we were going to Newhaven. We travelled with one other man who was Iranian. They put Tara and me in a prison room with two beds with filthy military style blankets. Tara was ill. I spent the whole night awake with her on my lap, covered with my coat. We were not given anything to eat. We told each other stories so we didn't think about our hunger. Tara could sense my anxiety and she kept saying: 'Don't worry, Mummy.'

We had been told we would be picked up by 10 a.m. but we were still there at 4 p.m. An interpreter came and told us we were going back to London to Heathrow Airport. A bus came to pick us up. I had no idea why we were going back to an airport and that was worrying me.

At Heathrow, they introduced us to the Refugee Arrival Project (RAP). Everyone there was so kind and supportive. We told them we had not eaten for twenty-four hours. They gave us a juice and a coffee and some biscuits.

At the sound of an aeroplane at Heathrow, I thought it was military planes coming to bomb us and I started to shake before I remembered that we were in the UK. The people from the project calmed me down and told me to talk to an interpreter.

I took the telephone and a man spoke to me in Kurdish.

'Hello, Diana. My name is Amir. I'm your translator.'

'Hello, Amir,' I said, immediately recognising this voice although we hadn't spoken in seventeen years.

'Is this Galavezh?' he asked me.

'Is this Azad?'

'I will come there quickly.'

I couldn't believe it. I had avoided Azad all this time. I had refused to speak to him. I had been running from him for years. Now we were forced to speak.

When Azad arrived at the RAP office, I began to shiver; my tongue seemed frozen and I couldn't talk properly.

Azad also appeared shaken but he pulled himself together quickly. He had aged a little, but he was mostly the same man I had loved before.

'You are in a safe country now,' he said. 'All will be OK. You will get a home. I will help you in any way that I can.'

It was wonderful to see him and talk to him, yet my bitterness had not faded, even after all these years. I realised I still loved him and was hoping that he would be there for me, but on the other hand, I wanted to push him away and refuse him as my interpreter. Yet I felt safe with him. He was one of us. He knew our story and our life. He was the best person to help us.

Tara and I were sent to a big hotel run by a refugee group and given a room. It housed hundreds of asylum seekers from many different countries. It was 11 p.m. at night when we arrived and I was worried because Tara hadn't eaten. I asked for food but they told me the kitchen was closed.

An Afghan boy, aged about eighteen, was voluntarily interpreting for us. He brought us jam and toast. The bread was all soft. I wasn't used to this bread and I'd never tasted jam like this before; I'd only eaten runny marmalade. This jam wasn't like normal jam. It was hard. I tried to spread it but it would not spread properly. Instead, I made a hole in the bread.

'I'm sorry, Tara. This is all that we have.'

'Let's pretend it is chicken,' she said.

I couldn't eat the bread. It stuck in my throat. I thought of my father's thin, fresh, crispy bread back home. Focused on survival, I had not had one second to think of my family since I left Iraq. Now thoughts of my mother and father were overwhelming.

At around 1 a.m., the Afghan boy came and knocked on the door and said: 'I am here, don't be afraid. I can come and sleep in your room to protect you.'

'No thank you,' I said angrily. 'I don't need you.'

I shut the door in his face.

After a few days, the council gave us a room in a hostel in north London. There were two beds in the room with a shared toilet and bathroom. The whole place was filthy and all the showers were blocked. Azad took us to the town hall and he managed to get us rooms in a different hostel, which was much better.

After we had been in London for a little while, Azad invited me and Tara to dinner at Pizza Express. We couldn't talk much in front of Tara, but after a while he looked at me directly.

'Why did you send me that letter?' he said. 'Why did you want to end our relationship when everything was so good?'

I looked at him, startled. 'It wasn't me that finished it. You sent me a message through your sister that you wanted to end it.'

Azad put his head in his hands. 'I never once said such a thing to her.'

I was shocked. All this time I had believed that he had sent his sister to end things between us. I was too upset to say anything more.

Later, when I was on my own, I thought for a long time about mine and Azad's relationship. We had had opportunities to talk to each other over the years but I had avoided him. Why had we not spoken to each other properly before? Was it a deep fear of rejection or the strict code of honour that had kept us apart? Perhaps it was both. We had suffered tremendously for our pride. I berated myself for having avoided Azad. There were so many unanswered questions. Would we have the courage to speak honestly this time?

Epilogue

I am sitting in Trafalgar Square.

Tara is jumping and playing and touching the water. I am holding Azad's hand for the first time in years. I love him as much as I always did. I am angry and heartbroken for all that we have lost.

I sit, almost in a trance, on the steps in Trafalgar Square, watching everyone around me. Everything is new. I look at how happy people are here. They are moving freely. I see a young couple kissing and laughing. The woman's hair is blowing wildly in the wind. Her jeans are tight at her waist.

I think about my brothers and sisters and all the young people in Iran. Kissing someone once means you have to marry. A boy and a girl cannot walk together in the street without the fear of being arrested. Going out without a hijab can lead to a woman being lashed.

Why can't Iranians enjoy simple pleasures? Do we not deserve the same human rights?

I begin to sob, and once I start I cannot stop.

I cry for my mother and my father, my brothers and sisters. I cry for everything we have fought for, for all the friends that we have lost. I cry for beautiful Iran and the mountains of Kurdistan. I cry until I am exhausted and there are no more tears.

Azad holds my hand.

I look at Tara, jumping and playing and touching the water. She is laughing. She is so full of joy. She is free.

Authors' Notes

It has always been my dream and passion to write my life experience.

Girl with a Gun is not only about me but is the story of thousands of women and girls who couldn't tolerate injustice and became involved in political activities to make changes in their country and in other people's lives. This is the story of many who risked or lost their lives to protect others and to create a safer environment for them. This is a short but strong history of sacrifice. I admire all those who fought for justice, freedom and equality and will always remember those who lost their lives fighting for a safer and better future for others.

Although this book is based on true events, names and place names have been altered to protect those who cannot be named for their safety.

In the writing of this memoir, taking a deep dive into these traumatic moments in my life has taken me right back to those situations and I have suffered emotionally and mentally. I would like to thank my wonderful daughter, Tara, my sister, Shaesta, and my co writer Karen Attwood for being there for me throughout. Without their tremendous emotional support, I would not have been able to finish this.

My heartfelt thanks go to other people who helped me to remember issues that I had forgotten, especially my sister, Shaesta and my dear friend, Galavezh Hosseini, who hosted gatherings in Stockholm and in Gothenburg, inviting many of my fellow comrades and friends into her own home. It was extremely helpful and I was delighted to see them after years of separation.

I spoke to my father a couple of months after my arrival in the UK to wish him Happy New Year. I told him I was safe and that

I would invite him to the UK. He started to cry, saying: 'Where is my fifteen-year-old daughter? I miss you so much. I don't know anything about your daughter, your new life and city.'

I promised him that he would be able to visit me in the UK. Sadly, he died a short while later. I never got the chance to see him again.

My dear mother died in February 2025. While I was unable to see my mother for many years, we kept in regular contact with video calls. Following her death, Shaesta and I were able to spend time together in order to celebrate our mother's life and remember her unwavering love and support. She sacrificed herself and put her own life in danger trying to keep us safe from being arrested so many times when the Islamic Revolutionary Guards raided our home in Iran. I wish I could hold her hands and hug her and thank her. Her memory will stay alive with me and Shaesta forever. I miss her so dearly.

As for my name, Galavezh, I am still known by this by close friends and in my community. Diana is my official recorded birth name and I use it professionally and in my work with the Iranian and Kurdish Women's Rights Organisation (IKWRO), the charity I founded.

The fight against Islamic extremism in Iran continues to this day. We have seen the Taliban, Hezbollah, Al Shabaab, Al Qaeda, ISIS in Kurdistan and many more. The Peshmerga men and women continue on the front line, sacrificing their lives so that others can live in freedom.

I would like to express my gratitude to my fellow Peshmerga women in the region of Baneh: Shaesta Qadernejad, Galavezh Hosseini, Masom Shafei, Galavezh Kermanshah, Djamila Shafei, Nazira Mehmari, Rabi Fathi, Djamile Fathi, Nasrin Bahrami, Halale Taheri, Parvane Ahmadi, Fatemh Eghdami, Soraya Fatahi, Sara Daliamin, Shirin Watankhah, Nahid Fatehi, Homa Ahmadi, Atifa Fatehi, Farideh Amini, Freshteh A, Rabea Kamali, Jamileh Azadi, and many more that for confidentiality and for reasons of safety I cannot name.

I used to think that in European countries women's rights would be respected, fully implemented, and you would never hear of violence against women and girls. But when I came to the UK in 1996, I found that the reality was different. I had an interpreter who helped me to enrol my daughter in primary school. She was a very lovely Kurdish woman. Twice she took us to the school, and then she didn't turn up to our third appointment. I called her office and they told me that she was dead. I learned that her husband had suspected that she was flirting with a colleague, so with his brothers he plotted to take her to Kurdistan and she was murdered there. Afterwards, he came back to the UK and carried on with his life. He remarried and had children, and later he returned to Iraq. Of course I was shocked by this news and decided to do something for her. With the help of a friend I called the police in London and explained what I had heard from her colleagues. They said they couldn't investigate the case because her death didn't happen in the UK. I told them that she was a British citizen and that it was an 'honour' killing, but they told me this was a cultural issue and that they had to respect it otherwise our community would call them racist.

I was astonished by the police response. A woman had been murdered – a British citizen – but the police weren't interested. 'Honour' killing is a crime and should be treated as such. Culture or religion cannot justify it.

My interpreter had lived in the UK for eleven years and was educated and spoke English fluently. If she could be killed, what about the women who couldn't speak English, or didn't know their rights, or were afraid to seek help? The police didn't know what 'honour' killing was and they didn't seem interested in women from minority communities. I felt that if my interpreter had been a white British woman, they would have investigated, as indeed they ought to. I heard about other cases where the police would not address violence within minority communities because they believed it was their 'culture' or their religion, and that if they did, they would be accused of racism. This was cultural relativism, and as a result of it, women from black and minority communities were being discriminated against and their lives were being sacrificed.

I kept thinking about setting up an organisation to help women like my interpreter and to campaign against 'honour' killing and other forms of violence against women and girls. I wanted to raise awareness of this brutal practice, both within the communities and among police officers and other professionals, and to put an end to acceptance of unacceptable cultural relativism.

With the help of some friends and other organisations I established IKWRO in August 2002, working from home, and established the Stop Honour Killings campaign in the UK.

IKWRO soon became a trusted organisation for women and girls within Iranian, Kurdish, Afghan and Arab communities in the UK and abroad. While our activities and campaign faced huge challenges, it found its great supporters in women's rights activists, human rights activists, governments, and women who were victims and survivors of 'honour' based violence. IKWRO soon became a well-known organisation by providing free, holistic, in depth and confidential advice and advocacy to women and girls in community languages, offering them counselling, training and for providing refuges and safe houses for women. We continue to campaign for better laws and policies in support of women.

Diana Nammi, September 2025

The murder of Mahsa Amini in suspicious circumstances in Tehran in September 2022, after she was arrested for inappropriate dress, ignited the Women, Life Freedom movement which demanded the end of oppression of women in Iran. The worldwide protests that this sparked drew greater attention to the tyrannies of the Islamic Regime. With the oppression of the people of Iran continuing, the story told in Girl with a Gun remains as important as ever.

We are therefore deeply grateful to Gadfly Press to be publishing for the first time a paperback and audiobook of Girl with a

Gun along with a new ebook in order for this story to be brought to a wider audience.

Thank you to Lale Inceoglu for the most fantastic audio recording and to Tom Sanderson for the new and very impactful book cover.

Thank you, most of all, to Diana for trusting me to help to tell this powerful story. Reliving some of your most painful experiences hasn't been easy, I know.

Thanks also to Shaesta – this story is as much yours as Diana's, as it is the story of all the Peshmerga women who made great sacrifices to help others.

A huge thank you to my husband Charlie – who has changed my life immeasurably since we met. Also to my parents, my brother Shaun, my mother-in-law Anne for all of your support and to my wonderful children Yasmin and Isaac for all of the joy that you bring.

Karen Attwood, September 2025

Notes on the Authors

Diana Nammi is a human rights and women's rights activist. In 2002 she founded IKWRO (the Iranian and Kurdish Women's Rights Organisation). Ten years later she was named as one of 150 women who shake the world by Newsweek and the Daily Beast.

In 2014, she was honoured with a Barclays Woman of the Year Award and was included in the BBC's 100 Women series. In 2015, she won the XX1 Premis Ones Mediterrania Award in Spain. Diana has received honorary doctorate degrees in law from the University of Essex in 2016, and the University of St Andrews in 2019.

In a twenty-year career as a journalist, Karen Attwood's work has been published in all UK national newspapers as well as many international publications. She is a former staff writer at the Independent, the Independent on Sunday, Abu Dhabi's The National, and the Press Association. She currently works in communications and is working on her first novel.

Karen Attwood's mother's debut book is also available world-wide on Amazon!

Blue Plastic Cow: One Woman's Search for Her Birth Mother

By Barbara Attwood

This is the true story of Barbara's adoption by a family who lived in a town on the banks of the River Mersey. They were a loving family but Barbara always felt different. Her mother, Florrie, never wanted her to know the truth. At age 12, after Barbara accidentally discovered that she was adopted, Florrie lied to her about her birth mother, Carole, and the facts surrounding her birth.

As a teenager, unable to deal with the shock of what she'd learned, she rebelled against her parents, finding solace in the exciting 1960s' Liverpool music scene. Against her parents' wishes, she got a job in Liverpool as a secretary. She went to lunch time sessions at the Cavern where she saw The Beatles, and often stayed out late in Liverpool drinking.

Decades later, Barbara discovered tear stained letters from her birth mother, containing heart-breaking words that would send her on a challenging 26-year quest to find Carole and discover the secret of the blue plastic cow.

www.ingramcontent.com/pod-product-compliance
Lightning Source LLC
LaVergne TN
LVHW051254080426
835509LV00020B/2962